140

Death and Dying

Contributors

LEONARD PEARSON, Ph.D., is associate professor of psychology at Sonoma State College, Rohnert Park, California.

ROBERT KASTENBAUM, Ph.D., is professor of psychology at Wayne State University, in Detroit, and research associate at the Institute of Gerontology (University of Michigan/Wayne State University).

LAWRENCE LE SHAN, Ph.D., is research associate at Mills College of Education, in New York City.

CICELY SAUNDERS, O.B.E., M.R.C.P., is medical director of St. Christopher's Hospice, in London.

RICHARD A. KALISH, Ph.D., is associate professor in the Division of Behavioral Sciences, School of Public Health, University of California at Los Angeles.

ANSELM L. STRAUSS, Ph.D., is professor of sociology at the San Francisco Medical Center of the University of California.

Death and Dying

CURRENT ISSUES IN THE TREATMENT OF THE DYING PERSON

Edited by Leonard Pearson

1969
THE PRESS OF CASE WESTERN RESERVE UNIVERSITY
CLEVELAND & LONDON

Copyright © 1969 by The Press of Case Western Reserve University,
Cleveland, Ohio 44106. All rights reserved.
Printed in the United States of America.
Standard Book Number: 8295-0153-3 (cloth).
8295-0154-1 (paper).
Library of Congress Catalogue Card Number: 67-11483.

*For those
who are enriching my living:
Lillian, Andrea, and Seana*

Preface

I FIRST BECAME AWARE OF DEATH as a clinical entity with special psychological impact when consulting at a home for the aged in Chicago some years ago. One day one of the residents failed to appear for our group-therapy session. When I asked about him, the staff member serving as cotherapist with me looked startled. With her face reddening, she said she would tell me about it "later." Then one of the other residents calmly spoke up: "He died last night." This led to a discussion of attitudes toward death as well as toward the dead man. It became apparent that most of the older persons had made some resolution of their feelings toward death. Subsequent talks with staff members, however, revealed much reluctance to discuss the concept.

Despite the universality of death, the subject has long been viewed as a taboo area, especially by the professionals in the health field who are closest to it—physicians, nurses, social workers, and others. As recently as 1963, a book on taboo topics of research was published which included the landmark paper by Dr. Herman Feifel on the meaning of death.[1]

As my conviction grew that the subject of dying and death had an important place in a graduate-school curriculum, I developed a course dealing with the psychological issues involved in dying and death in our society at Case Western Reserve University. Soon, I became the object of a curious interest on the part of colleagues. At a social gathering of faculty one evening, the host greeted me at the door and led me to the living room, where he introduced me: "And here is our Minister of Death." Students who were studying with me began to acquire a campus reputa-

---

1. N. L. Farberow (Ed.), *Taboo Topics* (New York: Atherton Press, 1963).

tion as eccentrics, as they often asked questions of friends about death, attitudes toward bereavement, and so on.

Now it is becoming apparent that there is a growing interest in the science of death, or "thanatology," as a legitimate area for study and research. The professional literature has begun to reflect the shattering of the "glass wall" (Lawrence LeShan's term) that has traditionally surrounded the scientific investigation of dying and death as a psychological and sociological process. An increasing number of journal articles and books on the subject are being published. A free quarterly newsletter, *Omega*, is being issued to facilitate communication among "death workers" (scientists and clinicians dealing with the psychological and sociological aspects of dying and bereavement).[2] The University of Minnesota has established a center for thanatological studies, and the Johns Hopkins University School of Medicine now has a suicidology program. In 1965, the first federally sponsored conference on terminal illness and impending death among the aged was held, and the 1968 class of medical students at Case Western Reserve University organized a symposium entitled "Death in Medicine: Treatment of Terminally Ill Patients," at which the speakers included a psychologist and a philosopher!

In order to present the current thinking of eminent clinicians and scientists in the field of thanatology to a wide audience of students in psychology, medicine, social work, nursing, speech pathology, religion, sociology, and other fields, I arranged a lecture series in Cleveland under the auspices of the Case Western Reserve University Department of Psychology.[3] The speakers in

---

2. R. A. Kalish & R. Kastenbaum (Eds.), *Omega: A Newsletter Concerned with Time Perspective, Death, and Bereavement* (Detroit: Wayne State University Psychology Department).

3. Supported by a grant from RRT-5, Rehabilitation Research and Training

that series are the contributors to this book. From their disparate backgrounds in medicine and nursing, sociology, and psychology, they have focused on existential aspects of dying and on the psychological and sociological aspects of the interaction between the dying person and the significant people during the last phase of his life—his healers and his family.

Leonard Pearson, Ph.D.
Berkeley, California

Center, Case Western Reserve University, funded by Social and Rehabilitation Service, U. S. Department of Health, Education, and Welfare.

Contents

Psychological Death

ROBERT KASTENBAUM

PSYCHOLOGICAL DEATH? This peculiar term refers to just one province within a most peculiar realm, what is coming to be known as the psychology of death. This larger realm of inquiry includes problems such as the following:

1) How does the idea of death develop from infancy through the entire lifespan?

2) How do ideas about death influence the way in which we conduct our lives?

3) How does the way in which we conduct our lives influence the timing and manner of our deaths?

4) What is the impact of impending and actual death upon the social structure that surrounds the individual?

5) What are the psychological structures and functions that operate during the preterminal or dying process?

This partial list includes some of the most significant questions in the psychology of death. The available answers are quite inadequate. At present we must rely overmuch on scattered research findings based on rudimentary and flawed techniques. Our interpretations or explanations tend to be vague and self-contradictory. Distinctions among facts, opinions, and formal hypotheses often are blurred, and seldom do we find systematic bridge-building between this wobbly new field of research and general psychology.

Some of the material presented here was derived from work supported by USPHS Mental Health Project MHO-1520 at Cushing Hospital, Framingham, Massachusetts.

The situation is even more unsatisfactory with regard to the topic of psychological death. Here we have merely a phrase, not an established, delimited content area. It is tempting to by-pass or dismiss this topic; there is already an abundance of elusive material in the more established subareas. Why should we perplex ourselves further with an odd assortment of observations and anecdotes? Well, perhaps we should not! There is no guarantee of an eventual "pay-off" in practical information, and little prospect of making substantial contributions on short order. Perhaps, however, we are capable of tolerating the uncertainties of such an exploration, allowing ourselves to be lured onward by the intrinsic interest of the subject matter even though most of the "data" lack proper credentials at present. Perhaps a temporary relaxation of our grim scruples will result in no lasting harm to our cognitive apparatus. Perhaps we can begin simply by making ourselves receptive to vague images of psychological death. Here comes the first image now.

Picture to yourself, if you will, that you are in contact with a dead organism, whether human or subhuman. You walk away — and a few minutes later the "dead" organism does likewise.

And here is a second image. We are coming into contact with an organism, creature, person who we know very well is alive. However, by the time the contact has been completed we have developed the strong impression that our partner in the transaction is not "really" alive. Legally and administratively there is no question that this person is alive; yet we cannot entirely persuade ourselves to regard him as a living soul.

Still another image. What we see now is a person whose behavior strikes us as being entirely stereotyped and routinized. He seems to be "going through the motions" and nothing more. We doubt that he is *experiencing* very much of either his inner or his outer world.

And just one more image. Bring to mind the image of somebody who appears to be much more than merely existing and carrying out the routine of life. Rather, he might be described as violently alive—unusually responsive, unusually spontaneous, displaying an extra zest, a true *joie de vivre*. In fact, our contact with him makes us feel, by comparison, stodgy and only partially alive.

These are among the images that should be clarified by the study of psychological death. Description of the phenomena generally is the first step in a new field of scientific investigation, a step that is followed eventually by efforts at classification. Still later, we would expect to discover empirical laws that relate the various phenomena to each other and to phenomena in other fields. Development of an integrative theoretical framework and applications to practical affairs usually await an advanced state of knowledge, although not invariably. Right now we are at the earliest possible stage of inquiry: the very existence of our subject matter has yet to be established! Thus we will be forced to deal with the topic of psychological death in a rough and preliminary manner, seeking mainly to describe its phenomena as they have impressed themselves upon us from various prescientific sources.

THANATOMIMESIS

Let us review the first image. This was the paradigm of an organism that is defunct, according to Observation A, but subsequently proves to be alive, according to Observation B. A phenomenon as formidable as this obviously deserves some long, fancy, and classical-sounding name. Accordingly, we have combined two Greek terms—*thanatos*, death, and *mimos*, imitation —into the designation *thanatomimesis*. We will define thanatomimetic phenomena as those which are likely to arouse in the perceiver the *false* impression that he is in relationship with a dead rather than a living organism.

Thanatomimesis has been observed in two-, four-, six-, and eight-footed creatures who occupy widely separated rungs on the ladder of life. No less an observer than Darwin, for example, recorded that some spiders, when intimidated, behave as if they had been struck dead. Darwin recompensed his experimental subjects by murdering them with camphor, which produced "an easy, slow death [Carrington & Meader, 1911, p. 56]." He concluded that spiders that he personally dispatched or that were found "naturally dead" did *not* assume the same positions as those that had given rather convincing thanatomimetic performances. These little studies gave Darwin new respect for spiders and, no doubt, gave spiders new respect for Darwin. Nevertheless, one might be hesitant to attribute death-feigning dynamics to a creature that is generally assumed to have no dynamics at all.

When we ascend several rungs on the ladder, however, it becomes possible to test the proposition that thanatomimetic behavior is adaptive or "purposeful." The animal most famous for "playing possum" is, of course, the opossum. Recently a trio of scientists in Los Angeles recruited fifteen opossums and planted electrodes in their skulls. The marsupials were then made central characters in an experimental drama. An artificial dog-jaw clenched and shook each opossum in his turn, the effect of realism being enhanced by the playing of recorded dog barks and growls through a high-fidelity system. All the opossums behaved in the expected way, i.e., they instantly transformed themselves into inert-looking balls of fur, putting on an entirely persuasive set of thanatomimetic performances. But during the time that an opossum was being thus terrorized, the continuous electroencephalographic recordings from his skull indicated that he was maintaining an *alert* cortical state. It was definitely *not* the case that the opossum had fallen into some type of involuntary, reflex-like condition. Additionally, the animals seemed to "know" when the danger had passed. Norton, Beran, and Misrahy (1964) replicated this phenomenon with a new set of "naive" opossums and a new set of dog-jaws that belonged to real dogs. Once again, it was found that the performance was accompanied by a heightened mental state, thereby strengthening the argument that subhuman organisms can use the appearance of death as an adaptive device to avoid actual death.

Human thanatomimesis is naturally of greater interest to us. Occasionally a person will feign death in the service of the same impulse that prompts the opossum. We are thinking, for example, of the wounded soldier who is attempting to avoid a fatal bayonet thrust when his position is overrun by the enemy. Deliberate feigning on the part of an untrained human is likely to be much less convincing than the thanatomimetic behavior that seems to come so easily to a number of animals. (Even with regard to the latter, however, it might be instructive to study the possibility that the death-feigning behavior is learned or imprinted.)

Paradoxically, it would appear that the most persuasive examples of human thanatomimetic behavior often are those which are inadvertent, i.e., the individual gives the impression of being dead when this was not his intention at all. Perhaps you have seen or read about some of the peculiar coffins that were designed and marketed in the United States, not very long ago. One such coffin featured a chain that was carefully placed in the hand of its tenant. Should the "corpse" return to life he would be able to tug at the chain, which in turn would sound a little bell. If one were to believe everything that has been reported about premature burials, then we would have to imagine the typical graveyard as being alive with feeble dings and dongs on a warm summer evening. Admittedly, it is difficult to believe *everything* that has been reported on this topic—but it is impossible to dismiss the copious and varied documentation of premature burials as being merely the product of a few superstitious, ignorant, or pathological minds.

This is not the place to exhume every report of interrupted or completed premature burial; a partial survey of this literature has been reported elsewhere (Kastenbaum & Aisenberg, in press). Perhaps it will be sufficient to offer a few generalizations that the interested reader might wish to pursue further:

1) There have been many reports in the medical, paramedical, and popular literature to the effect that people have been "taken for dead" and processed for burial when in fact they were still alive. Such reports were especially prevalent toward the end of the nineteenth century and in the early years of the twentieth.

2) Although many of these reports are to be doubted, it is probable that a substantial percentage of them were accurate.

3) Some of these instances probably can be attributed to shortcomings in medical knowledge and practice per se. It also seems likely, however, that *culturally sanctioned patterns of behavior* contributed to the frequency of thanatomimetic situations. We have particular reference to states of being that now have a rather old-fashioned aura around them, for example, "catalepsy," "trance," "ecstasy." Young women were simply performing in accordance with the fashion when they swooned with emotion. A good swooner and a hasty undertaker made a bad combination.

4) Somewhat apart from the question of how prevalent genuine premature burials might have been, it seems clear that many

people were disturbed by the possibility that such an error might be made in their own case. Trick coffins were among the precautions that made sense to people who had been exposed to direct experiences or unnerving reports of inadvertent thanatomimesis.

5) We are probably justified in accepting the reassurances given to us by contemporary physicians, funeral directors, etc. Nevertheless, what has already come to light does emphasize the point that direct perception and even examination by professionals can be in error.

Thanatomimesis of the sort that may have once launched premature burials seems to be a phenomenon that is rapidly becoming buried in the past. However, the traditional assumption that death is a forthright and monolithic condition—something that one can determine at a glance—is coming in for even more substantial attack. New developments in the art and science of resuscitation—for example, the recent advances in heart transplants—are leading to continuous revisions in the definition of death. Every time a new method of intervention is introduced we have also a new perception of the (possibly) deceased organism. Where a physician or biologist would have judged "dead" a few years ago, we now sometimes hear the significant variant: "*clinical* death—on with the next step!" The concept of clinical death is supported by literally hundreds of experiments, most of them recent, and most of them summarized by Negovskii (1962). In retrospect, then, many souls who were consigned to the graveyard *properly* on the basis of then current knowledge may have been only in the state of clinical death by the most advanced standards of today. Viewed in this way, it is not inconceivable that the reported number of premature burials was an *under*-estimation (and perhaps still is).

As we turn this first image of psychological death over and

over in our minds other facets continue to appear. Let us catalogue two more of them for future reference:

1) Deliberate self-induction of a thanatomimetic state as an exercise in "mind-over-body" mastery. The highly accomplished practitioner of yoga would be an important example here, although not the only example (Herbert, 1961). And he would have to be carefully distinguished from the skillful "magician" who may succeed in providing the thanatomimetic impression by illusion without actually inducing any substantial alteration in his psychobiological functioning.

2) "Playing dead" by children and possibly even by infants. It would be especially instructive to examine these behaviors with regard to their role in working through emotional challenges and helping the child come to terms with the concept of death.

In summary, we have taken a first look at a phenomenon that occurs in a wide variety of organisms and under a wide variety of circumstances. The unifying thread is a matter of discrepant perceptual frameworks: (for whatever reason) an organism yields the impression (to whatever observer) of being dead (however the observer defines death). But a second set of observations (second observer, same observer a second time, or whatever) yields an impression contradictory to the first. This is what we mean by thanatomimesis. The hard empirical and conceptual work lies ahead.

PHENOMENOLOGICAL DEATH

The second image of psychological death involves the recognition that we are in contact with an organism that is *not* dead, but complicated by observations which lead us to doubt that the organism is *really* alive. This condition might be classified as a special form of thanatomimesis in that we derive the impression of a deathlike state as it applies to one sector of the organism: its inner life or phenomenological state. However, it might be clearer for the present purposes to consider *phenomenological death* as a separate condition. It is one of the two major conditions which, in our opinion, make up the second image of psychological death.

Let us first consider an "ideal" case of phenomenological death. The body of a human being is "alive enough" to forestall the completion of a death certificate. Yet the feeble indices of life are being maintained only by so-called heroic measures, administered by a hospital staff that has the latest equipment at its disposal. The person inside the body gives absolutely no indication of his continued existence. He does not utter sounds either spontaneously or in response to our words. As far as we can determine, all attempts to communicate with him fail completely. To make this picture even more definitive let us say that electroencephalographic recordings indicate that all forms of cerebral activity associated with phenomenological life are absent. And so it is that we feel unable to classify this body as dead, but also unable to classify this person as alive.

This in-between condition generates numerous medical, administrative, legal, ethical, psychological, and social problems, most of which are far from resolved (see, for example, Fletcher, 1960; Hamlin, 1964; Kalish, 1965). Applying a designation such as phenomenological death to the condition does not solve any of the problems. But it does help to establish the condition as having a certain definable status in its own right instead of being merely a vaporous neither-this-nor-that. And we are more likely now to discover continuities between "all-alive" and "all-dead."

A person can also give us the impression of being phenomenologically dead even if the circumstances are not as extreme as those we have used for illustration. Observers may differ widely in the criteria they require before they consider that phenomenological death is an appropriate appellation. Personnel who work intensively with the chronically ill encounter many situations which raise the question of phenomenological death. Here are a few examples from our experiences with geriatric patients at Cushing Hospital:

1) The possible effect of psychotropic drugs on elderly patients was studied in a controlled and fairly intensive manner. The investigation involved a series of clinical interviews and testing procedures administered before and during periods of drug administration (Kastenbaum, Slater, & Aisenberg, 1964; Slater & Kastenbaum, 1966). Apart from specific clinical and test findings, a number of the interviewers showed qualitative changes in the way they viewed their patients. In essence, they were saying, "I am *now* dealing with a person." One of my own patients gave me a clear example of this alteration. During the pre-drug sessions this octogenarian widow spoke only in stereotyped phrases and generally seemed to be in a fog. She would seem to attend briefly to my remarks or the test materials, but soon would withdraw into picking invisible objects off her dress or into a vacant immobility. Withal, she did not strike me as being depressed or anxious; the woman simply "wasn't there," as other interviewers sometimes reported about their patients.

In general, the drug effects were provocative with respect to their theoretical implications, but quite modest with respect to their direct therapeutic benefits. The relevant point for us is that a minority of patients, including this woman, gave the impression of a return to life. It took a few minutes before the realization dawned on me that I was now in contact with a real person. She had feelings, opinions, fragments of memory, and an interest in the immediate situation. Not only did her thought and behavior still bear the signs of obvious impairment, but she now was a troubled person—indignant, lonely, affection-craving, bewildered. Although her phenomenological life would have to be described largely in negative or dysphoric terms, there was no longer any question that "something was going on" inside.

Experiences such as these made us realize that there were times when we had in fact assumed the presence of phenomenological death without making this judgment explicit in our own minds. It was our occasional witness to a revival performance that brought this condition to our attention.

2) In clinical practice with institutionalized geriatric patients one occasionally has an encounter similar to those which emerged from the drug study. The most salient example in my own experience concerns another octogenarian widow. "Mrs. Kiley" suffered from hypertensive heart disease, cerebral arteriosclerosis, and chronic brain syndrome. She had been grossly disoriented since her admission three years earlier. Her verbal behavior (one would hesitate to describe it as conversation) consisted largely of alternating between two stereotyped phrases, delivered in a high-pitched, whining voice: "I'm cold, cold!" and "I want to go home, home!" Unlike the woman previously described, Mrs. Kiley did show affect (regressed), and a bright, intent quality in her eyes suggested that she maintained an interest in the immediate situation.

We would not have described this person as being phenomenologically dead. But *somebody* had suffered a phenomenological death, namely , the person that Mrs. Kiley once had been. An unusually persistent clinical interview finally succeeded in breaking through the stereotypy: "In what probably would have been my final effort to 'get through' to her, I started to move away from her, then came back, drew very close, and said, 'You are alone and grieving, and nobody knows how miserable you feel.' The voice in reply said, 'I *am*.' It was a well-controlled, low-pitched adult voice. There followed . . . an actual conversation in which Mrs. Kiley spoke clearly about her grief over the death of husband and son. However, this depressed but 'normal' conversation was interrupted several times by squirming, shivering, and whining—alterations with State One. Mrs. Kiley would return to her more mature self when I gained permission through her dominant, regressed self. In subsequent interviews I have generally succeeded in contacting the more mature self by simply requesting, 'Speak to me in your *real* voice' [Kastenbaum, 1964, pp. 17–18]."

The most relevant point for us is that (for whatever reason) a person can lose (temporarily or permanently) the distinctive qualities by which we know him. These qualities can be replaced by an alternative psychological organization so different from the previous one that we consider ourselves to be in contact with quite another "self." In the case cited, we had been under the impression that the original and relatively normal or mature self had departed permanently. Its replacement was not even a reasonable facsimile of the former Mrs. Kiley, but it did seem to possess at least a rudimentary form of phenomenological life.

3) With the valuable assistance of three colleagues,[1] I was able to conduct a small but systematic inquiry into the situation of geriatric patients whose functioning was on the low end of the behavioral spectrum. As this clinical investigation has now been described in some detail elsewhere (Kastenbaum & Aisen-

---

1. Paul T. Costa, Jr., William Dalton, and William McKenna.

berg, in press), let us just consider the basic procedure and major impressions. Preliminary observations were made of the least responsive, most impaired patients in this 650-bed geriatric hospital. We then developed a typology of Low Level Behavior Syndromes. Four patterns of behavior were distinguished, each pattern being reduced to a set of readily observable conditions. The lowest levels (Type I and Type II) were regarded provisionally as "the living dead"—i.e., it was with such patients that the question of phenomenological death and other forms of psychological death was most apt to arise. The definition of the Type I syndrome is given below to exemplify the approach; this definition also served as the guide for observers' classification efforts.

A patient was classified in Type I when he met the following criteria:

1) In bed
2) Supine
3) Mouth open
4) Eyes closed or with empty stare
5) Head tilted back
6) Arms straight at side
7) Absence of adjustive movements, fidgeting, speech, verbalization, etc.
8) General impression of having been fixed or molded into position

More than two hundred patients were observed both morning and afternoon on three successive days (supplementary studies were later pursued). Each rating session had two clearly demarcated phases: Observation and Confrontation. In the first phase the rater approached the patient but did not attempt to initiate an interaction. In the second phase the rater did attempt to engage the attention of the patient and develop at least a rudimentary sort of relationship. Separate ratings were made for each phase.

What did we learn? Perhaps the most significant finding was that the impression of phenomenological death—no matter how convincing the external behavior or posture may be—cannot be taken as a trustworthy index of the subject's actual inner state. Roughly half the time that a Type I or Type II patient was approached, his response to the contact was sufficient to call for a revised (upward) rating for the Confrontation phase.

Observations in the realm of psychological death are not always innocuous or academic. If we judge "dead" when we are beholding a thanatomimetic performance we may inadvertently become accomplices in hastening death. Similarly, if we judge "phenomenologically dead" and are mistaken, then we are all too likely to do harm that we do not intend. Unfortunate effects of a false positive judgment include omissions: the physician, nurse, chaplain, or relative refrains from words, deeds, contacts that might have registered upon and comforted the patient. Errors of commission are also more prevalent than they need be: the patient's condition or other emotionally loaded topics are discussed cynically or inappropriately in his presence, as though he were not there; he is handled as an object rather than as a person.

SOCIAL DEATH

Much of what has already been said about psychological death requires careful attention not only to the condition of the subject, but also to the words and actions of those who are in relationship with him. Suppose that we were in a situation that provided us with an inadequate vantage point. We know that a human body is in the vicinity but are unable to determine with our own eyes whether this is a living person or a corpse. A concrete example would be the receiving room of a busy general hospital that has just taken delivery of several people who were involved in an automobile accident. How would we attempt to judge the condition of any particular human body? Most likely we would fix our eyes upon the hospital personnel. What are they doing? Do they communicate an air of urgency or of indifference? Do they treat the patients as people or as objects? Naturally, we might misinterpret the actions of the staff in either direction. The point, however, is that the behavior of others comprises an important dimension of psychological death. We will say that a person is *socially dead* when there is an absence of those behaviors that we would expect to be directed toward a living person and the presence of those behaviors that we would expect when dealing with a deceased or nonexistent person.

Voodoo death, so-called, is a dramatic example of social death, although we seldom see it in obvious forms in our own culture. Action taken by a powerful individual in the community or by the community as a whole can amount to a symbolic execution. There may even be a mock (but serious) funeral ceremony performed while the "deceased" is still very much alive physically and phenomenologically. After the funeral, the place of the "deceased" in his community is declared vacant; his property, titles, privileges, obligations, etc., pass to other hands. Physical death of the victim is said to occur as the usual consequence, but without any direct attack being made upon him. He perishes for lack of shelter and sustenance, perhaps, or, more romantically, because of anomie, a broken heart, existential despair, or sheer determination to conform to social expectations. Whether or not the victim does in fact perish and for whatever reason, the phenomenon of social death is complete on its own level. Interesting suggestions have been offered regarding the mechanisms of so-called voodoo death (Barber, 1961; Cannon, 1942) and the possibility that we might sometimes be "hexing" each other in daily life (Weisman & Hackett, 1963), but we cannot pursue these bypaths here.

Social death can also be in evidence when there is still general agreement that the person in question is physically and phenomenologically alive. An individual might be "cut dead" by his peers, even by his intimates, if he is thought to have committed some fundamental breach of conduct. This process of excommunication does not require a mock funeral or other elaborate ritual. We simply do not admit the offender to our dwelling place or seek him out. We have no more communication with him than we would have with a dead person. An adolescent may approach his classmates only to find them looking away or past him, continuing their conversation as though he had not appeared on the scene. He is socially dead (for the moment, at least). It is obvious that social death (one component of which is "the silent treatment") can be an effective way of influencing the behavior of group members who have not conformed with the dominant values.

Any course of events which removes an individual from community life to institutional residence also has the possibility of rendering him socially dead. Since they took Joe up the hill (or up the river) we do not speak about him any more. He is "as good as dead" behind the thick walls of ————. (Here we fill in the name of any institution which, in our own social circle, is regarded as a symbol of shameful withdrawal from the proper patterns of human existence. The "lunatic asylum" has often been such an institution, but by no means the only one.)

A person may come to be classified as socially dead precisely because he has *not* died. We are thinking of the man who has lived well beyond his prime. Ripe in age, he may find himself increasingly detached and disenfranchised from his social context. The built-in protection that has helped to maintain the social integration of elders in so-called primitive societies (Rosow, 1967) seldom applies in our society. Instead, the elder is becoming ever more a candidate for placement in a special setting, a rest home, nursing home, geriatric hospital, or whatever. This is not the place to analyze the gerontopolis per se (Bennett & Nahemow, 1965; Kastenbaum, 1969). We simply wish to call attention to the observation that "significant others" may regard the elder as being socially dead once he has been admitted to an age-segregated institution. When the implicit judgment of social death accompanies institutionalization, we are likely to see that families and acquaintances now make a variety of decisions that once would have involved the opinions and desires of the elder. He is no longer consulted, even if it is his own pet dog or cat that is involved. Communications with the elder are likely to become attenuated and may vanish entirely except for required administrative or legal purposes. The elder himself is likely to experience keenly his new status as being dead to the outside world. Let me emphasize that these dynamics are not inevitable, nor do they occur in all cases; furthermore, social death of the elderly, when it does take place, can often be reversed.

There is an important and little-understood variation on the theme of social death. Here is one example that comes to mind: In central Poland there existed a small town whose population was largely Jewish. The residents viewed the rise of Nazi Germany with an apprehension that proved all too justified. During these months of apprehension, several important members of the Jewish community died of natural causes. But the community did not accept these deaths, much in the way that a corporation or government might refuse to accept a letter of resignation. The deceased citizens remained socially alive. They retained their vote and their opinion in community matters (by proxy and inference, of course). The same care was taken to treat these valued dead as being socially alive as is taken in other circumstances to treat devalued living as socially dead. It was as though the community could not afford to lose the strength represented by these people.

Does this reaction have anything in common with our own thoughts, feelings, and behaviors in the wake of President Kennedy's assassination? How many of us found it difficult to believe and behave in accordance with the sudden reality of his death? How often, in fact, does news of a death elicit the response, "Oh, no—it couldn't be." Acknowledging the death of a valued and significant person is not a simple and automatic adjustment. Perhaps we *always* must work through a phase during which we maintain the emotional belief that the deceased is still alive, and during which this belief conveys itself in our actions. For the suddenly bereaved, the physically and phenomenologically dead may remain socially alive.

ALIVE AND LIVELY

The first two images of psychological death led us to brief exploration of thanatomimesis, phenomenological death, and social death. Even more briefly, the last two images will take us beyond psychological death per se. Now we are concerned with the quality of lived experience in people whose physical, phenomenological, and social life is not in serious question. The third image, as you will recall, was that of a person whose behavior strikes us as being entirely stereotyped, routinized. He is merely going through the motions. The ability to classify him in this manner is dependent upon our appreciation of a fourth and, if you like, higher image: the person who is vibrantly or violently alive, enjoying a high rate of exchange with his environment, zestful, responsive, and spontaneous. Had we no direct or indirect experience with the final image, then we might be willing to accept the condition of "not dead" as equivalent to "fully alive." But there is a difference.

The distinction between merely plodding along and being fully alive has been celebrated by many poets and philosophers. Curiously enough, it is also a pertinent theme in contemporary "mass culture." Billboards invite us to "Come alive!" by drinking a sweet, carbonated beverage. Other invitations to achieve the same purpose are issued *sub rosa*: "Want to be turned on, man? Try this . . ." Marijuana, LSD, and other drugs may have particular appeal for people whose phenomenological life has been clouded by depression and other negative affects. Feeling themselves to be "numb" or even "dead," they may be hopeful that a simple, almost magical, act will raise them from the depths to the heights. Numbed by despair, these unfortunates sometimes appear to occupy a place on the life-death continuum slightly above phenomenological death per se, but below that of routine, functional consciousness.

But the prospect of being "turned on" also seems appealing to many people whose level of experiencing is what would ordinarily be regarded as "normal" or unimpaired. Some are lured by psychedelia, others hearken to messages delivered via "respectable" mass media. The common element seems to be the implication that the solid citizen is missing something. It is no longer enough to be a "success." The person who has attained the traditional middle-class goals—education, a good job, status in the community, "wholesome" family life—is now invited to doubt whether all this is enough. Is there perhaps another and somehow more valuable or higher level of functioning that is just beyond one's reach? Has "success" become a "drag" rather than the state of true self-fulfillment?

It is obvious that not everybody has these doubts, but it does seem to me that doubters are becoming ever more numerous, perhaps in direct proportion to the number of people who are "making it" in terms of the traditional goals of success in middle-class United States. Perhaps the old-fashioned "quest for human perfection" has returned to its starting-place—inner experience—after a lengthy and rather successful affair with material reality. Rather than inflict my murky and convoluted ideas upon the reader, let me simply suggest that an explanation for the heightening concern with inner experience might be sought in the vicissitudes of the so-called Protestant ethic (Weber, 1948). In short: for many years we have been influenced by the belief that our "salvation" is to be attained through material achievements, and we have tended to judge ourselves and others by this standard. The astonishing development of technological production during the last hundred years or so might then be regarded as a product of a psychological need that is "spiritual" in character.

Without unrolling the whole blanket of speculation, may I simply suggest the following points to bring the Protestant ethic up to date:

1) Technological development is now more or less taken for granted. Accordingly, it has lost much of its character of a "new frontier" and its attraction for our imaginations and energies.

2) Yet we are likely to retain the restless sense that we must

"move ahead" along some dimension. This attitude is so deep-rooted that we (the present generation) feel uneasy or guilty if we are not working toward "bonus points" for achievement. (Later generations might well be less subject to this attitude.)

3) And we are also likely to be struck by the discrepancy between our own inner experience and the external forms of the society we have helped to create. It is one thing to feel exhausted or dulled after a long day of routine but demanding work, whether in the fields, at the factory, or at home. But what if one feels empty or bored in front of the color television set or racing along the highways in an "exciting" new car? It is as though the experimental animal has finally reached its goal box but now does not enjoy the meal it worked so hard to reach.

4) We might then expect that the products of our society would be promoted increasingly on the basis of their alleged resonance with desired qualities of inner experience (psychological aliveness) rather than upon external qualities (e.g., status-value). This trend seems to be in evidence already. Note how many soft drinks, automobiles, toothpastes, etc., are being dubbed with qualities that are appropriate for *human* experience. The soft drink is "wild," the car is a "youngmobile," the toothpaste has "sex appeal." We drab, under-living creatures can have some of these desirable attributes rub off on us by magical association. Who will be the first to market Nirvana Toothpaste?

5) Accordingly, an increasing number of us may be experiencing what is virtually a sense of moral necessity to get "with it." The "it" now has something vaguely to do with our own level of experiencing life rather than with material accomplishments.

Let me pretend that I am not embarrassed by the simplifications and distortions involved in the preceding outline, and conclude with a quick suggestion as to the attitude one might take regarding the "Come alive!" movement, if such there be.

The easiest attitudes to adopt are those of amusement, disapproval, or condescension. Some of us flounder pretty badly as we seek to enrich our phenomenological lives. We can wag our heads at those who explore psychedelia, practice yoga, embark upon risky activities such as parachute-jumping, or obey the current suggestions for self-fulfillment offered by the mass media. But is there not a more appropriate and productive attitude to take? In point of fact, neither psychology nor any of the other behavioral and social sciences have done much to clarify the nature of psychological aliveness. It is scarcely recognized as part of our subject matter. We do not know precisely what it is (though often enough it seems to be a function that diminishes markedly from spontaneous childhood to staid adulthood), nor do we know what methods and conditions might be most conducive to creating such a state of being. Lacking the knowledge that would permit us to move directly and unerringly toward a greater degree of psychological aliveness, we might do well to keep an open mind on the subject, looking for opportunities to learn. Almost anything that a person might do to increase his phenomenological life could look peculiar to somebody else. Perhaps we should be tolerant of the groping efforts that we ourselves and others are making. It is too much to expect perfection in the pursuit of perfection.

FOR THE FUTURE

Virtually every statement that has been made in this preliminary exploration of psychological death requires much further explication and verification. Furthermore, most of the implications for theory and practice have been passed by with little or no comment. These defects will not be remedied here. Instead I would like to invite critical attention to several interrelated propositions that have been offered.

It has been suggested that life and death might be regarded as a continuum rather than as a dichotomy. This proposition is closely linked with the assumption of epistemological relativity: we know something only through the specific operations we have employed in entering into contact with it. Thus, a person may or may not be known as dead (in any of the senses of this term) depending upon the specific observational framework involved. The very definition of death becomes limited to specifiable sets of perceptual observations. Another way of saying this is that "death" (and "life") become of decreased scientific value as general concepts. We have as many degrees of deathness or lifeness as we can support with careful observations and as we find useful to recognize. If we accept the assumption of epistemological relativity, then we are also, in effect, agreeing that life and death are relative. No single definition based upon a single observational framework could be selected as *the* death perception.

The principle we are talking about is, of course, quite familiar in the philosophy of science and seems to have won acceptance in most fields of investigation. But when psychological inquiry is our focus, it seems necessary to elaborate upon this position in one particular direction, the interpersonal. Our observations about life and death (especially in the senses used here) depend upon somebody's perception of somebody else. On the strict interpretation we are not entitled to say: "Person A is dead." This statement implicitly locates "death" inside Person A, or makes "death" in some way wholly an attribute of A. What we can conclude is: "Death occurred between Persons A and B." In other words, that pattern of behaviors or "nonbehaviors" which we have agreed to define as death was manifested during the time that B, the observer, was in contact with A. An observer who is located outside the A-B interaction will have still another observational framework to contribute. His conclusion might be: "No behavior characteristic of life was witnessed during the period of observation. Hence, a death situation prevailed (behaviorally defined)." If we press him to tell us, "But *who* was dead?" then he would simply report the logical alternatives: "A was dead—perhaps; but it could be that B was dead. Or that both were dead. All that I can properly conclude is that a death *situation* prevailed; the terms lose their moorings to direct observation when I try to attribute an aspect of the total situation to one element within the situation."

We have far from exhausted the logical possibilities of this approach to defining and observing death, although we may be perilously close to exhausting the patience of the reader. But it should be clear that the very definition of death can be psychologized to the extent that we have no absolute, a priori knowledge to fall back on—and all this in the name of science. This leads us to another related point: the nonreversibility of death. Several of the examples given earlier involved an apparent "return to life." The traditional way of interpreting these phenomena would be to maintain that Observation A ("He is dead") was in error *because* Observation B ("He is alive") was made more recently or made from a different level of perception (e.g., detection of faint heartbeat). But if the line of reasoning offered here were to be applied relentlessly, then we would have to say that we have two different observations that cannot be reduced to either one. We are assuming that what we mean by death (whether in the physical, phenomenological, or social sense) has been carefully specified for the occasion. A person *is* observed as dead using the most precise and stringent procedures to meet the consensual criteria. But other, equally trustworthy, observations indicate that the person is alive. We cannot overrule either observation and still pretend to be consistent with our own ground rules about scientific methodology.

Employing this approach we might have to abandon the deductive (and absolute) conclusion that a person is dead—if by death we still mean "nonreversible." We would be limited to inductive probability statements (just as in other areas of research). We cannot rule out the possibility that the "dead" person could be observed by some frame of reference not presently available or known to us (e.g., a more refined biochemical test, or ordinary perception five minutes or five years from now.) Absurd-sounding possibilities abound here. One might argue that we do not know *for sure* that anybody has ever died. If death is a nonreversible state (i.e., a state whose existence could not possibly be contradicted by any observation that might be made at any level by any observer at any time), then we would have to wait until the final observation has, in fact, been made. Judgment Day?

We suggest a simpler alternative: do not confound the empirical definition of death as we wish to use this concept in psychological, medical, sociological work, etc., with the nonempirical, formalistic definition of death. This latter definition has its place, but perhaps not in the scientific investigation of death. Let us limit the concept of death (physical, psychological, or whatever) to those observations that actually are within our purview. "Nonreversibility," in any absolute sense, is not within our purview.

Perhaps these remarks have merely served to conform to your expectations that psychological death is a murky, forbidding, and unrewarding area of inquiry, if, indeed, it may even be said to exist. Yet it is difficult to see how we are ever to attain a complete psychology of the human person without taking very much into account the extremes of functioning from the vibrant, exhilarating heights to the last flickerings within the phenomenological world.

References

Barber, T. X. Death by suggestion: A critical note. *Psychosom. Med.*, 1961, *23*, 153–155.

Bennett, R., & Nahemow, L. Institutional totality and criteria of social adjustment in residences for the aged. *J. Soc. Issues*, 1965, *21*, 44–78.

Cannon, W. B. "Voodoo death." *Amer. Anthrop.*, 1942, *44*, 169–73.

Carrington, J., & Meader, C. *Death, its causes and phenomena.* New York: Dodd, Mead, 1911.

Fletcher, J. The patient's right to die. *Harper's Magazine*, October 1960, pp. 139–43.

Hamlin, H. Life or death by EEG. *J.A.M.A.*, 1964, *190*, 112–14.

Herbert, C. Life-influencing interactions. In A. Simon, C. Herbert, & R. Straus (Eds.), *The physiology of emotions.* Springfield, Ill.: Charles C Thomas, 1961. Pp. 187–209.

Kalish, R. A. The aged and the dying process: The inevitable decisions. *J. Soc. Issues*, 1965, *21*(4), 87–96.

Kastenbaum, R. Multiple personality in later life—a developmental interpretation. *Gerontologist*, 1964, *4*, 16–20.

Kastenbaum, R. Beer, wine, and mutual gratification in the gerontopolis. In D. P. Kent, S. Sherwood, & R. Kastenbaum (Eds.), *Research, planning and action for the elderly: The power and potential of social science.* New York: Behavioral Publications, 1969.

Kastenbaum, R., & Aisenberg, R. B. *The psychology of death.* New York: Springer, in press. (See Chapters 2 and 3 especially.)

Kastenbaum, R., Slater, P. E., & Aisenberg, R. B. Toward a conceptual model of geriatric psychopharmacology: An experiment with thioridazine and dextro-amphetamine. *Gerontologist*, 1964, *4*, 68–71.

Negovskii, V. A. *Resuscitation and artificial hypothermia.* New York: Consultants Bureau, 1962.

Norton, A. C., Beran, A. V., & Misrahy, G. A. Experiment summarized in *Sci. Amer.*, 1964, *211*, 64.

Rosow, I. *Social integration of the aged.* New York: Free Press, 1967.

Slater, P. E., & Kastenbaum, R. Paradoxical effects of drugs: Some personality and ethnic correlates. *J. Amer. Geriat. Soc.*, 1966, *14*, 1016–34.

Weber, M. *The Protestant ethic and the spirit of capitalism.* New York: Scribner's, 1948.

Weisman, A. D., & Hackett, T. "Hexing" in modern medicine. In *Proceedings of the Third World Congress of Psychiatry.* Montreal: McGill University Press, 1963. Pp. 1249–52.

Psychotherapy and the Dying Patient

LAWRENCE LE SHAN

Death is a dialogue between
The spirit and the dust.
"Dissolve," says Death. The Spirit, "Sir,
I have another trust."

Emily Dickinson

W E HAVE NOT AS YET FOUND a useful way of conceptualizing the life and death forces within the individual. We are forced by a wide variety of clinical data to assume that some individuals "wish" to live more than others and that this desire has—at least in certain instances—a definite effect upon the resistance of the body to stress and to disease processes. These data appear to indicate the existence of a "will to live," but it has not been possible to further define this in ways that would be widely accepted and pragmatically useful.

The limits of the effect of the patient's desire to live—upon his body in health and disease—are simply not known. All we know is that these limits are much wider than was generally be-

Expanded from D. M. Kissen & L. L. LeShan (Eds.), *Psychosomatic Aspects of Neoplastic Disease: The Proceedings of the Third International Conference of the International Psychosomatic Cancer Study Group.* International Psychosomatic Cancer Study Group, 1964. Pp. 109–20. This work was made possible by a research grant from Frederick Ayer II. The writer wishes to express his deep appreciation to Marthe Gassmann, M.D., who served as control therapist for these psychotherapies and contributed greatly to these formulations. Eda LeShan, M.A., also has made major contributions to this work and has the writer's gratitude.

lieved twenty-five years ago. Most physicians today believe that the patient's will to live is an important factor in the pathogenesis of serious illness at least. In addition to clinical data, a wide variety of reports, ranging from studies of voodoo death to Weisman and Hackett's excellent paper on "Predilection to Death" (1961), to Booth's important papers on disease (1962a and 1962b), and to studies of the effect of personality on cancer (e.g., LeShan, 1959), all attest to the importance of this factor.

Although our basic concepts in this area are very far from clear, there *are* certain things we can say.[1] In this essay, I shall be concerned with the problem of increasing the will to live in the physically ill patient. It is drawn from twelve years' experience with a wide variety of cancer patients, including over five thousand hours of intensive individual psychotherapy (see, for example, LeShan, 1952–1960, 1964; LeShan & Gassmann, 1958; LeShan & LeShan, 1961; LeShan, Marvin, & Lyerly, 1959; LeShan & Reznikoff, 1960; LeShan & Worthington, 1956a, 1956b).

In addition to the possible effect on pathogenesis, a second consideration in mobilizing the patient's will to live is the personal value to the patient. In the growth, self-exploration, and self-acceptance which the attempt itself brings (LeShan & Le

---

1. Beecher (1962), in an excellent discussion of the problem of psychological factors in disease, has stated: "It is rather paradoxical that, while the group of non-specific forces which surround disease remains ill-defined, it is now possible to deal specifically, precisely, even quantitatively, with some of the components of the group. . . . Thus we can state a new principle of drug action: some agents are effective only in the presence of a required mental state. . . . These matters lead us inescapably to certain ethical problems. When the absence or presence of disease, when the efficacy or failure of treatment can be determined by those non-specific factors, we clearly have no right to escape the obligation to plan our diagnosis and therapy on a sound basis which takes into account these non-specific factors insofar as this is possible today."

Shan, 1961), he becomes a fuller and richer person. He does not die defeated and beaten by life, but as a stronger and more complete individual.[2] The growth of the self is of value irrelevant to the passage of chronological time. If we believe in the value of the individual and the sacred character of human life, our concern does not stop as death approaches. The responsibility of the psychotherapist (or of the physician or of the pastor) is not limited to certain stages of development.

In a special sense, we come here to the philosophical problem of the relationships between life and death. It is not possible within the confines of this essay to enter into a serious discussion of this central problem. However, it is essential in this work for the therapist to have come to terms with it for himself. His view will have critical consequences for his work with seriously ill patients. The general medical viewpoint that death is *never* appropriate must be examined carefully. If held in this work (with its implication of an absolute separation between the two), it also tends to prevent the greater acceptance of life. The psychotherapist becomes more concerned with blocking death than with enriching life. The viewpoint that has seemed to make the most sense to the writer is that life and death are both aspects of the same *vital* center, the same existence. (Who would save Socrates from the hemlock or Winkelried from the spears?)[3] In working to increase the will to live, we are also

---

2. Bell (1961) quotes Seneca: "The longest necessary life is until a man is wise." Our goal is not only to reawaken the inner life, but also to help liberate those inner forces which can enable the patient to experience as fully as possible the meaning of his life and death.

3. Consider these lines of Emily Dickinson:
> A death-blow is a life-blow to some who,
> Till they died, did not alive become;
> Who, had they lived, had died, but when they died,
> Vitality began.

working to increase the "being," the "person," the "soul," in whatever aspect it is or it will exist.

Edgar Jackson (1963, p. 48) has contrasted the views symbolized by Asclepius and Hygeia. The approach of Asclepius was toward healing the sick person through the medical arts of repairing damage and restoring disordered functioning. Hygeia, on the other hand, symbolized that quality of wholeness that moved a person toward the realization of his nature as a being endowed with health. In work with the seriously ill it appears to be one task of the psychotherapist to bring Hygeia to the aid of Asclepius—to help the patient explore his own inner nature, his own potential, not only because the exploration can have meaning for the patient but because it may enable him to cooperate more fully with his physician. We can help the patient find and accept his own being and path; to sing his own individual song, to play in life the special music of his unique personality. As the individual moves asymptotically in this direction, his fear of death lessens even though his physical condition may stay the same or become worse.

The patient whose will to live is very weak in a catastrophic situation (except where this has been brought about by extreme physical fatigue and debility) is almost invariably an individual whose will to live was weak before he became ill.[4] The "presenting symptom" does not give a true picture. An attempt to solve the problem as if it were a result of the illness will have little success. Help is really needed in terms of how to live, not how to die. It might seem that it is a strange and wrong time (when the patient is severely ill) to tackle the deep problems of how to make the most of one's being. This is far from the truth. It is only

---

4. Kierkegaard (1954): "If a person is at one moment in despair, this shows he has been in despair his whole life."

by going as quickly as possible to the real problems of the patient's life, to the questions of his existence that he has been unable to answer in a satisfactory way, that the will to live may be awakened and mobilized. The therapist must show himself, by his approach, not daunted by either the minor problem (the fear of death) or the major problem (the fear of life). If he can make this clear, the patient can frequently begin to move—often with surprising rapidity—in the search for his own strengths and what has blocked them.[5]

Therapy should not raise false hopes. The concentration should be more on the expansion and freeing of the self than on physical recovery. Where the therapist has the courage to say in effect, "We do not know what the outcome will be, but we do our best; the psychological work you and I do here can only be beneficial in any case," he will generally find this acceptable to the patient.

Patients may fight for life for different reasons. The two reasons we see most frequently are the fear of death and the wish to live. Clinical experience seems to indicate rather strongly that, in serious physical illness, the fear of death is not a very powerful tool. It does not appear to bind the resources of the individual together and to increase host resistance to pathological processes. The wish to live appears to be a much stronger weapon for this purpose and to bring more of the total organism of the patient to the side of the physician. In mobilizing this wish to live we must have goals in the future which are deeply important to the

---

5. This approach—the search for the patient's strengths and what has blocked them—makes far more sense to these patients than does a therapy attitude which concentrates on the search for psychopathology and its causes. It gives the patients much more self-respect, strength, and hope—hope not so much for physical improvement but for that spiritual improvement (in Maslow's term, "self-actualization") that is the real core of our concern for ourselves. Shortly before she died a patient sent her therapist a Christmas card. On it she wrote simply, "Thank you for being my ally." She did not mean ally against her husband or others but in the battle for her own being.

patient. We need an ideal to work toward. Maslow (1962, p. 4) has pointed out that each culture has its ideal individual. These include the "hero," the "saint," the "knight," the "mystic," the "gentleman." In our time we tend to have given these up. Our ideal is rather the "well-adjusted man." But who would work hard and long, suffer pain, fight for life in order to be "well-adjusted"? The ideal, however, of the full, rich self, the development of one's own being in one's own special way, the freedom to be oneself fully without fear—this is a goal acceptable to our *Zeitgeist* and worth fighting and suffering for. It is literally a goal worth living for. Patients, once they grasp this goal, seem to find it so.

It is not easy (or, with present knowledge, always possible) to make this goal seem attainable to patients who may long since have given up hope of achieving it. Generally patients who have lost the wish to live have already judged and condemned their inner selves. One patient, for example, had been told that he had a fatal malignancy and was going to die by a certain date. Under a new type of treatment (E. Revici's "guided chemotherapy"—Revici, 1961) his cancer diminished and disappeared. As he was about to be discharged from the hospital, he said to his physician: "Doctor, you may not be aware of it, but my biggest problem was not that I was going to die. It's what to do with my life now that I've recovered."

With another patient, the following exchange took place:

THERAPIST: "Isn't it time you started being concerned about *you* and stopped being concerned about people's reaction to you?"

PATIENT: "But they're important. That's our job. What I have to do."

THERAPIST: "Sometimes one's job is to cultivate one's garden. The garden in one's backyard, in the front, or the one in one's heart."

PATIENT: "What's the use of cultivating a little patch of rocks surrounded by high, thick hedges?"

THERAPIST: "That's how you see your heart?"

PATIENT: "Yes."

The approach by logic and reason does not seem to be a useful one. The deep concern and involvement with life which is central to the wish to live is not amenable to logic. As a statement to a patient, "You have every reason to live" may be perfectly true, but even when buttressed with a list of assets, it is not very convincing.[6] The approach must lie deeper, in an arousal of faith in the self and concern with the self. Despair with life must be countered by something just as deep—here is the therapist's ultimate concern. Only the therapist's faith in the patient is strong enough to fight the patient's faith in despair.

When I write here of "faith" in the patient, I use the term as Paul Tillich (1957) uses it: "Faith is the state of being ultimately concerned [p. 1]." Ultimate concern means primacy; other concerns—in this context the therapist's concern for himself and his own ego, for his hurt if the patient dies, for his pride and his persona—are secondary and must sometimes be sacrificed. By his faith, the therapist tries to lead the patient to give up his concern about "success" and the opinions of others, to overcome his fears and anxieties, and to become ultimately concerned about his own inner development. The therapist expresses *"Fides quae creditur"*—the faith which is believed. This, of course, must be real, it cannot be faked.[7] When the patient begins to respond with faith in himself, he begins to live.[8]

---

6. "An emotion can only be controlled or destroyed by another emotion contrary thereto, and with more power for controlling emotion." (Spinoza, *Ethics*, part 4, proposition 2.)

7. This is one of the reasons that the patient load—the number of this type of patients treated at one time—must be kept small. It is far too great a strain on the therapist to have more than a few patients with this problem at one time. Ideally, those doing this type of therapy should have other types of patients or other types of work also. Even so, the emotional drain is considerable. It is important that the therapist be aware of his own inner resources and their limits. Once one starts work with a patient in this situation, it is not wise to stop in the middle, since abandoning the therapy is quite likely to precipitate a strong depressive reaction in the patient. It is better not to start than to start and not finish.

8. "He who enters the sphere of faith enters the sanctuary of life [Tillich, 1957, p. 12]."

Basic to this arousal of faith is the approach of the therapist to the patient. Moustakas (1956) has pointed out that the careful person is only one step away from the paltry person.[9] So it is with this type of therapy. It needs intense concentration, almost absolute caring and acceptance—but not carefulness. If the therapist has reservations about meeting the patient fully, the patient will sense that something is being held back, and his own reservations about meeting life and meeting himself will be reinforced.

Basic is insistence on a real "encounter"—a real contact between the patient and the therapist. (This seems the best way to the unexpected experience that will cause the patient to confront the world again and decide to re-enter it—like the bray of the donkey that awakened Prince Mishkin to life in Dostoevski's *The Idiot*.) If the encounter can be made without carefulness on the therapist's side and without second thoughts (which the patient usually catches), the breakdown of the wall between the patient and life has begun.

The fact that there is a human encounter between patient and therapist does not mean that the therapy is kept on superficial levels. To understand the patient's problems in the present, one must frequently explore the past. This, however, can be done without the therapist's having to remain anonymous and without the elaboration of a transference neurosis. Defenses can be explored and worked through as thoroughly as in an orthodox psychoanalysis. The intense human contact seems to enhance rather than preclude depth exploration.

The honesty of the encounter rules out kindness. (Usually, kindness not only has self-protective qualities for the therapist but also carries an implication of a superior position.) The encounter needs empathy, not sympathy. And the empathy must

---

9. Or, as E. Jackson (1962) has put it, "The good is often a hazard to the best."

go both ways. One must be in full contact with the patient before the patient can accept being in contact with himself and with life.

Said a patient, after the therapist had answered some questions about his work and discussed some of the difficulties and satisfactions he had with it, "Up to now I've been saying to myself that the things you told me were very nice and exactly what I would tell someone else who was in my position [i.e., very ill]. But now I see that you mean them and live them. So it *is* possible."

We might make here an analogy with a psychotherapeutic problem that arises in working very intensively with schizophrenics. Between the unconscious of the therapist and the unconscious of the patient there is only the therapist's ego. He is thus in danger of being drawn into a schizophrenic reality. In the type of work we are describing here, there is only one defensive system between the patient's ego and the therapist's ego— the defensive system of the patient. The patient is thus in danger of being drawn into the world he basically wants so much to enter, but is afraid to.

Fisher (1962) has written well of the training the psychotherapist receives *not* to meet the patient openly and fully. He tells the story of the schizophrenic girl being seen in a hospital staff conference. When asked, "How do you like the people here?" she replied, "There are no people here. There's just doctors, nurses, and patients." Gordon Allport (1959) has noted that the usual psychotherapeutic training may produce

. . . a kind of contempt for the psychic surface of life. The individual's conscious report is rejected as untrustworthy and the contemporary thrust of his motives is disregarded in favor of a backward tracing of his conduct to earlier formative stages.

The therapist who works with seriously ill patients must not be too ready to analyze each statement the patient makes (Le Shan, 1962). He must listen and accept the probability that the patient knows what he is talking about. The shoe is as likely to be pinching in the present as it was in the patient's childhood. Once when I was working with a cancer patient, I listened to his complaint about a relationship and quickly went to an exploration and analysis of its deeper meaning, pointing out that the complaint was unrealistic, citing contrary examples, and examining it in terms of the patient's past. As a result I missed the entire point and ignored an important clue. Some time later, when —in another context—the point was reopened, both of us recalled the original incident. The patient (who had previously had several years of orthodox psychoanalysis) said: "You goofed badly there, Doc. But you're usually very good about this. Generally you assume that when a patient has a complaint, there's something real that's really bothering him."

"Pain," wrote Daudet (1934), "is always something new for him who suffers but banal to those about him. They will all get used to it except myself [p. 15]." This illustrates one aspect of the psychological isolation that frequently surrounds the severely ill patient—an isolation so profound that, as Tolstoi describes it in *The Death of Ivan Ilyich*, he could be at the bottom of the sea or on the other side of the moon. This isolation, in itself, appears to weaken the ability to deal with stress, to cope with pain, and to fight for life. Until new relationships are built, the therapist himself may have to serve as the major relationship the patient has.

The naked encounter makes it plain to the patient that the therapist accepts him without reservation and therefore without fear. He can thus begin to question his own fear of encountering himself. Once this full "meeting" has been made, the process of psychotherapy in a more usual sense of the term can really get under way. Only then is it real to this kind of patient. Without this he is often cooperative and may work hard at the therapy, but it is all ego action only. It does not touch him in his vital centers.

The therapist insists that the patient must constantly search his own being for the sources and directions, the channels and paths of his self.[10] The proof of the value of this approach is in its results as one proceeds. The patient tests as he goes. (The analogy of the artist applying paint to his canvas is often useful.) If the development makes him dislike himself less, understand the world more realistically, feel more and more at home in the universe, the therapy is worth while and moves well. It should be made clear to the patient that the goals of therapy are these practical goals, and that he should verify them experimentally as he goes along.[11] The patient is trained to listen to his inner sources, to lower his internal threshold and listen to the almost inaudible whispers which say "I enjoy this," "I like doing this," "I do not like this," etc. The idea of this "listening" may sound naive, but in my experience these patients tend to understand it, to "get it" quickly—it helps to turn their orientation to a genuine acceptance of, and concern with, the self.

In the old tale, the wise man said to the king, "*I* am the most important person in your life—because you are talking to me *now*." (One patient put his view very clearly: "I always lived as

---

10. "Everyone, as Pliny says, is a good doctrine to himself, provided he be capable of discovering himself near at hand." (Montaigne, *Essays*, Book 2, Chapter 12.) And elsewhere: "It is an absolute perfection and, as it were, divine for a man to know how to enjoy his own being loyally."

11. This point has been made by Maslow (1962, p. 5) and by Jackson (1963).

if there were only tomorrow and yesterday. Today didn't exist.")
It is this sense we try to give the patient: the importance of the
only moment in which he can ever live—the *now*. Living in the
now and being *engagé* in it makes it possible for the life force
to flow more fully.[12] This point of view is part of what Jourard
in an important paper (1964) has written of as setting in mo-
tion "a general hope syndrome," which seems to him to decrease
the entropic level of the body and raise the level of the spirit
("increase spirit-titre") so that the patient can "move toward
wellness."

An important step in the development of overcoming despair
is the point at which the patient exchanges his static goal in life
for a growing and moving one. Usually the goal has been seen
in static, utopian terms—"and they were married and lived
happily ever after." It is much more realistic and helpful, however, to view life as a dynamic process of reception, expression,
action, searching, growing. A viewpoint is advanced that sees
life as an opportunity to become more than one is, to become
less "blind." The goal of life becomes a continuing process of
inner expansion rather than a series of external accomplishments. Patients seem clearly to recognize the difference between
these two viewpoints and to find the dynamic much more possible of acceptance.

Just as the therapist tells the patient to search and examine his
own goals and values, so he himself must keep up with the
search, examination, and re-examination within himself. It is too
easy to believe that the truths we bring to the patient are *the*
truths—to become smug and satisfied with our own approaches

---

12. It is true, as Weisman and Hackett (1961) point out, that genuine relationships can be built to the dead as well as to the living. Nevertheless, it is in
the *now* that these operate and are effective.

and answers. This can blind and blunt our own inner awareness, can block the *sensus divinatatis* by means of which we try to perceive the essence of the patient and his universe. Once we cease searching ourselves, we are telling the patient to do one thing while we do another. This is quickly sensed and our effectiveness is severely damaged.

Psychotherapy with these patients should move strongly. The therapist thus shows both his grip on the seemingly hopeless situation and his confidence in the patient. It may help the therapist to keep in mind the Toynbee-like concept of the overwhelming challenge that the patient has been unable to meet. Life, for these patients, has been dominated by a problem they must solve but cannot. The failure of the life force seems generally (in my cases invariably, except where a terminal physical state had produced overwhelming fatigue) a result of this other failure. Said a patient, speaking of a period five years before the first signs of her cancer, "If I looked ahead in life, there was nothing I could see unless I kidded myself." Another patient had a favorite saying which, it seemed to her, symbolized her whole life: "If the rock drops on the egg—poor egg! If the egg drops on the rock—poor egg!" It is important for the therapist to come to grips with this problem as soon as possible. In this, he can push harder with these patients than might seem indicated by the patient's life history or the therapist's "feel" of ego strength. The therapist should push rather hard as long as the patient is not fighting him. The approach of death seems to give a much greater ego strength and the likelihood of a psychotic break is greatly lessened *if therapist and patient have become* engagé *and both are clear about their goals.* During the seventh session between a therapist and a patient, the following exchange took place:

PATIENT: "I'm afraid of my cancer. I want to live."

THERAPIST: "Why? Whose life do you want to live?"

PATIENT: "I detest it! I've never lived my own life. There was always so much to do at the moment. So much to. . . . I never got around to living my life."

THERAPIST: "You never even were able to find out what it was."

PATIENT: "That's why I drink. It makes things look better. Not so dark."

THERAPIST: "Maybe the better way would be to find out what is your way of life and start living it."

PATIENT: "How could I do that?"

THERAPIST: "That's what we are trying to do here."

There is a good deal of evidence (LeShan, 1952) that deep psychological isolation, the loss of ability to relate and to love, lowers the ability to fight for health. Paul Federn (1932) put it: "All that is living must be loving so as not to die [p. 130]." Freud (1946) wrote: "In the last analysis, we must love in order not to fall ill and must fall ill when, in consequence of frustration, we cannot love." The inability to relate, however, must be overcome in ways that are organic and syntonic to the patient's personality. Attempting to reach solutions in other ways is *worse than useless*, since it increases the patient's feeling that his efforts really to relate are hopeless and are doomed to failure. It brings no feelings of reward and meaningfulness. Further, since the trail is a false one, it increases the energy going into facade and surface, reinforces the patient's feelings of self-alienation and despair, and decreases the relating of deeper personality levels and behavior and the progress of the patient toward wholeness and health.

Each person has ways of relating which spring naturally from his total personality gestalt. He has his special song to sing, his own music to beat out. When he discovers this, and puts his energy into relating accordingly, he finds that his relationships bring him feelings of being "right" and "good," that he has zest and enthusiasm for them, that they refresh rather than exhaust him. When he accepts himself as he actually *is*, rather than as he feels he *should be*, he can relate in his own ways.

It is often a problem to help the patient realize how thoroughly he has rejected himself and is out of contact with his real feelings. For instance, a therapist once pointed out to a woman patient that she had accepted her perception of her parents' rejection of her and agreed with it. When she protested that she did not know what he was talking about, he asked her to recall the incident in childhood in which she had been most unfairly treated and hurt. She was able to recall and visualize it in great detail, even to a description of the clothes she had been wearing. The therapist then asked her to imagine that there was a "time machine" (she knew the H. G. Wells story) in the office. She was to get into it and, in her present person, travel back to the room where the painful incident had occurred:

THERAPIST: "You now enter—as you are now—the room in which the little Arlene is crying on the bed. You walk into the room. She looks up at you. What do you do?"
PATIENT: "I'd hit her!"

The amazement and shock that she felt on hearing herself say this was the first step toward a major orientation to the self. This "time machine" technique, borrowed from Arthur Laurents' superb play, *A Clearing in the Woods*, has proved useful with a variety of these patients.[13]

---

13. This play, with its brilliant understanding of modern psychotherapy and the search for the self, is one which—either read or seen—has often proved very helpful to patients. It presents clearly, artistically, and with excellent taste what the therapeutic program is all about. Another often useful work is Hermann Hesse's great existential novel *Steppenwolf*. This—on a more subtle and symbolic level—does the same thing. One patient said after reading it: "I didn't understand what it was all about, but after I finished it, I couldn't stop crying for two

Another patient, a woman with breast cancer, was asked—as it is often important to ask repeatedly—what she really wanted in life. At first she spoke only of her illness and her wish not to die. When, however, the therapist asked: "If you were completely well physically, would you want to go on living with your husband or would you prefer living alone?" she started to answer, stopped, looked puzzled, and then said with much surprise in her voice: "I don't know." From this point she was able to go to work more seriously on her psychotherapy and appeared to be in much better spirits.

The basic self in these patients has generally been so rejected that they are either completely cut off from it or else view its wishes and impulses as completely unacceptable. (This is one reason why Hermann Hesse's *Steppenwolf* is often so helpful for them to read.) A patient with a deep love of nature—with a great understanding of flowers and gardens—rejected these interests because she saw only "intellectual" pursuits as valid. She felt that her love of growing things was something shameful and "childish." She felt herself inferior because she did not read the latest professional journals and was not interested in discussing abstract theories. Another patient had been a successful actress. Only on the stage had she felt completely at home and at ease. She had given it up, however, since acting was "like children dressing up in their parents' clothes and pretending." Since then, her life had consisted of a constant social whirl, arguments with her husband, and an empty feeling of uselessness and hopelessness.

---

hours. But they were not sad tears, only bittersweet." Later, in referring to the meeting between the two parts of the hero—Harry Haller and the wolf—she told how struck she had been by the fact that "the wolf had such beautiful eyes and was sad. I guess maybe what I've hated so in me maybe also has beautiful eyes and is sad."

In psychotherapy of this type, we are concerned with freeing zest and enthusiasm rather than with determining the causation of mental symptoms. Symptoms are viewed as results of the inability to be oneself freely and as behavior patterns which continue to block such expression. As Maslow (1962) has stated it: "It seems quite clear that personality problems may sometimes be loud protests against the crushing of one's psychological bones; of one's true nature [p. 7]."

In this work we are concerned neither with mental pathology (the psychotherapeutic search is for strengths, not weaknesses) nor with preparation for death. Rather than a *Sein zum Todt*, we are oriented toward a *Sein zum Leben*. Patients seem to grasp this point of view quickly; even those with long experience in classic psychoanalytic therapy seem to find the philosophic approach syntonic and stimulating.

Rosenthal (1957) in her important paper (a work of much value to anyone working in this field) has stated, "One way to reduce the patient's fear of death is to re-arouse his creative impulses." We would only add that these creative impulses have often been so withered by life that it is frequently necessary first to *find* them. The rearousal of which she speaks can give the patient goals in life that are meaningful and real to him, can reawaken his hope, and appears to increase his ability to bear pain and stress and organismically to fight for his life. This is similar to the doctrine of Pelagius: *"Velle, posse, esse"*—"the wish, the ability, the [sense of] being."[14]

One part of the problem is to help the patient turn from concern with the opinions of others to concern with the needs of the self. Jung (1933) writes of this as taking place usually between

---

14. This similarity was pointed out by Ensor Holiday in a personal communication to the writer.

the ages of thirty-five and forty-five. Those who have made this development do not need our help at this time. They are with life and for it and a part of it. Those who need our help in the catastrophic situation are the many who have not achieved this step. To them, the opinions of others (the "shoulds" in the sense that Horney uses the term) still come first: their primary orientation is—in Riesman's concept—"other-directed." It is this neglect of their own inner development that seems related to the weakness of their will to live. Not only do they suffer the long-term exhaustion that comes from investing one's psychic energy into ways of expressing and relating which give one no inner satisfaction; they are also robbed by physical illness of even the little support that they receive normally. When one is ill, one is alone with oneself. The supports of status, prestige, the opinions of others diminish considerably in importance. The patient is pulled to concentrate on his vital centers. He is largely deprived of those aids to his feelings about himself which come to us reflected in the behavior of others. The patient is, generally speaking, restricted to the psychic supports that come from his inner life, and it is just these supports he has neglected. When these patients are able to turn their efforts inward, the will to live seems to show a considerable increase.

Sometimes the attempt fails. The flame of the life force seems too weak. It flickers, but will not burn brightly. A patient with advanced metastatic breast cancer told the therapist after three months of intensive psychotherapy a dream she had had:

"Something happened in my office. In order to get away from it, I went outside the window and stood on a ledge outside. It was very high and I intended to jump. Then someone reached out a hand from inside my office window. I turned to take the hand to go back inside, but it was too late. I tried as hard as I could, I stretched out my arm, but I couldn't quite reach your hand. I almost touched it and then fell off the ledge. As I was falling, I woke up."

The therapist who works with patients in a catastrophic situation may find to his surprise that there are real rewards in the work that he did not expect. There is a dealing with "the dimension of seriousness and profundity of feeling (or perhaps 'the tragic sense of life') . . . [Maslow, 1962, p. 11]." Little effort or time is spent on the superficial, the petty vanities, the superstructure of life. Although strong relationships (coupled with realistic dependency) are the rule, transference reactions which must be "worked through" are rare. Usually patient and therapist can come quickly to the basic problems of the human condition.

Further, one discovers something that is rarely mentioned in the textbooks of psychology and psychiatry. One sees clearly the strength and dignity of human beings, the deep altruism, the positive qualities that exist at all levels of personality. Working with people who are under the hammer of fate greatly increases one's respect for them and makes one proud of being a human being.

References

Allport, G. W. The right to be believed. In S. J. Beck & H. B. Molist (Eds.), *Reflexes to intelligence*. Glencoe, Ill.: Free Press, 1959.

Beecher, H. K. Nonspecific forces surrounding disease and the treatment of disease. *J.A.M.A.*, 1962, *179*, 437–40.

Bell, T. *In the midst of life*. New York: Atheneum, 1961.

Booth, G. Disease as a message. *J. Religion Health*, 1962, *1*, 309–18. (a)

Booth, G. Healing the sick. *Pastoral Psychol.*, 1962, *13*, 11–27. (b)

Daudet, A. *Suffering*. New Haven: Yale University Press, 1934.

Federn, P. The reality of the death instinct, especially in melancholia. *Psychoanal. Rev.*, 1932, *19*, 129–51.

Fisher, G. M. On the pseudo-humanistic education of the psychotherapist. *J. Humanistic Psychol.*, 1962, *2*, 19–22.

Freud, S. On narcissism. In *Collected papers*. Vol. 4. London: Hogarth Press, 1946.

Jackson, E. Mediating the faith that makes whole. Manuscript, 1962.

Jackson, E. *The pastor and his people*. Manhasset, N.Y.: Channel Press, 1963.

Jourard, S. M. The role of spirit and "inspiriting" in human wellness. In S. M. Jourard, *The transparent self*. Princeton: Van Nostrand, 1964. Pp. 79–80.

Jung, C. *Modern man in search of a soul*. New York: Harcourt Brace, 1933.

Kierkegaard, S. *The sickness unto death*. In *Fear and trembling* and *The sickness unto death*. New York: Doubleday, 1954.

LeShan, L. The safety prone: An approach to the accident free person. *Psychiatry*, 1952, *4*, 465–69.

LeShan, L. A psychosomatic hypothesis concerning the etiology of Hodgkin's disease. *Psychol. Rep.*, 1957, *3*, 565–75.

LeShan, L. Personality states as factors in the development of malignant disease: A critical review. *J. Nat. Cancer Inst.*, 1959, *22*, 1–18.

LeShan, L. Some methodological problems in the study of the psychosomatic aspects of cancer. *J. Gen. Psychol.*, 1960, *63*, 309–17.

LeShan, L. Contemporary trends in psychoanalytic psychotherapy. *Ment. Hyg.* 1962, *46*, 454–63.

LeShan, L. The world of the patient in severe pain of long duration. *J. Chronic Dis.*, 1964, *17*, 119–26.

LeShan, L., & Gassmann, F. L. Some observations on psychotherapy with patients suffering from neoplastic disease. *Amer. J. Psychother.*, 1958, *12*, 723–34.

LeShan, L., & LeShan, E. Psychotherapy and the patient with a limited life span. *Psychiatry*, 1961, *24*(4), 318–23.

LeShan, L., Marvin, S., & Lyerly, O. Some evidence of a relationship between Hodgkin's disease and intelligence. *A.M.A., Arch. Gen. Psychiat.*, 1959, *1*, 477–79.

LeShan, L., & Reznikoff, M. A psychological factor apparently associated with neoplastic disease. *J. Abnorm. Soc. Psychol.*, 1960, 60, 439–40.

LeShan, L., & Worthington, R. Loss of cathexes as a common psychodynamic characteristic of cancer patients: An attempt at statistical validation of a clinical hypothesis. *Psychol. Rep.*, 1956, 2, 183. (a)

LeShan, L., & Worthington, R. Some recurrent life history patterns observed in patients with malignant disease. *J. Nerv. Ment. Dis.*, 1956, 124, 460. (b)

Maslow, A. *Towards a psychology of being.* New York: Van Nostrand, 1962.

Maslow, A. The need to know and the fear of knowing. *J. Gen. Psychol.*, 1963, 68, 111–25.

Moustakas, C. *The self.* New York: Harper, 1956.

Revici, E. *Research in physiopathology as basis of guided chemotherapy.* New York: Van Nostrand, 1961.

Rosenthal, H. Psychotherapy for the dying. *Amer. J. Psychother.*, 1957, 11, 626–33.

Tillich, P. *Dynamics of faith.* New York: Harper, 1957.

Weisman, A. D., & Hackett, T. P. Predilection to death: Death and dying as a psychiatric problem. *Psychosom. Med.*, 1961, 23, 232–56.

The Moment of Truth: Care of the Dying Person

CICELY SAUNDERS

THE TITLE I HAVE CHOSEN, "The Moment of Truth," includes far more than the question "Who should tell—or should you tell—a patient that his death is near?" I think that the title includes many more of the realities and challenges of the situation. It is a situation that concerns all of us, whether we are doctors, nurses, psychiatrists, psychologists, social workers, or theologians. (I have deliberately made the list alphabetical, because all are of equal importance.) Perhaps most of all, the situation concerns us when a member of our family or a friend is dying. This is, or should be, a "moment of truth." It is not a matter of mere words, of who says what; it is a moment with many implications, not only for research and treatment, but implications for the whole of life, and its meaning, implications for us as well as for the patient. But it is the patient who is, or who should be, in the center. The question is *his* because it is his situation and he is the person who matters. This is why the second part of my title is "Care of the Dying *Person*" and not simply "Care of the Dying." I think that with the increased interest in this problem there is a danger that the dying may, in a sense, be put in quotes, and I believe it is very important that they should not be. The expression, "moment of truth," was taken by Boros, a philosopher and theologian, for a book about death. But apparently the phrase comes originally from the Spanish, and is a technical term referring to the moment at the end of a bullfight when the matador is alone with the bull. The whole audience, and everybody else in the ring, are secondary. It is just these two together, and the person is absolutely in the center. This is what I want to do now—put the patient in the center. This is why I am going to tell about people I have known in my seven years at St. Joseph's. I am not going to describe my work there very much—I think it will describe itself.

When I arrived at St. Joseph's, I had the good fortune to be given responsibility for some forty or forty-five patients (out of their total capacity of 150) who came with malignant disease, and with a prognosis of three months or less to live. They were sent to us by other centers when the stage of active treatment was over. They were having pain or distress, or had no family to look after them, or had some other complication that made home care impossible. This hospice had a link with the National Health Service and so did the patient, so there was no charge for their stay, and no "parking meter," as it were, ticking away beside the bed. Once a patient came, this was his bed and he could stay. What I must try to do as we proceed is distill the many teaching sessions we have had during these seven years with various groups of students; to try to encourage you, as I encouraged them, just to look at the patients and listen to them to learn from them what they had to teach us. It was far more important that the students should go alone and informally round the wards, and be able to talk to people than to have the usual formal rounds, and then afterwards to sit down over tea discussing the questions that arose. After these informal visits, often they would see the patients in a totally different way, be concerned with the individual people they had been meeting, learn respect and regard for them, and the beginnings of understanding.

Though I do not consider training in psychotherapy a necessity for this kind of work, I do believe that we need all the understanding we can acquire of the patients, who are, after all, people similar to ourselves. Of course, we cannot understand exactly how a dying person feels; death is totally unknown until a person comes to it. But I do think that we can talk of the implications of what individual patients say or do. Moreover, we do not need to have had the same experience as another person in order to enter into it to some extent. We just need to have *had* our own experiences and not to have slid past or, as it were, ducked out from under any hard fact of reality that happens to have hit us. Having had these, we can begin to look at this "moment," which is as much a part of life as any other part, and, for very many, the most important. It is a time of summing-up, a time of final decisions for this person who is the patient. Since our work at St. Joseph's is completely person centered, the criterion of success is not how our treatment is working, but how the patient is; what he is doing; or, still more important, what he is *being* in the face of his physical deterioration. Our attitude toward the dying patient betrays a good deal of our attitude toward people in general, and, of course, of our interpretation of the meaning of life. So often, it is *we* who need rehabilitation, not the patient, just as it is the psychology of the seeing rather than the psychology of the blind that is the problem.

I speak from a special viewpoint, but, because this is such a very personal part of caring, I do not think it will be too difficult for you to find relevance to your own situations. What I want to discuss concerns attitudes much more than details. I want somehow to convey the sort of atmosphere that I have seen as being very helpful to these dying patients—the attention, the security, the hospitality of St. Joseph's. St. Joseph's is a sectarian religious foundation, but welcomes patients of all sorts and kinds, and welcomed me as a staff member of a different denomination. All are welcomed with a confident sense of strength and peace, with the immense strength of a recognized shared purpose—full-time concern for the patient.

PROLONGING LIVING AND PROLONGING DYING

I want to talk about the personal achievement of the dying. It is people and the look on their faces that matters, because from the look on their faces we learn both their needs and their achievements. I think we must learn to recognize the moment when our treatment turns into "care of the dying person." To go on pressing for acute, active treatment at a stage when a patient has gone too far and should not be made to return is not good medicine. *There is a difference between prolonging living and what can really only be called prolonging dying.* Because something is possible does not mean that it is necessarily either right or kind to do it. One often sees a great weariness with the sort of pain and illness that brings our patients to us such as that of Sir William Osler who, when he was dying, said, "I'm too far across the river now to want to come back and have it all over again." I do not think he would have given a "thank you" to someone who pulled him back at that stage. Recognition of this stage is not defeatism either on the part of the patient or on that of the doctor. Rather it is respect and awareness of the individual person and his dignity. When one patient came to us, she described her situation by saying, "It was *all* pain." Another patient said to me, "Well, doctor, it began in my back, but now it seems that all of me is wrong." And she went on to describe the physical pain, her feeling that nobody understood how she felt, that the world was against her, that she could have cried for pills and injections but knew that she should not, that her husband and son were having to stay off work to look after her—and that it was wonderful to come to St. Joseph's and begin to feel safe again. She began by talking about her physical problems and her many symptoms but went on to describe mental pain, emotional distress, financial problems, and this need for security. They are all interwoven, tied together, so that you cannot say at one moment that you are treating one problem and not the other. The treatment at St. Joseph's is designed to relieve the pain. Yes, one _can_ do that, to enable the patient not only to die peacefully but to live fully until he dies, living as himself, neither swamped with distress nor smothered by treatments and drugs and the things that we are doing; nor yet enduring in sterile isolation. Now, this is the very opposite of doing nothing, and one _can_ do it.

The patient who had described her world as "_all_ pain" showed a remarkable difference just a few months later when she was relieved and relaxed; when she had given up her flat and organized all her affairs and when she had really forgotten that the medicine she was taking was for pain, because, as she said, "Now it's gone and I'm free," adding, "Doctor, do you think I could leave off the medicine because I really don't much like the taste of gin?" (Our normal pain medication does have gin in it— a good mild sedative.) She did not even remember that it was for that purpose. This was two weeks before her death.

FAMILY CONSIDERATIONS

If we could, we would want to look after a patient at home. But many patients have so much distress that this is not possible. I have two photographs of a patient, photographs that tell a story. In the first, taken in his ward at St. Joseph's with his wife soon after he arrived, he is sitting up with tense alertness; his face betrays his anxiety, and his wife's face, her despair and guilty feeling of inadequacy. In the second photograph, taken after he had been under our care for a time and was on a diamorphine mixture, he looks as I think a patient ought to look: peaceful and comfortable. He is filling in his football pools (a mild English form of gambling) while his wife sits nearby, her relief at *his* relief showing in her face. I remember the wife of another patient stopping outside the ward and saying to me, "Oh doctor, I won't hurry in. I'll just stay here and look at him. I haven't seen him look like this for weeks!"

If we can give this kind of comfort to the patient and his family, then we have given them back something in this last time. It is of great importance to both of them. A patient can still be part of his family when he has to be admitted—and he can also fail to be part of his family while he is still at home. Wherever we are looking after these patients we have a tremendous responsibility to help them know they are still part of life and still a part of their own family. We have a photograph of a patient and his wife taken for their golden wedding anniversary only forty-eight hours before he died. Though he did not have the energy to smile, the picture shows his peacefulness and his feeling of closeness to his wife. I recall that when he came to St. Joseph's he was confused and did not recognize his wife or anything else. But after a short while with us he was himself once more. When his wife visited they were as close as they had been at any time during their fifty years of marriage. It is very important to share this "moment of truth" in whatever way one can. It is very important to say "Good-bye." Good-byes matter. We all give importance to saying "Good-bye" when we go on a journey—how much more meaning "Good-bye" has now. We can do a lot to create this sort of quiet togetherness for a couple by telling the patient that we can help him cope with the pain as it comes and letting him know in advance that the moment of death itself is quiet. Then he can, as far as possible, have this moment alone with a relative, shielded from the things that the staff can do something about. You cannot take away parting and its hardness, but you can help it.

Dr. Lawrence LeShan has spoken of "the wall of glass between the patient and other people." My thought is more of a vacuum around the patient, in part created by the anxious family who keep pulling themselves up and wondering, "Have I let something out?" Then all communication ceases and they are just not able to relax and talk about "something else," let alone real things. This can be a vastly important time, and often family members bitterly regret afterwards that they were not in touch. To get them to talk together, we may first have to do a lot of listening to both sides. We find it easier to do this separately, and we say to the family, who are usually the ones who are concealing their awareness, "You know, he really does realize." We point out that they must not come in being too cheerful and say, "You know, you're going to get better," because the patient is saying, "They won't even let me say 'Good-bye' to them." Usually, this sharing of awareness happens quietly, without fuss, and in its own time. I sound as if I take the line of least resistance all the time, but we have found that in our atmosphere at St. Joseph's, this problem resolves itself spontaneously, especially after pain and distress are relieved and we have listened to the anxiety. Sometimes a family member will say, "I can't talk to him. I just can't. I can only keep going without." Then perhaps the patient can talk to us, and then at least he is sharing it with someone. The nuns listen to the families more than I do, for they are always available. They do not have a day off and they are always there, or on call. There is a strong feeling of "Sister's there and I can always talk to her." They often do. But we share together as a group. Conditions in the typical general hospital do not apply in the same way here.

I think it is particularly important to try to help a dying parent say "Good-bye" to the children. I have seen mothers with quite young children saying "Good-bye" not in so many words, but deeply all the same. I have seen mothers doing something special for a daughter. I remember going out to buy a copy of *The Messiah* for a patient of mine to give her daughter as a last present—a gift which obviously is going to be unusually precious. Sometimes, when patients are failing, they have said to me, "Oh, there's nothing I can do now." You can say to them, "You know, she isn't ever going to forget how you were loving, how you were patient, how you did this, that, or the other while you were so ill."

I know this is true from my own memories, and I have two tape recordings of patients, one in her forties leaving two children who had both been problems, and another separated from her husband, leaving a son about sixteen. They both say the same words, repeating before they died, "I've done what I can." One went on, "I've said what I wanted done, and I have written it all down in my will." The other dictated a letter to me for her children. This was of immense help to them, to feel that they had done all that they could. They could then trust that their children would be cared for, just as they trusted that they would be cared for at St. Joseph's. It is a long way to come, to this place, and as soon as a young patient with a young family comes in, we know that this is going to take special time. We know we are going to feel awed by having to try to help this person face something much harder than anything we ever had to cope with.

The fact is that while this is, indeed, sad work, yet when you come to the bedside you are not saying, "How can *I* help Mrs. So-and-so?" but rather, "This is St. Joseph's and I just happen to be the one here at the moment. And it will be all right."

COMMUNICATING WITH THE DYING

At St. Joseph's, there is one nun in charge of each ward, but the rest of our nurses are not nuns. Most of them are young Irish girls who come over and do apprentice nursing with us before they go and get further training elsewhere. Since they have not yet been taught to hurry, as many a trained nurse will, they are well suited to work with dying patients. You cannot hurry the dying. You cannot hurry them to realize what is happening; you cannot hurry them to turn over in bed quickly; you cannot hurry them to eat faster than they can manage. Within this slow speed, their own speed, they often make a great deal of improvement. Certainly they are quieter and easier.

I recall being with a patient with a cerebral tumor about two weeks before he died. He had been blind for about six months and was very slow now. His wife tried to get him to look up as I got ready to take their photograph, but he could not manage it and sank back again. She looked up at me and the picture shows the tremendous grace and maturity that I have seen again and again, both in patients and in their families. You might ask, "What is the point of looking after a man for fifteen months since he's going to die at the end?" But there are no short cuts to this kind of maturity. Though there may not be a long time available for a couple to be together, time is a matter of depth and quality rather than length. At this period I remember asking his wife, "Does he always know you?" And she said, "Oh, yes, he does." Then she added, "The other day when I came in I said to him, 'Who's here?' and he said, 'I don't know.' When I said, 'It's me,' he just said, 'Ah, but you're always there!' " It was marvelous how she had gotten across to him the sense that she always was there with him, by her faithfulness, by coming whenever she could, even though she was working at the time. And he, who was a gentle and courteous person by nature, was giving her this absolutely perfect "thanks," and still responding in his own character to the reduced information that his senses were now giving him. He was still much the same person, unique and irreplaceable.

I remember another patient, who, like so many, showed that her heart was still loving though her mind could no longer grasp much at all. A picture of her shows her loving response to an unsophisticated little nurse who is just enjoying her as she is, demonstrating her pleasure in just meeting her, somehow still the same person as ever. Now, this simplicity is a quality we too often lose, but I notice that the young seem to have it almost by nature, if they choose to come into this kind of work. This quality is, I think, important for a relative to observe and feel—to see this person as himself, indefinably the same, still with his own worth until the moment he dies.

AWARENESS OF DYING AND "TELLING"

Now I have to consider the old question of what to tell the patient. In the first place, I am sure I have to make a distinction between telling somebody his diagnosis (that it is a malignant disease) and his prognosis (that he is not going to get better as far as we can see). I think we have to remember that the degree of insight a patient has into his condition is not under our control.

It does not depend just on what we tell him. There are many other factors in the situation—his intelligence, his courage, what is happening in his own body and what this is saying to him, what he overhears. *I know that some fifty per cent of my patients not only knew that they were dying but talked about it with me.* Of the remaining fifty per cent, there were some who were senile, some who had cerebral tumors, and some who were just not able to have insight. There were others who, I think, recognized but did not choose to talk about it—at least not with me. The choice should be theirs. The real question is not, "What do you tell your patients?" but rather, "What do you let your patients tell you?" Learn to hear what they are saying; what they are not saying; what is hidden underneath; what *is* going on. Incidentally, only a very few of our patients did know at first that they had been sent to St. Joseph's as the last stage of their journey. Usually they had been told something such as "You need specialized treatment for pain," or "You need longer-term nursing than we can provide in a general ward." Later some of them told me that they had a pretty shrewd idea that it was something like this when they came in. They do not often discuss their diagnosis, which seems often to be irrelevant at this stage, but they do talk about their prognosis, about what is happening, and they all do it differently. Since giving a general description is difficult, all I can do is describe a group of people and tell you what happened to each one of them.

I recall one young woman who had been with us for two months. She and I were quite friendly. I thought she "knew" and that she had chosen never to mention it. She just kept her own counsel until one day she suddenly looked up at me and said, with courage and determination in her voice, "Doctor, where did all this begin?" I pulled the curtains round and sat on her bed (as an ex-nurse, rejoicing in the fact that I was no longer bound by the rule that nurses do not sit on beds!). This is important for communicating: standing at the bedside, I would tower over a patient. In this two-way traffic, I want to be on the same level. Then she went on, talking about her family, and soon got to her real question: "Is it wrong for me to let my children come up and visit me now that I'm getting so thin?" She said that she had "known" since her operation six months before, adding, "I haven't talked to my husband about it and I think it would be so hard for him when he realized that I've been carrying this on my own all this time. I just don't know quite how to begin." I told her, "Well, you know, it will just happen, quite easily, and you've been sharing it together anyway." And, of course, having talked to someone else she found herself talking with him the next day. At last it was possible for them to share openly. About a week later she died, but in her face she showed a quietness and acceptance that upheld her whole family.

Other patients are quiet and objective and unworried. I remember one old man saying, quite unexpectedly, "Of course, doctor, I realize this isn't a question of cure now, is it? It's just a matter of jogging along." He was quite sure that it would be all right, that it was his family who needed reassuring. But there are common questions and common fears that lie beyond the one big question that we seem to talk of as if it were the only one. Many are concerned about their families. Many ask, "Will it be very long?" "Will I have pain?" "What will it be like in the end?" Or, "I hope it will be in my sleep." Now, we can be reassuring about it all. If we refuse to discuss it openly, or smother their questions in a kind of blanket of reassurance, they still know very well what is happening. What we have said to them, in effect, is, "I'm afraid to discuss it." They want to talk about the other questions, and they will do it when they are ready if only we will let them. We can also help them without doing so in every word. Effective communication can take place indirectly. Discussing symptoms with a patient, often a way out of having to talk openly, can also be a way to begin. It can give reassurance, understanding, a feeling of "I will be here."

It can be a great release to be frank. I remember one man saying to me, "You know, I've had it all out with my wife and now we can relax and talk about something else." I think that is important too.

Rather unusually, one family took complete control and told a young woman patient so that she could share her knowledge of dying with her husband all the way through. For the two months or so that she was with us, she maintained an air of serenity until the end. Of course, this would not work for every family. With another family and another patient the situation is completely different.

I remember one old woman telling me, very firmly, "And when I'm going downhill, doctor, I don't intend you to tell me!" (That reminds me of another patient who, looking at me rather sideways, said, "I know you know how much chance I've got, doctor, but I'm not going to ask you.") Such feelings are to be respected; it is the patient's choice and we should honor it. When the woman was beginning to go downhill I saw her sitting pensively with her great-grandchild on her knee, realizing—but not telling. At St. Joseph's we certainly admit, allow, and welcome children into the ward. They are very important to *all* our patients, not just the ones they are visiting. The patients need to have this sense of continuity, to know that life is going on. A child, just because it is a child, should be welcomed in this sort of ward.

We all know the very anxious patient who has, as it were, an invisible extra pillow: she can never rest her head right back on her pillow, she is constantly in some kind of tension. Such a person will tend to deny what is happening, will talk only about her symptoms, and has to be reassured by practical things—being given this or that drug or treatment. Not only is every patient different from every other patient, but the same patient will have a different face on a different day. One particular patient made her will with a fair amount of drama one day, and then a week or two later confided to me, "Doctor, you know what I *really* need is a new set of false teeth." Care of the dying person is a changing situation, and we have to time the help we give to the right moment. Patients will reach out to us on two levels at the same time. And they, too, want a day off! Mankind cannot bear too much reality. There is a day when you think you see a crisis coming and think, "Ah, now we're going to talk about it." Not at all—the patient only wants to talk about the weather, and naturally should be allowed to. The rule is that there are no general rules here except that you must listen. You must be ready to listen; you must be ready to be silent; and you must just be committed.

Sometimes one gets a very direct question. One man asked me a direct question at a stage when I knew him very well and when it would have been an insult not to have fully answered him. Often I give a rather open or perhaps two-way answer and the person can pick up whichever one he really wants. But when this man asked, "Am I going to die?" I just said "Yes." And he said "Long?" and I said "No." He said, "Was it hard for you to tell me that?" "Yes, it was." He just said, "Thank you. It's hard to be told, but it's hard to tell too." His comment was, I think, truly significant. In the first place, it shows how extremely courteous and outward-looking these patients are. And secondly, it should be hard to tell. You just should not be doing this easily. It *should* be hard because you are trying to bring everything you have of understanding to hear what this patient is really asking you. Then you should be concerned that he does well with what you give him, and that you really are committing yourself to helping him in every way you can, helping him right up to the end. I remember also asking him, "What do you look for most of all in the people who are looking after you?" He thought and said, "Well, for someone to look as if they are trying to understand me. I'm hard to understand." He asks not for success but for somebody who looks as if he cares enough to try. I think that is the fundamental thing. Of course, when you are a student, and when you are a nurse, the patient must know that you really do not know the answer, but this gives you all the more opportunity to try to learn by listening, to ask yourself, "What does the patient really want to know? What is it he's worried about?"

PAIN

A great deal of my time has been spent with patients who have severe intractable pain. This is really where my interest in this work began. I remember one patient who, when she was admitted, simply could not think of anything but pain. In a tape recording made at the time she said, "I love my family but I couldn't bear to have them in the room because I couldn't think of anything else, and they would have seen the pain in my face." That sort of pain we can control, nearly always without rendering the patient sleepy. Later in her stay at St. Joseph's I looked in on her and found her peacefully writing a letter.

Chronic pain of this kind is a very complicated condition, different from acute pain. One woman had a whole variety of symptoms and problems including a very large, open wound. She was restless and in severe pain. Upon admission the referring doctor had written on her form, "Mainly stuporous now." But that was due to drugs, and not her mental condition. Three months later, she was sitting up in a chair, organizing the ward and so on. When she was finally dying it was she who told me at what stage she thought she really ought to take to bed. I think that to be in such control can be a psychologically healthy and reassuring situation.

I recall a girl newly admitted. When I went in to talk to her she just burst into tears because she expected to be hurt so much the moment anybody came near her. She had chronic pain that went on the whole time but also was exacerbated by movement. The situation held her, as it were, in a vise. As she described it, "The pain was all around me." This is so different from the protective, warning pain of a kitchen burn or of the symptom that brings a patient for diagnosis or the postoperative pain which has a reason and which you know is not going to go on for very long. This is a *chronic* pain which seems to be timeless and endless as well as meaningless. Now, it is important to realize that many patients make their pain worse by anticipating it. Consequently *we* should do the anticipating. At St. Joseph's we use our drugs to prevent the pain from ever happening rather than trying to get on top of it once it has occurred. This means a careful analysis of the total situation—the other symptoms, attention to details, a lot of careful nursing, and just listening so that we know what their sensation is like, and so that they know we are interested. I had a patient say to me, "And then I came here and *you listened*. The pain seemed to go by just talking." She was not just trying to be polite; her perception of pain had really been influenced by our attention and time.

I stopped to talk with a girl about six weeks before she died, and she had the rather "yonderly" look of someone who is beginning to let go. Preparation for dying seems to begin in the subconscious. How much was conscious for her at any stage I do not really know. I had hoped we might get her home again, but when I saw her face that day I knew it would not be possible. The surgeon came up to consult again and told us that nothing more could be done. She had been in our ward for five and a half months, and when she died she was on the same dose of narcotic at which we stabilized her when she first came in. This can be done. The problems of tolerance and dependence can be almost eliminated by the way in which the administration of drugs is managed. It should be part of the whole process of caring for the patient. The aim is that the patient should be alert—alert and himself, and that he should be independent. If every time the patient has a pain he must ask somebody else for something to relieve it, it reminds him that he is dependent on the drug, dependent on another person. But, if instead, the staff can anticipate the occurrence of pain, at St. Joseph's by a system of regular giving of adequate medication to cover the chosen routine time, the patient does not continually have to ask for relief. He can stay alert, thinking of other things, and "forgetting" the pain.

Relief from pain should be given all the way to the end. If it is, the patient can remain himself. I remember talking to one woman who clearly demonstrated the capacity for meeting person-to-person that we so often see in the very ill. This was five days before her death. This woman was Jewish: she was deaf and dumb and she had lived in the east end of London all her life. She could not have had an easy life. But just by looking at her, we knew a great deal about her as she truly was. Our job was to control her distress and pain so that she could be herself until the end.

After this patient died, I remember the woman in the next bed confiding to me, "She didn't suffer. They don't here. I think the motto of this place is 'There shall be no pain.' It makes you feel very safe." This is a safety which gives independence, not dependence.

BALANCING CLARITY AND REDUCTION OF PAIN

To give enough help up to the end without making a patient sleepy is a problem of delicate balance. If you balance your drugs for the control of incipient confusion, anxiety, and depression the patient will not be sleepy and confused. It is often more difficult to get the balance of the tranquilizers and sedatives than of the analgesics but all the more rewarding for that.

Alcohol remains our best sedative, especially for the elderly. Most of us feel better after a drink; why should the patient be any different? We are allowed to give alcohol in the National Health Service and we are allowed to give gin as part of our favorite pain-relief cocktail, and "it's on the house." Also we encourage relatives to bring in alcohol if they know the patient would enjoy it. I mean quite honestly that a bottle of whiskey may be more valuable than a whole great basket of oranges. A little of what the patient likes does him good. I know you have a problem with alcoholism in the United States as well as with addiction, and perhaps you feel differently, but I have not noticed that Americans feel any differently about serving drinks. I am not suggesting that I have my patients high on alcohol. I am not trying to produce a high positive euphoria. But they come in with a heavy burden, which makes them feel lower than the next person, and we are trying to reduce their burden to manageable proportions. As visitors often remark, our patients look like ordinary, relaxed, serene, cheerful people. I heard one of the students explain the atmosphere this way: "It's the kind of atmosphere that makes one feel that death really isn't anything to be frightened of, but a sort of homecoming." I think she summed it up very well. You just go on. You go on trying something different. You go on listening. You keep coming in, day after day, trying to get the balance right. With some patients you have to keep on trying. With others, you get them balanced and it remains perfect for them to the end.

Personal, caring contact is the most important comfort we can give. It is not necessary always to pay a long visit. Often we are very busy, but there is always time for a brief word. Above all, we must never let the patients down. Never just go by. The dying will lie with their eyes shut just out of tiredness when they are waiting for you. If you then fly past the end of the bed, rather pleased to find them asleep, they have lost that precious moment for which they were waiting. In a Chinese poem of the ninth century A.D. are the lines: "Tranquil talk was better than any medicine. Gradually the feelings came back to my numbed heart." Once a patient knows that you are really interested, he also knows well enough when you are in a hurry. Some of the things to which you listen are not particularly fine, maybe, and some are jolly good grumbles. But I think it is essential that the aggressive person who wants to grumble should be able to do it to you and not to other patients. Somebody who is basically a "doing" sort of person, such as one old patient I remember, a former flyweight boxer, finds it very hard having things done for him. If he is going to let his frustration out and blow some of it off by grumbling away about it, then he should be allowed —not indulged—but allowed to do so.

THE IMPORTANCE OF CHOICE

If a patient chooses to be out and about, as far as possible we let him. If he says, "Oh, I really must take to bed," we usually find that he is right. He knows what he can manage. On the whole, we really do let him make the choice. I think this is valuable, but it is usually difficult to do in a general ward, where the whole process is geared to getting the patient out, getting him going, and so on. You may see some poor old man propped up in a wheelchair when you know he is just longing, "Please put me back." When a patient does not have much energy, he may want to save it for talking to relatives at visiting time, and not use it being gotten in and out of bed. As far as the control of physical symptoms and the control of pain are concerned, some of our patients say, "I don't want to get used to it." We can always reassure them that what we are using will go on being effective. I find that patients are more often fearful about taking something for sleep than about taking something for pain. I say to my patients, "Now, I'm going to give you something for your restlessness and something for this and something for the other." I do not tell them exactly what the drugs are—they would not remember, anyway. But I do tell them what I am trying to do, and I try to involve them in the situation. I also try to change only one drug at a time, because if you change three drugs and the patient feels sick, which one is responsible? As the guides to public speaking advise, "Tell them what's going on." There is a paper written by a patient who says that he had received many pills and many medicines in his various visits to hospitals and nobody had told him what any one of them was for. He said, "I could have at least added one minim of faith if I'd been told in what direction to project my faith."

THE ISSUE OF EUTHANASIA

I am in the happy position of not being able to carry out drastic life-prolonging measures because we just do not have the facilities at St. Joseph's. Other people have made the decision, at a prior stage, that this is a patient for whom such procedures are not suitable or right or kind. This makes it very much easier for us than for the staff of a busy general ward. I think that it is extremely important that the decision be made by a person who has learned all he can about the family, about the patient himself, and about the whole situation. The further we go in having special means at our disposal, the more important it is that we stop and think what we are doing. Of course we must consider the facilities available in the particular institution and the demands on them, but the most crucial consideration is the welfare of the individual patient. In England there is a society that works to get euthanasia legalized. They are specially concerned with the problem of the patients that I work with, those with terminal malignant disease. Though these are not necessarily the most difficult patients to look after, I will stick to them because they are the ones I know best. I have had much correspondence with the former chairman of the Euthanasia Society in Great Britain, and I took him round St. Joseph's after I had been working there some eighteen months. He came away saying, "I didn't know you could do it. If all patients died something like this, we could disband the Society." And he added, "I'd like to come and die in your Home." I do not believe in taking a deliberate step to end a patient's life—but then, I do not get asked. If you relieve a patient's pain and if you can make him feel like a wanted person, which he is, then you are not going to be asked about euthanasia. It is sad that so many patients still do not die in this condition. However, there is no situation in which you cannot get across to a patient that he is a person you care about. Even if you are in a hurry, you can do it; I have seen it happening again and again. This is the positive side of the issue. The idea of euthanasia, legalized killing, is to me morally wrong. But if my own standard of morals, or code of ethics, does not make sense for the other person, I am not going to change his mind by saying that. I think that euthanasia is an admission of defeat, and a totally negative approach. One should be working to see that it is not needed. The great responsibility that we have, those of us who think it is wrong to relieve all pains by euthanasia, is to see that the pains *are* relieved. After all, this is no more than the total responsibility that you take on with any patient under your care.

WARD DYNAMICS: DEATH OF A PATIENT

The patient who is upset when another patient dies is usually the one who has just come in, and who does not yet know us or trust us. The patient who has been with us for some time, and knows that the other patient is ready, takes it far more quietly, not carelessly but with a compassionate matter-of-factness which one sees, of course, with the nuns. The nuns have this quality par excellence: this capacity to be matter-of-fact and to go on doing things while showing deep compassion. We do not move our patients away when they are dying. We have one single room on each floor, but we do not move patients into it unless, perhaps, family tradition dictates that ten members of the family sit around the bed for ten days on end or something like that. But apart from such occasional crises the patients remain in their own beds during their final days. This is vital. I have worked in a setting where patients were always moved out, and the other patients were then far more disturbed. You could see them thinking, "What is it like? We never see it. It must be awful." By contrast, when people die in the ward, it isn't "awful." It is always quiet. "It's as quiet as blowing a candle out" is how patients have described it to me. Often it is because they have seen somebody else die quietly that they are finally able to talk about death themselves. They talk not because they have an extra weight of anxiety but because they feel "Oh! Now it seems that it isn't quite so frightening." What counts the most is that they can see that they are not alone. Since we take care that the nuns say the "last prayers" at the last moment, we have to be good at knowing when this last moment is. We try hard to see to it that patients are not alone at the end. And so they are in the ward, they do have their cubicle curtains drawn at the last moment, and more often than not Sister is actually there, saying her prayers at the very moment that the patient dies. Often the family is there too. While you may think that this sounds disturbing, it is not. It is aloneness that our patients are most afraid of. It is also essential that we should be good at making the end peaceful. The patient should not be confused, fighting for breath, crying out, and that sort of thing. The end is always quiet and peaceful, and nearly always the patient is in a state of sleep or unconsciousness. The patient who dies fully conscious is rare, but a few do.

Another feature is that one must always let the other patients talk about it, if they want to. We do not force talking upon them, but neither do we say, "She went home in the middle of the night," or "We moved her out into a single room," or some other deception like that. I found out that one old lady was mending her nightdress forty-eight hours before she died because the patient in the bed opposite told me. Then we talked about her.

Sometimes patients become extremely fond of each other and they have much to give each other, including emotional support and a great deal of individual helping. But—love costs. It always does. It is hard when somebody you are very fond of goes but more than once a patient has said to me, "You know, I gave her her last drink." There is a special communication here.

Sometimes we may have several patients who die, one right after the other. Because we have only about forty-five beds for dying patients out of a wing of seventy-five, the others having long-term illness, we are able to move some around and release the tension. Of course, this is a problem but there are problems in every hospital. My final point on this topic is, we are not afraid of dying ourselves. It is quiet on the ward; there is no sense of panic; it is all right.

HELPING THE GRIEVING FAMILY

We always tend to feel guilty in bereavement. Indeed, feelings of guilt are part of bereavement. We go back in memory until we find ways that we let the person down. We remember things that we did and now cannot undo. To know that it is natural and ordinary to feel this way can be very helpful. I think that the nurses can do a great deal for the grieving family. The nurse who said to me, "He didn't open his eyes again after you left, you know. You *were* the last person he saw," helped me more than anybody else. This really did matter to me.

One of the ways we try at St. Joseph's to help the bereaved is just to listen. If a relative wants to say, "Why did God do this to me? Why did He let this happen? Why did the doctor operate?" you must let him do it. You must never stop him. You must never argue. You must let him talk, because expressing these thoughts begins to help toward healing. He may have to express his anguish again and again, but the listener is the person who is needed, and especially the listener who is not a member of the family. The listener from outside can help in a way that another family member cannot. But if we are to learn to help as listeners, we have to learn to accept people as they are. Once when I was complaining about a particularly disturbing and troublesome patient, Sister looked up at me and said simply, "He is himself." People who can allow us to be ourselves are helpful, particularly in bereavement.

One sees that mourning is not just forgetting. It includes a sense of going back to all the ties, and undoing them, and taking out what is really valuable, until in the end what is finally left is no longer grief in the same way, since much has been resolved. This part of the family time together is very important and can make a crucial difference to the whole grieving process.

THE MEANING OF DYING

A feeling of meaninglessness can be the hardest pain of all for a dying person to bear. Now, you can never impose your own meaning upon another person and his situation, but in a place like St. Joseph's where other people are convinced of the meaning of living and dying, it is easier to find your own way. Sometimes another patient is more help than anybody else. Sometimes the staff have to bear their inability to understand, to feel as if they are not helping at all, yet still go on staying close to the patient. We tend to feel that if we are bringing nothing, then we had better go away. But I think that is just the moment when we have simply got to stay. And if this is the moment when the patient feels that there is no meaning in life and that the weariness of it all is more than he can cope with and we are feeling helpless too, well, we are very much on the same level there. In that place where you share helplessness—there, perhaps, you can help more than you realize.

"Yes, doctor, you can show my photograph to anyone you like," I remember a patient saying, "and you can say to them 'It was all right.' " When she had been admitted to St. Joseph's, it was not "all right" for her, but as she found her way it was she who was telling us the meaning, not the other way around. The answer is found by meeting fate, not by demanding "Why?" but by asking "How?" "How do I live in this situation?" It is like Viktor Frankl finding meaning in the life of the concentration camps; like Dag Hammarskjöld deciding to say "Yes" to life; learning from Pierre Teilhard de Chardin to accept our own passivities at the deepest level. But for the woman photographed it was not complicated like that at all. The answer for her was just simple, loving obedience to the daily demands of what was going on in a place where she was continually finding help and meaning, finding that love casts out fear.

THE ROLE OF RELIGION WITH THE DYING

Though there are many similarities among patients who are facing death, each has his unique way of responding. Religion is a real and living thing for a number of our patients, and its meaning grows deeper as death nears. But many of our patients are extremely indifferent to religion, or at least detached from it. I have heard one of the Sisters say kindly of a patient: "His religion's pretty harmless." I doubt that the really aggressive atheist ever reaches us, because the family, knowing that the hospice is run by nuns, would be likely to decide to go somewhere else.

In any case, we certainly never do any imposing. I remember one incident when the Sister reported to me, "You know, I went round the ward the other day and I found Mrs. So-and-so reading the Bible and I said to her, 'My goodness, Mrs. So-and-so!' and she said, 'It's all right, Sister. It's just for the crossword puzzle!' " The fact that we could all enjoy this as a joke is indicative of the atmosphere at St. Joseph's.

Whatever the religious background of our patients, I often see in them something that could be called "reaching out trustfully." They come to remember things from the past, things that they have been too busy to listen to before, and as death approaches, they find that things begin to make sense. They bring a new attention to the old truths. This is something entirely different from plucking at straws, and is an extremely personal matter for each patient.

What I see over and over again with dying persons, and not only because I hope to see this, are the fruits of the spirit—"love, joy, peace, long-suffering, gentleness, goodness, faith, meekness, self-control." For me this is "truth," and this I continually see. The nuns, I think, represent Christianity in general rather than Catholicism in particular. What we have in common is much more important than what we disagree about. What I see in patients is to be read of in Martin Buber, the Jewish theologian and philosopher, in Teilhard de Chardin, the Catholic, and in many others—they are talking to each other. I am trying to pin down the intangible. If you have seen it—if you have been with these patients—then you will recognize what I am trying to say.

Patients are often shy to ask for spiritual help; at least, they are in Great Britain. So all the more we have to serve as a link. It is often easier for a patient just to mention it to or to have it mentioned by an ordinary person. Perhaps they can accept this kind of help only from an ordinary person. You have to go quietly and very slowly, but you do need to know, I think, about their need for spiritual help, and classify this term as widely as you like. When professionals talk about the care of the dying, they are often careful to omit this topic completely, or they may say, "Well, it's an individual matter." I believe there is a responsibility on us here; otherwise it is just deciding by default. It is part of total care, even if it is not called by that name, or even recognized. At St. Joseph's I have had the good fortune of working with nuns in an atmosphere where religion is totally integrated into all that we do and think, but never forced on anyone who enters. It is there, largely without words. Florence Nightingale, I think, is the one who said, "You should carry the bedpan for the glory of God." Many would prefer to say, "I'll carry it for the dignity of man." But, you know, the two belong together.

I have been trying to talk, in several ways, about "being present" to these people. Underneath there has been a belief in the person in the midst of life and death and in God as the Truth of the moment of truth. Personal, compassionate trust is really what is behind the atmosphere at St. Joseph's.

In my work one is continually seeing people at their most mature. One could look thus far in this work and say that to recognize this moment of greatest maturity, of the greatest depth of individuality, is a totally satisfying and positive aim and ending. But Eissler, in his book *The Psychiatrist and the Dying Patient*, talks about the need for the psychotherapist to have some sort of feeling about the immortality of his patient. I would add: perhaps something more than just "some sort of feeling."

I remember watching one man who could concentrate totally on the white hyacinth plant by his bed. I saw in him the relief of that moment of pure pleasure. Somehow it seemed to be saying to him, "The world to which you also belong is good and can be trusted."

I recall the gaiety of that man and of many others. It was not a euphoria induced by drugs and alcohol. It was the gaiety of having gone through doubts and fears and questions and having come right out on the other side. This, I believe, is why one can go on working with these dying patients, day after day, and month after month.

One patient moved from severe anxiety and denial to an emotional stage where one day, when I was sitting on her bed, she suddenly said to me, "You know, doctor, I couldn't ever really imagine myself dying, but there does come a time when you are ready to lay it down." This reminds me of the always uncanny moment when the body, which even in confusion and pain expresses the person, is suddenly empty. To me, the mind and body are absolutely interwoven, but appear to be no more than the tools of the spirit, which is of much more importance. The spirit seems to lay down the body and the mind when death finally comes.

I recall so many who have been truly ready for meeting this "moment." These patients show man's ability to sum up all that he is in this one moment, this moment of truth. In life, we are always looking ahead and never quite getting there. We are always aiming too far, or we are always tipping over into the depths of self-concern. Even so, we bring all that we are into every moment. The "reason why we're here" is a summing up of everything that has happened before. At this stage, and I have seen it again and again, somehow there is a moment that is fully personal and everything is summed up. When Pope John was dying, he said, "My bags are packed and I can go with a tranquil

heart at any moment." This is the "moment" of the bullfight—
the whole thing summed up.

I remember talking with a patient the day before her death.
Her face showed all the quietness and the weariness of dying.
Yet she consented to my taking her picture, knowing that I
would use it for lectures. She was a warm person who had been
in our wards a long time, and she enjoyed meeting students.
That afternoon, she was easily able to talk about death and also
to ask me to say one or two things to her family for her. Our students used to come round to visit her. She was the sort of person
who was helping our work, and she knew it. She could teach far
more during just a short visit by sharing her experience, in whatever way she wanted to at the time, than ever I could do in my
talking about it. People who are dying often have a tremendous
capacity for meeting, or encountering, because they have put
aside the mask that we tend to wear in everyday life. Now they
are ready to meet, just as themselves, and I am sure this is why
you can get to know these patients in an extraordinarily short
time, in fact, even in a brief meeting. As students going round
the ward said, "She taught us a great deal of wisdom which we
will never forget."

The answer to the question of preparation for this kind of
work is that *you learn the care of the dying from the dying themselves.* But only if you look at them with respect and never
merely with pity, and allow them to teach you. It is they who
show us that the fear of death is overcome. Seeing this, we, too,
can come to the place to which I have seen them come so often,
and which Ralph Harper describes vividly in his book *Nostalgia*:
"We cannot know what is beyond the end of our days, but we
can enter into an order of things which can make us say, 'I'm not
afraid.' "

The Effects of Death
upon the Family

RICHARD A. KALISH

Ray AND HIS WIFE have been close friends of ours for about eight years, in that sort of friendship where you can argue about basic values, snipe at each other's style of living, and remain close friends. Ray had accumulated a considerable net worth through careful investment and management and by living comfortably but far within his income, but had never had children. One evening at our home, he told us that they had decided to adopt a child; he suddenly realized that the substantial holdings he was building would not offer him the prospect of pleasure in his old age unless he could see someone else enjoy the use of the money and could know it would be used after his death by someone he loved. This was the first time we had discussed death, and it was obvious that—at his age of thirty-five—the inevitability of his death had suddenly become an emotional force in his life. The first decade of his work life had been directed solely at accumulation, but this was already appearing insufficient as a reason for being. Now he was seeking a more significant meaning for his existence, through the desire to see his money enjoyed by someone he loved. (He now has two children and has been talking about two more.)

Then, the day I began writing this paper, Ray and I were talking on the telephone. His wife had been hurt in a serious automobile accident, probably having her life saved by the seat belt. She had returned home after ten days in the hospital just in time to watch her mother fall downstairs and break her leg. In the telephone conversation, Ray mentioned almost immediately that the two accidents, especially his wife's, had caused him to change his mind about his style of living, that from now on he was going to live more comfortably and devote only a small share of his income to building his "fortune." He had encountered death in another way, and recognized that all his careful planning for the nebulous future was almost negated by a chance occurrence.

I mention this because of its salience to me at the moment of writing, but also because it is a dramatic example of how death, in this case an almost-death, provides an impetus for behavior change. How would Ray have reacted if his wife had died in the accident? The impact of death upon the family is the formal topic of my discussion.

BACKGROUND ASSUMPTIONS

First, by way of background, some speculation regarding the role of death in contemporary America. Let me make some of my assumptions explicit. These are somewhat controversial assumptions, and you need not accept them in toto in order to follow my subsequent thinking about the role of death and its impact upon the family of the dying and dead.

First, I will assume that Americans—at least by comparison with past generations—do not have a firm belief in an afterlife. They may halfheartedly accept the idea of some form of self-aware existence after death, or they may wish to believe that such exists, but the belief is neither firm nor dominant (Hinton, 1967). However, although the typical American does not fear hell or judgment, he does fear the possibility of a void. Hell, at least, can be discussed, thought about, argued about, perhaps discarded for theoretically logical or theological reasons, but how do you speculate about the nature of a void?

Secondly, closely related to the first assumption, is that God, if not dead, is pretty sick. In this statement, I am not presenting in any sense a theological argument, but the social-psychological point that when people no longer believe in God, God—in a sense—ceases to exist. Please do not misquote me—although after fifteen years of teaching I should be used to that—as stating an atheistic position; this is strictly psychological. All right, then: God in the traditional Judeo-Christian form is not the dominant, overpowering figure that He was to our grandparents. We go to church, perhaps, and enjoy services, but we talk about how good it makes us feel and about the values our children are learning and about the social-service and recreational functions of our church. We do not go to propitiate a God who wields tremendous power over us and frightens us, or to give grateful thanks, but to bargain a bit—we will give him our soul and our children's souls in exchange for a promotion, a more academically motivated child, or a peaceful solution to our urban conflicts.

Thirdly, that we have seen that the physical body, our shell, can remain in good condition for many decades, and rather like the idea. This is new. In past centuries, when death was always imminent, the minister represented the most important force in the world—the sacred force of God, which promised people a happier life "beyond." Unamuno quotes the statement of an elderly European peasant: "If there is no immortality, of what use is God? [cited in Barrett, 1958]." And, also, of what use is the minister? Since the body, not the soul, requires the most immediate care, it was inevitable that the custodian of the body would be elevated to the rank of priest. If you can accept the premise that religion is "man's ultimate concern," then physical health is most assuredly a religion, and the physician is its priest, and the rewards of believing in this religion are a long and healthy life.

However, whereas there was no way of empirically verifying the effectiveness of the more traditional priest in getting our souls to heaven, the impossibility of the task assigned the medical priesthood became only too painfully apparent. When the medical profession was found wanting in its imposed (and often gladly accepted) role as the new priesthood, an antimedical movement (comparable to earlier anticlerical movements) developed. The financial demands of the medical profession further outraged us, just as the financial demands of the clerics had in earlier times.

Fourthly, that we do not find the affluence we enjoy as fulfilling as we anticipated, even though it provides us with a vast array of material possessions and services. As with any element of the status quo, people soon begin to take for granted that "what is," is right and proper, and we have assumed that these possessions and services are part of our birthright. If, however, affluence and good health form "man's ultimate concerns" and therefore his religion, death is antireligious, because it makes these accomplishments—eventually and inevitably—meaningless. Even the funeral director's chemicals and the cemetery's noncombustible concrete vaults are not sufficient. It also makes meaningless some of our other gods, such as education and knowledge, warm human relationships, scientific advances, emotional stability, personal identity, artistic taste, and fame. Even being mentally healthy can only have temporary meaning as an "ultimate" concern.

Fifthly, that we are afraid, as the existentialists admonish us that this is an absurd world without meaning and that there is nothing to do but try to have the strength to accept death and subsequent nothingness. We have given these views some consideration, but the loss of earthly life is difficult to contemplate *even* when a future life is anticipated; when your religion preaches the desirability of material possessions and bodily health, the loss is overwhelming. We are compelled to find a meaning in life, and we seek it frantically.

Lastly, that, in our experience, death is for the very old, the accident victim, and the soldier. It rarely comes close to us. It occurs in the hospital, it occurs on the highway, it occurs in Vietnam. When it happens to a member of our family, chances are that the person who has died is physically away from us, in a retirement community, or in a nursing home, or in a hospital. Often toward the end our contacts with the person have not been frequent, and our emotional involvement has diminished. (Social gerontologists have written extensively about the disengagement of the elderly person as he and society withdraw emotionally from each other, but relatively little has been said about the disengagement of the relatives of the dying person.)

To try to pull these ideas together: the religious worship of God has, to some extent, been replaced by the worship of material goods and services, with secondary gods such as education, taste, knowledge, scientific advances, and human relationships. The method of gaining access to these gods is through physical and psychological health. This form of worship eventually ends in failure, since we all must die. Death, then, is the final insult, since it robs us of what we worship.

Viewed in this light, death is blasphemous and—using Geoffrey Gorer's word—pornographic (1956). We react to it and to its symbols in much the same way as we react to any pornography. We avoid it. We deny that it exists. We avert our eyes from its presence. We denounce it and send out squads of people to eradicate it. We protect little children from observing it and dodge their questions about it. We speak of it only in whispers. We consider it horrible, ugly, and grotesque.

And, logically, we push away from us those symbols of death

that remind us of this obscene and blasphemous matter. The terminally ill and the very old are carefully segregated so that their presence will not remind us that we shall some day find our God has also failed. We hope they will enjoy themselves—but away from us. The possibility that dying at home has merit is once again being discussed, but it is still far from popular with either the medical profession or laymen—and not only for the practical matters of the need for intensive care. A study I conducted recently indicated that dying people are more to be avoided as friends, neighbors, or even visitors to the country than are Negroes, Mexican-Americans, Jews, or other discriminated-against ethnic minority groups (Kalish, 1966).

I would like to add, parenthetically, that I think there are ways we can change these attitudes about death. I think the opportunity to read about the dying process, to think about it, and to talk about it is most helpful. Just as many of us pride ourselves on our ability to be able to talk about sex without blanching, without using euphemisms, or without being unnecessarily crude, we will eventually become comfortable with the topic of death. If I were to set up a training program for professionals who work with the dying person, it would provide ample opportunity for discussion, although not necessarily to the point of group therapy. Once such discussions can be held easily, the problem will be substantially reduced. I would also hope that the training of doctors and nurses, and perhaps also that of clergymen, psychologists, and social workers, would include being brought into an environment where people are dying. In three years of nursing school my wife saw a dying person only once, and then only by chance; and certainly there are innumerable medical students who rarely or never encounter the dying patient.

With this background as a frame of reference, I would like to discuss more explicitly the impact of dying upon the family, first the dying of the elderly person, then of the middle-aged person, and finally of the child. Many of my comments, of course, will be relevant to a substantial portion of the life span.

THE DYING OF THE OLDER PERSON

The dying of the elderly is, by and large, the least disturbing. In our society, the aged are not especially valued. I once asked a group of about two dozen Cambodian students in their mid-twenties whether, given the necessity for choice, they would save the life of their mother, their wife, or their daughter. All responded immediately that they would save their mother, and their tone implied that only an immoral or ignorant person would even ask such a question. I doubt whether 10 per cent of a comparable American group would give that response.

In a recent study, Kastenbaum (1964) asked nurses what they felt were appropriate time and energy considerations for saving the life of a twenty-year-old, an eighty-year-old, and a pet dog. The ratio of importance of the twenty-year-old to the eighty-year-old was greater than that of the eighty-year-old to the dog. Glaser and Strauss (1964) have consistently found that the lives of the elderly are not highly valued. Thus their deaths are not highly disturbing.

This situation is accentuated by modern living arrangements, in which the elderly most frequently live apart from their adult children, or move together only when the elderly person requires physical care or at least cannot safely live alone. In a society that regards independence in children as a "good thing," it is considered inappropriate for a child to continue to live with a parent beyond a certain age. Being tied to mother's apron strings is a major concern even with young children—although in traditional Japanese families this occurs in a literal fashion (Kalish, 1967).

Nor does the elderly individual wish to become dependent upon his children. Such a relationship will not only be perceived as a regression, but may rearouse the younger members' anxieties regarding dependence. The nuclear family has become a part of our culture, and the elderly person inevitably stands outside this unit. I remember a magazine advertisement showing a well-dressed, attractive elderly woman riding in the rear seat of a station wagon, facing out the back and looking most forlorn, with the children and grandchildren enjoying the ride together in the front seats. I believe the ad was for annuities—it was most telling.

Since most elderly people prefer, if with occasional ambivalence, to live outside the family units of their children, and since their children are usually only too happy to accord them this privilege of remaining independent, the close and continuing contacts of times past are not revived. The concept of the seventy-year-old man being the patriarch to whom others come for advice seems of historical rather than contemporary validity, though the often-cited desertion of the old by their middle-aged children may well be exaggerated in frequency.

To aggravate this situation further, geographical mobility often separates the elderly from their children by many miles and many dollars' worth of transportation. Retirement communities also contribute to this separation, as does our age-graded society in which social relationships tend to be among individuals of the same age group and family status, rather than among members of the same family regardless of age or status. In spite of lip service to the benefits of age integration, many Americans of all ages appear to prefer living near their own age peers.

In other ways, the role of the elderly has become less important and, thus, his death is less disruptive. His children are out of the home and are probably well ensconced in their own homes. The older person is responsible for handling the financial arrangements only for himself and his spouse (and frequently only for himself), so that his function as breadwinner has diminished greatly in importance. He is not respected as a decision-maker or adviser and, indeed, is likely to have less, perhaps much less, formal education than his children, so that he probably has difficulty considering himself essential to the welfare and emotional stability of his children. Nor is there a work organization or a bustling household which requires his (or her) wisdom and counsel. And his church activities have probably diminished, although—ironically—his religious beliefs have likely intensified (Moberg, 1965).

The importance of the elderly person to the world around him has diminished, and simultaneously he may be undergoing the process called disengagement, through which he is withdrawing from some of his involvements in the world. He and his community are moving socially and emotionally away from each other. Lack of contact with younger people, including his own children and grandchildren, social isolation accentuated by independent living and geographical mobility, a view of dependence as an admission of failure, and lack of importance to a work organization or a household, all these factors conspire to make the death of an elderly person less upsetting to his family and the community. Added to this, the likelihood of his dying at home is relatively slight, so that the family encounter with the dying process of an aged individual has less impact and is less disturbing. As Glaser and Strauss have claimed, there is indeed a "right" time to die (1968).

However, I have covered only part of the matter and from only one point of view. I have portrayed a picture in which young people (i.e., everyone under sixty—working in gerontology does wonders for your self-concept as you age) are unfeeling villains in the drama of their parents' dying. There is another side to the coin. The elderly person is likely to be dying of a degenerative disease. He is often in pain and has been for some time, although several sources assure us that the dying hours and minutes are rarely painful if proper medical attention is given (Worcester, 1940). His disease is irreversible and this has been known for some time. During the preceding weeks, months, perhaps years, he has undergone certain personality changes that—regardless of their cause—make him a less pleasant person to be with. He may be comatose, seldom lucid, unable to recognize his family. And illness and dying may well be cutting deeply into the finances of his children, not infrequently causing hard feelings between siblings.

Resentment over paying the expenses of terminal illness and guilt over this resentment are a common theme in the family of the dying. Often the child of the aged individual is himself planning for a retirement in the near future. Not infrequently the assets of the elderly fail to cover fully the costs of terminal illnesses, dying, death, and funeral preparations. Medicare will now take much of the financial burden from the elderly and their children, so that the financial problems and the resulting psychological and social problems will be reduced, although hardly eliminated.

I recently had the opportunity to observe a good example of hostility between two sisters, resulting from the dying process of their mother. The older sister and her husband were childless after sixteen years of marriage and lived comfortably, though hardly luxuriously. The younger sister had three children, and her husband was unstable in his job situation, although his own income was comparable to his brother-in-law's. The mother had lived with the older sister and her husband for fifteen of their sixteen years of marriage, and had recently become confused. She would wander away from home and be brought back by the local police, or they would receive a telephone call from a police station twenty miles away that Mama had reached without remembering how. Finally the older sister and her husband decided to make arrangements to have her mother placed in a geriatric facility. She explained to me that her younger sister refused to take the mother home for more than an infrequent visit, and that she also refused to contribute to the cost, because she claimed she had other financial responsibilities. However, when the decision to institutionalize the mother came up, the younger sister refused point-blank—would not even consider it. The older sister went ahead with the plan, in spite of increasing resistance; and the actual hospitalization marked the end of all communication between the two sisters. This situation had prevailed for almost a year when I conducted the interview.

The combination, then, of changing personality, lost role, social and psychological isolation, low social value, financial pressures, and possible physical suffering is used by family members to justify the death of an elderly person, perhaps even to anticipate it with positive feelings and to find it easy to rationalize these positive feelings as being appropriate. After the death, however, a sense of guilt frequently occurs, although perhaps with less intensity than after the death of a younger person. The guilt results from a number of feelings and occurrences, including the conscious or unconscious desire that the elderly person would die, or would hurry up and die, or would hurry up and die before all the money is gone, or . . . If the older person had an estate which the family desired, the wishes for an early and expedient death would be more intense and the resulting guilt would be greater. Feelings of guilt also spring from the younger person's awareness that he should have done more, written more often, gone to more family gatherings, invited the elderly relative for Sunday dinner more often, and so forth.

It is easy enough, however, to rationalize the death of an elderly person and even to rationalize one's wishes that the death would occur: He had lived a long, good life; or his life was long and wretched and he is better out of it; or how fortunate that he did not suffer any pain or any more pain or was able to gain release from the terrible pain. In giving these hypothetical quotations, I do not intend to belittle their validity, but merely to describe experiences we have all observed.

THE DYING OF THE MIDDLE-AGED PERSON

The dying of the middle-aged person provokes more emotional reaction. Such a death overturns the almost sacred goal in our society of a long and healthy enjoyment of affluence and material goods and services. Also, it becomes a reminder to the rest of us that we also are vulnerable, that this man's death represents the possibility that we also may die prematurely. If his death is accidental, we chalk it up to statistical probability, but with anxiety that our turn may be coming next, with the next drunk driver or faulty industrial machine or inadequately patrolled beach. If the death resulted from an illness, it is a strident reminder that a certain proportion of individuals die of so-called natural causes before the theoretical life span runs out, and the mortality tables take on a new significance. Recall for a moment my friend Ray, whose style of living changed so abruptly after the almost-death of his wife. Our accumulation of things is a bet against death, and when we observe someone who loses the bet, we wonder whether we are not letting too much of our life be thrown on the gaming table.

In addition, the middle-aged person still has important roles to play in life. He is probably still productive in his work; this I feel is a very important matter to the vast majority of Americans, who tend to place a high value on hard work and productivity. Second, people are still dependent upon him. His wife and children, especially, need him to play his role, and the role of a middle-aged parent is very difficult to replace. He may also have a role in various organizations, political, religious, social, and so forth. All in all, the dying and the death of the middle-aged individual are very distressing. He is perceived as having been cheated out of a portion of his birthright, and his absence causes an upheaval in his family and, perhaps, in his work organization and other groups. His children, if young, are deprived of a source of emotional stability and affection; they have lost a model for the development of sex-role behavior; their financial status is often abruptly altered. New roles must emerge in the family, perhaps with children taking over certain adult functions, perhaps with paid help, perhaps with other family members or close friends filling in, and perhaps—eventually— with a substitute parent.

I wish to consider briefly some typical patterns of emotional reaction to the death of a middle-aged person. Similar patterns may be observed following the death of a person of any age, but they seem to fit most appropriately here. The patterns I will mention include guilt, anger, displaced hostility, fear, sense of loss, and normal and abnormal bereavement.

First—guilt. No human relationship is perfect, and we all recognize—when pushed—that we have not contributed all that we might to any given relationship. We have ignored people when we should have offered love. We have hurt people by unnecessary and unfair harsh words. We have postponed occasions for enjoyment because of our selfishness. But through it all, we have perhaps felt that we would make it up later. Suddenly death eliminates the possibility of later. There is no longer any later, and we accuse ourselves of shortsightedness, of impatience, of failing to appreciate the worth of the dying or the dead. The ensuing feeling of guilt can be great, and there may be no one to afford absolution.

A particularly touching example of this feeling of guilt is shown, ironically in reverse, in a scene in Thornton Wilder's *Our Town*. Emily, a young wife, has died, but she has persuaded the powers-that-be to allow her one day back among the people she loved. She selects a happy day, her twelfth birthday, to relive. At once twelve years old and the shade of herself, deceased, Emily cries out to the members of her family to look at one another in their moment of happiness—to take notice of life as it speeds by. In this moving good-bye-world scene, Emily, as a person who has died, realizes the richness of life and the lost opportunities, but too late. The same words might well come from the living about their lost opportunities with the dead.

Feelings of guilt also arise from our wishes that another person would die. We all become angry with those we love, as well as with those we care little for. We all occasionally think life would be simpler or more pleasant if certain individuals were eliminated from the scene of our lives. If my father died, I could have his money; if my wife died, I could find a younger, more attractive woman who catered more to my whims; if my children died, I would be relieved of enormous responsibilities. These are mild death wishes (or desires that a person be eliminated, an end result for which death seems the most probable road). Stronger death wishes also occur: in the young man who greatly resents his older brother; in the wife who regrets a teenage marriage and a quick succession of children; in the middle-aged divorcee who remarries for security and finds only physical abuse. Yet, if the death occurs, we may feel that in a sense we willed it to occur. Even those who can honestly deny any superstitious feelings are likely to feel some guilt that their wishes were fulfilled.

In this context, I recall a personal experience that took place when I was in high school in Cleveland. I was talking with a small group of friends one Friday afternoon, when one of the girls, who had been courageous enough to take a physics course with the reputedly most demanding physics teacher in the county, exclaimed, "Damn it—I wish he'd drop dead!" The statement was made with great feeling. On Monday, when we returned to school, we learned that the teacher had had a heart attack over the weekend. Although he would recover, he would be out of school for some time. My friend was a wreck for the rest of the week. Though she could readily verbalize the total impossibility of any causal relationship between her statement and the heart attack, she was nonetheless strongly affected by a sense of responsibility for the event.

Children, of course, are much more susceptible to this feeling than adults or adolescents, since children cannot call upon the intellectual resources that would persuade themselves of their innocence. They still live in a world where magic and animism are frequent visitors. Children, as well as some preliterate groups, are less able to attribute acts such as dying to impersonal or chance forces; they apparently seek a different sort of reason. The mother who continually shouts to a child, "You'll be the death of me!" can evoke an understandably powerful sense of guilt if she does die in a way that, even by the most remote coincidence or distorted logic, the child might attribute to his behavior. Or the child admonished to be quiet during his father's illness may feel it his fault if his father dies following one of the demands for quiet—and he is likely to obscure the realities of time sequence in his recall. By no means do I wish to instill in parents any feelings of guilt for their exclamations or admonitions to their children—people cannot cover all possible contingencies for upsetting children, and I find too many parents too worried about what they do as it is. I merely wish to indicate a possible source of guilt feelings.

More important with children than these possibilities of chance is that children frequently express undisguised anger toward their parents. Accompanying this anger may be the wish, conscious or unconscious, to eliminate them. Thus if the death does occur, the child may feel that his acting out his anger produced the death. The logic of reasoning has little force.

Along with guilt, dying and death may elicit anger. Guilt itself, of course, may produce anger, since we tend to resent the source of our feelings of guilt, but other factors enter. Death is a type of desertion. Young children may perceive death as nothing more than desertion, but all of us feel that the dead person has left us, and we may have difficulty overcoming the unconscious feeling that he had a certain amount of conscious intent in his dying. We have difficulty overcoming the feeling that somehow—had he *really* wanted to—he could have chosen to live rather than die. Logic, of course, is often less important than feelings, and—since the end result of dying is much like the end result of desertion—it is not difficult to understand how even mature adults might unconsciously endow dying with some of the significance of desertion.

If you were to invest money in a friend's business, and your friend suddenly decided to leave town and take the assets with him, you would feel angry at the desertion. Similarly, when you invest much of yourself in another person, and he dies, thus taking your investment along with him—and leaving you with only memories—you are also likely to be angry. You have been punished for becoming dependent; you have been punished for offering your love and affection. These kinds of punishment are very painful and, for obvious reasons, are likely to elicit a form of anger in response to the extreme frustration they cause. Death of a family member may also induce feelings of helplessness and impotence that can lead to anger.

However, the anger need not be indirect. If there is an agent of some sort that may be identified as responsible, the anger may be directed against it: the driver of the automobile; the political leaders who are responsible for the war; the research scientists who spend so much time publishing in obscure journals and so little time finding cures for disease. The anger may also be directed against God, "the system," or the trick of fate that caused the person to take *that* road, *that* airplane, *that* medical treatment. There is often the need to find a "cause" which will enable us to understand a meaningless death. Without such a cause, the world may suddenly appear to lack an ultimate purpose; we would have to face the existential problem of a meaningless life followed by a meaningless death. This form of anger is likely to be a defense as much as anything else.

Anger can also be displaced, as some of the above examples suggest. You become angry with the doctor for not doing more, with the minister for misrepresenting God's powers, with the funeral director, whose presence makes you feel uncomfortable, with the nurses for not having taken better care of your mother and for not having made her final days more comfortable. It is very useful in times of bereavement to be able to rant and rail a bit at other people and institutions who—like you—fell short of their optimum performance in reviving and maintaining the life, and in making the weeks, days, and hours of dying a period of human warmth and good physical care.

Another part of the package is fear. Not only does the dying person evoke an uncomfortable awareness of our own finite nature, but we have an understandable fear of what the absence of the dying person will mean in terms of our own existence: new responsibilities, financial problems, loneliness, a new role in the community, a new work role, new types of arrangements to be made. A human relationship upon which we have depended and to a large extent accepted as an enduring part of our life will be missing, and there are many unknowns. When asked to indicate their greatest fears, college students ranked "loss of a family member" as number one. Their own death was far down on the list (Geer, 1965).

Our experience with separation is often an unhappy one. As children, the significant figures in our life, primarily our parents, would leave from time to time, and we were unhappy over the separation. These significant figures are such an important part of our life and their presence is so identified with emotional support and physical attention that their absence causes consternation. When significant figures are absent for vacations, hospitalization (especially if Mother returns with a new competitive baby brother or sister), business trips, and so forth, some sense of loss is engendered. The young child may rebel at sleeping at a neighbor's house or cry during the first nights at summer camp, until the new becomes a bit more familiar and predictable and the sense of separation is reduced.

I would speculate that these separation anxieties are revived during the dying of a close relative, even though the survivors may be mature people by that time. The loss through death of a parent, spouse, or sibling produces some reliving of the earlier anxieties emanating from the temporary loss of a significant figure. When the relative of the dying person is a child, I suspect the anxieties would be still greater. Also, if another important loss occurred during the early years, then the new impending loss will be even more threatening.

Although I had been of the impression that a child must be nearly a year old before such separation becomes a problem, I have read more recent material stating that as early as five or six months a child becomes distressed by a change in significant figures (Excerpta Medica Foundation, 1964). I believe that the feeling of loss due to separation is far underestimated by most people. In families where not only the parents but also grandparents and other relatives are close and familiar to the child, the temporary or even permanent loss of a parent finds a ready substitute, but a once-a-year grandfather is a minimal replacement for the nine-year-old whose world has been torn apart by the death of his father.

At this point I feel obligated to describe an incident that occurred with my own daughter to illustrate what I feel is a normal reaction to a separation. My wife and I left her with neighbors for a few days when she was two-and-a-half, the first time we had left her overnight. These neighbors had four children, and

Leah seemed almost as much a part of their family as of ours. When we returned, she appeared at the top of the staircase, looked down, said "Hi," and disappeared back into a bedroom to play. Her hostess used this and her uncomplaining behavior as evidence that she had not missed us, and that my worries had been unnecessary. My interpretation was different. About ten minutes later she returned, and this time she came down quietly and kissed us, but remained quite subdued. After about thirty minutes my wife suggested we go home and unpack. At this point Leah asked, "Are we going home now?" I nodded. And she ran up to me, threw her arms around my neck, and hugged me tightly. Subsequently she responded in her usual spirited fashion. To me this was obvious evidence that she had withdrawn from us and was waiting for us to indicate our worthiness to be relied upon, before she would allow herself to reinvest her ego with these deserters.

Children are more vulnerable to fear—at least overt fear—of dying in other ways. Not understanding the nature of death or the causes of death, a child can quite easily see death as a punishment. As a matter of fact, we all probably consider death as a punishment, at least to some extent. The child, however, is more likely to be confused by believing that death was a direct punishment for improper behavior, and may worry that his naughty behavior will be similarly punished. Recall the Biblical admonition, "The wages of sin is death." Another not infrequent reaction of children is to direct anger, fear, or even hatred against God for producing the death. That death is the result of chance or of natural causes is incomprehensible to children, and they often have a need to understand death in animistic terms, or with some one or some thing as responsible.

I mentioned previously that death is an obscenity, and that we wish to protect children from obscenities. Therefore, the modern middle-class child, who may be able to describe the human anatomy and the sexual act with frightening accuracy, is likely to be as shielded from death as his counterpart of a century ago was shielded from human sexual behavior. The child's contact with a dying person is usually severed early in the process, and even discussion of the dying and the death is conducted in whispers and abruptly stops when the child enters the room. This behavior is guaranteed, I feel, to frighten and distress the child, probably even more than comparable behavior regarding sex and human anatomy. He knows something is going on; he knows it is horrible; and he has only the vaguest notion of what it is. Fast and Cain (1964) described children who were terribly frightened by lies and euphemisms concerning death. Perhaps you can speculate upon possible childish interpretations of such statements as "God took her"; "He went on a long trip"; "She is up in the sky." One child came to hate and fear God; another became very much frightened whenever anyone in the family went on a trip; and the third was concerned that the deceased would be eaten by birds.

Children become interested in death during their third or fourth year (Spock, 1957), and they frequently bring it up in conversation. My personal response has been to discuss death with my daughter as though it were not a scary, blasphemous topic. I do not pretend to suggest that she understands all the implications, but I do hope she will be better prepared to cope with the implications when the time arises. A common parental reaction that I have noticed is to say, "Oh, let's not talk about things like that."

I will not dwell on a most obvious reaction to death—the sense of loss—or with normal and abnormal bereavement. These are described in the literature and they are commonly observed. A fine article by Dr. Erich Lindemann (1944) is still the landmark for a description of bereavement. And while mentioning reading possibilities, I would heartily recommend the excellent volume by Dr. Alfred Worcester entitled *Care of the Aged, the Dying, and the Dead* (1940).

Before going on to discuss the impact of child deaths, I should comment briefly upon some of the later effects of a death in the family. There is no need to elaborate on the problems facing the children and the remaining spouse in a one-parent home—we hear much about broken homes today and need only the reminder that a home is just as "broken" after death as after divorce. The problems of sex-role identification for the children can be just as difficult—perhaps more so, since they do not even have a father once a week. Later remarriage is a common resolution, but not always a satisfactory one. The new parent frequently has a very difficult time gaining the acceptance of the children.

There has been some interesting research along these lines. Studies have shown, for example, that children who have lost a parent early in their lives are more likely to be hospitalized later for mental illness and alcoholism (Hilgard & Newman, 1963; Barry & Lindemann, 1960). Numerous factors may contribute to this, but one interesting study focuses upon the anxiety associated with the death and dying, rather than with family problems caused by the death.

Another matter that has been investigated is the higher rate of delinquency in children who have lost a parent (Shoor & Speed, 1963). The authors concluded that the delinquent acts of violence, theft, and sexual promiscuity were outlets for grief that could not be released through the normal channels and for guilt that could not be absolved in a more healthy fashion.

Even physical health is affected. A series of studies in England (Parkes, 1964a, 1964b) has indicated that requests for psychiatric and nonpsychiatric medical treatment of women increased substantially immediately after their bereavement. This occurred both in young widows and older women, but was much more pronounced among the younger women. Bereavement also appeared to lead to an increase in the probability of mental hospitalization among adults. The impact of a death upon the family, like every other major event in a person's life, has a dynamic influence upon the remainder of his life and—undoubtedly—upon his own later attitudes toward the death of others and of himself.

I feel strongly that some of these later problems might be avoided if our culture did not frown on overt expressions of grief. A few years ago I asked nurses how they talked to the bereaved family (Kalish, 1963). The nurses indicated to me that what they tried to do in most cases was say, in effect, "Now, be brave and go home." The implication was "Get out of here." One of the nurses, concerned about the problem, suggested that wards where people are terminally ill should have a room set aside for the bereaved, just a room where the family could go and express their sorrows without disturbing the other patients or their relatives. I would certainly encourage the family to express their grief, their anger, their feelings of guilt in whatever way they can. This seems particularly important for children, who cannot understand a death intellectually.

THE DYING OF THE CHILD

The younger the dying person (exclusive of infants), the more distress is caused. One physician reported that the death of a child upsets the entire hospital, and the staff members are visibly affected. The life of a child has great social value. He has not had a chance to live, and we feel he is entitled to this. Also, his general helplessness moves us. In addition, we have been accused —justly, I feel—of focusing much attention upon the young. Also the uniqueness of death between the ages of two months and fourteen years intensifies its impact. No longer does a sixty-year-old mother say, "I had twelve pregnancies, bore seven children, and raised three of them to adulthood." This mother may now report four pregnancies, three live births, and three grown children.

Another factor is that we do not attribute the death of a child to "his own fault," to inevitability, or to a style of living of which we disapprove. The smoker who dies of lung cancer, the reckless driver killed in an accident, and the octogenarian who dies of heart failure are seen as partly responsible for their own deaths, either through their behavior or merely from having been around for so long. The child who dies in contemporary American society is not considered mature enough to be responsible for behavior leading to his death, and, unlike the elderly man, he cannot be considered to have died inevitably.

The death of a child has a tremendous impact upon the family constellation. The parents are very likely to feel guilty, not only for some of the reasons mentioned earlier, such as the feeling that they failed to give the child enough love and attention, but because they may hold themselves responsible for the death. If the death resulted from their carelessness, their feeling of guilt will be great, but what if the death could have been prevented by seeking medical attention sooner? Perhaps the child would have died anyway, but there is no way to be sure. In a similar situation, an adult is considered able to make his own decisions and to be responsible for them—although relatives might feel guilty for not having brought more pressure upon him to see a doctor—but with a child, the parents are expected to make decisions and are, therefore, responsible for errors in decisions.

Sometimes the cause of death involves hereditary factors. Once again the parents are likely to feel intense guilt, although nothing in their behavior—other than not having had a child—could have prevented the condition. I once observed a bitter argument between the parents of a mentally defective child, each insisting the other's heredity was at fault. And the responses that I discussed before, anger, displaced hostility, fears (which may be intensified by the belief that the other family members and friends will blame them), sense of loss, and normal and abnormal bereavement, all can occur with the death of a child, as with the death of a person of any age.

Other parallels may be observed. Just as the forty-year-old widow may consciously decide to remarry as soon as feasible, the parent of a recently dead child may decide to have a substitute child, either through an immediate pregnancy or through an adoption. Some such cases have been described in the literature (Cain & Cain, 1964) when they came to the attention of psychotherapists. Although there is no basis for assuming these to be a random sample of all substitute children, the dynamics were nonetheless interesting. In extreme instances, the new child was given the same name as the dead child, and was expected to be as much like him as possible; deviation from this expectancy was met with disapproval. The substitute child therefore had a tremendous burden, since he could never fully be himself—his identity was always a matter of uncertainty.

I have had recent contact with two such individuals, one a history professor and the other a student. The former, consciously planned for as a substitute child, was born less than a year after the death of his sister. Fortunately for him, he was of the opposite sex from the dead child, and in time seemed totally able to gain his own identity. The student was a different matter. She had been adopted very shortly after the death of the other child, also a girl. When I talked with her, she said that she had never felt she was herself, but was always someone else. She said that she loved her parents but felt that they did not love her, preferring the dead sister for whom she was merely a living symbol. The problems are obvious.

Reactions of children to the death of siblings (Cain, Fast, & Erickson, 1964) and to maternal miscarriages (Cain, Erickson, Fast, & Vaughan, 1964) are also discussed in the literature. One case describes a boy who went with his twin brother on a forbidden trip to the beach; the twin wandered off and was drowned. The parents blamed this boy, and he later became actively delinquent (Shoor & Speed, 1963). The well-known problems of sibling rivalry often invoke death wishes; when these are accidentally enacted, the feeling of guilt must be tremendous.

The parents, of course, are also trying to make some sense out of the death of their child, and the sibling makes a good whipping boy, if he did share some of the responsibility. In such circumstances, parental rejection can, at least temporarily, be an understandable result. An alternative, however, regardless of the circumstance surrounding the death, is for the parents to overprotect the remaining child. Their guilt and their fears combine to motivate them to overextend devices for protecting this child from the harm that befell his brother. Unfortunately, such behavior has other negative results.

The City of Hope, a hospital for certain chronic illnesses, near Los Angeles, conducted a study of hospitalized terminally ill children (Hamovitch, 1964). They encouraged parents to spend as much time as possible with these children. Although there were incidents of unhappy effects upon the other siblings, the investigators concluded that both the dying children and their parents benefited greatly from the intensified and personal care provided by the parent, and from the reduction in separation anxiety produced by avoiding the pattern of isolating the dying child from the family constellation. The parents, of course, had the opportunity to spend much time with the child, to persuade themselves that they were really doing something significant for the dying child (which, in truth, they were), and to give and receive satisfaction from the remaining time allowed the relationship. And, to the surprise of many, the hospital routine was improved and the increased problems encountered by the personnel were more than compensated for by the more efficient and more effective care received by the patients.

Just a brief word in concluding. Those of us who work in the social and medical sciences and arts are just beginning to express a willingness to look at the significance of death in modern America. I personally do not believe, as does one friend, that this is in the nature of a fad. I feel that the willingness to talk and write and read about death and its impact is an important first step, one that is beginning to make a difference in the kind of care and attention we can give the dying patient and his family.

References

Barrett, W. *Irrational man.* New York: Doubleday Anchor, 1958.

Barry, H. H., & Lindemann, E. Critical ages for maternal bereavement in psychoneurosis. *Psychosom. Med.*, 1960, *22*, 166–81.

Cain, A. C., & Cain, B. S. On replacing a child. *J. Amer. Acad. Child Psychiat.*, 1964, *3*, 443–56.

Cain, A. C., Erickson, M. E., Fast, I., & Vaughan, R. A. Children's disturbed reactions to their mother's miscarriage. *Psychosom. Med.*, 1964, *26*, 58–66.

Cain, A. C., Fast, I., & Erickson, M. E. Children's disturbed reactions to the death of a sibling. *Amer. J. Orthopsychiat.*, 1964, *34*, 741–52.

Excerpta Medica Foundation. Colloquium on maternal deprivation. Vols. 1 & 2. New York, 1964.

Fast, I., & Cain, A.C. Fears of death in bereaved children and adults. Paper presented to the American Orthopsychiatric Association, 1964. Mimeographed. Pp. 16.

Geer, J. H. The development of a scale to measure fear. *Behav. Res. Ther.*, 1965, *3*, 45–53.

Glaser, B. G., & Strauss, A. L. The social loss of dying patients. *Amer. J. Nurs.*, 1964, *64*, 119–21.

Glaser, B. G., & Strauss, A. L. *Time for dying.* Chicago: Aldine, 1968.

Gorer, G. The pornography of death. In W. Phillips & P. Rahv (Eds.), *Modern writing.* New York: Berkeley Press, 1956. Pp. 56–62.

Hamovitch, M. B. *The parent and the fatally ill child.* Duarte, Cal.: City of Hope Medical Center, 1964.

Hilgard, J. R., & Newman, M. F. Early parental deprivation in schizophrenia and alcoholism. *Amer. J. Orthopsychiat.*, 1963, *33*, 409–20.

Hinton, J. *Dying.* London: Penguin Books, 1967.

Kalish, R. A. Dealing with the grieving family. *R.N.*, 1963, *26*, 81–84.

Kalish, R. A. Social distance and the dying. *Community Ment. Health J.*, 1966, *2*(2), 152–55.

Kalish, R. A. Of children and grandfathers: A speculative essay on dependency. *Gerontologist*, 1967, 7, 65-70.

Kastenbaum, R. The interpersonal context of death in a geriatric institution. Paper presented at the 17th Annual Meeting of the Gerontological Society, Minneapolis, 1964.

Lindemann, E. Symptomatology and management of acute grief. *Amer. J. Psychiat.*, 1944, *101*, 141–48.

Moberg, D. O. Religiosity in old age. *Gerontologist*, 1965, *5*, 78–88.

Parkes, C. M. Recent bereavement as a cause of mental illness. *Brit. J. Psychiat.*, 1964, *110*, 198–204. (a)

Parkes, C. M. Effects of bereavement on physical and mental health—a study of the medical records of widows. *Brit. Med. J.*, 1964, 2, 274–79. (b)

Shoor, M., & Speed, M. H. Delinquency as a manifestation of the mourning process. *Psychiat. Quart.*, 1963, 37, 540–58.

Spock, B. *Baby and child care.* New York: Pocket Books, 1957.

Worcester, A. *The care of the aged, the dying, and the dead.* (2nd ed.) Springfield, Ill.: Charles C Thomas, 1940.

Awareness of Dying

ANSELM L. STRAUSS

AMERICAN PERSPECTIVES ON DEATH seem strangely paradoxical. Our newspapers confront the brutal fact of death directly, from the front page headlines to the back page funeral announcements. Americans *seem* capable of accepting death as an everyday affair—someone is always dying somewhere, frequently under most unhappy circumstances. To account for this absorbing interest in death (even death by violence), one need not attribute to the reading public an especially vigorous appetite for gruesome details. Death is, after all, one of the characteristic features of human existence, and the people of any society must find the means to deal with this recurring crisis. Presumably one way to deal with it is to talk and read about it.

Curiously, however, Americans generally seem to prefer to talk about particular deaths rather than about death in the abstract. Death as such has been described as a taboo topic for us, and we engage in very little abstract or philosophical discussion of death.[1] Public discussion is generally limited to the social consequences of capital punishment or euthanasia.

Americans are characteristically unwilling to talk openly about the *process* of dying itself; and they are prone to avoid telling a dying person that he is dying. This is, in part, a moral attitude: life is preferable to whatever may follow it, and one should not look forward to death unless he is in great pain.

---

1. Herman Feifel, "Death," in Norman L. Farberow, *Taboo Topics* (New York: Atherton Press, 1963), pp. 8–21.

This moral attitude appears to be shared by the professional people who work with or near the patients who die in our hospitals. Although trained to give specialized medical or nursing care to terminal patients, much of their behavior towards death resembles the layman's. The training that physicians and nurses receive in schools of medicine or nursing equips them principally for the technical aspects of dealing with patients. Medical students learn not to kill patients through error, and to save patients' lives through diagnosis and treatment, but their teachers emphasize very little, or not at all, how to talk with dying patients, how—or whether—to disclose an impending death, or even how to approach the subject with the wives, children, and parents of dying patients.[2]

Similarly, students at schools of nursing are taught how to give nursing care to terminal patients, as well as how to give "post-mortem care," but only recently have the "psychological aspects" of nursing care been included in their training. Few teachers talk about such matters, and they generally confine themselves to a lecture or two near the end of the course, sometimes calling in a psychiatrist to give a kind of "expert testimony."[3] Although doctors and nurses in training do have some experience with dying patients, the emphasis is on the necessary techniques of medicine or nursing, not on the fact of dying itself. As a result, sometimes they do not even know they are treating or caring for a dying patient.

Although physicians and nurses may thus exhibit consider-

2. These statements are the result of a secondary analysis of field-notes from a study of the University of Kansas Medical School; see Howard S. Becker, Blanche Geer, Everett C. Hughes, and Anselm L. Strauss, *Boys in White* (Chicago: University of Chicago Press, 1961).

3. Jeanne C. Quint and Anselm L. Strauss, "Nursing Students, Assignments, and Dying Patients," *Nursing Outlook*, Vol. 12 (January 1964); also Jeanne C. Quint, *The Nurse Student and the Dying Patient* (New York: The Macmillan Company, 1966).

able technical skill in handling the bodies of terminal patients, their behavior to them otherwise is actually outside the province of professional standards. In hospitals, as in medical and nursing schools, discussion of the proper ways to manage dying patients tends to be only in strictly technical medical and nursing terms. Also, staff members are not required to report to each other, or to their superiors, what they have talked about with dying patients. As we will discuss later, they are "accountable" only for the technical aspects of their work with the dying.[4]

Medical and nursing personnel commonly recognize that working with and around dying patients is upsetting and sometimes traumatic. Consequently some physicians purposely specialize in branches of medicine that will minimize their chances of encountering dying patients; many nurses frankly admit a preference for wards or fields of nursing where there is little confrontation with death. Those who bear the brunt of caring for terminal patients tend to regard its hazards as inevitable—either one "can take" working with these patients or he cannot. Physicians and nurses understandably develop both standardized and idiosyncratic modes of coping with the worst hazards. The most standard mode—recognized by physicians and nurses themselves—is a tendency to avoid contact with those patients who, as yet unaware of impending death, are inclined to question staff members, with those who have not "accepted" their approaching deaths, and with those whose terminality is accompanied by great pain. Staff members' efforts to cope with terminality often have undesirable effects on both the social and psychological aspects of patient care and their own comfort. Personnel in contact with terminal patients are always somewhat disturbed by their own ineptness in handling the dying.

---

4. Anselm L. Strauss, Barney G. Glaser, and Jeanne C. Quint, "The Non-accountability of Terminal Care," *Hospitals*, 38 (January 16, 1964), pp. 73–87.

The social and psychological problems involved in terminality are perhaps most acute when the dying person knows that he is dying. For this reason, among others, American physicians are quite reluctant to disclose impending death to their patients,[5] and nurses are expected not to disclose it without the consent of the responsible physicians. Yet there is a prevailing belief among them that a patient who really wants to know will somehow discover the truth without being told explicitly. Some physicians, too, maneuver conversations with patients so that disclosure is made indirectly. In any event, the demeanor and actions of a patient who knows or suspects that he is dying differ from those of a patient who is not aware of his terminality. The problem of "awareness" is crucial to what happens both to the dying patient and to the people who give him medical and nursing care.

From one point of view the problem of awareness is a technical one: should the patient be told he is dying—and what is to be done if he knows, does not know, or only suspects? But the problem is also a moral one, involving professional ethics, social issues, and personal values. Is it really proper, some people have asked, to deny a dying person the opportunity to make his peace with his conscience and with his God, to settle his affairs and provide for the future of his family, and to control his style of dying, much as he controlled his style of living? Does anyone, the physician included, have the right to withhold such information? Someone must decide whether to disclose, and when to disclose, but on whose shoulders should this responsibility fall —the physician, the family, or the patient? The rationale for making such decisions, as well as for designating who will make them, is not based on technical reasoning alone but also on various ethical, moral, and human considerations.

5. Feifel, *op. cit.*, p. 17.

Both the human and the technical aspects of the awareness problem are becoming increasingly momentous, for at least two reasons. One is that most Americans no longer die at home. Last year in the United States, 53 per cent of all deaths occurred in hospitals, and many more in nursing homes.[6] The family may be present much of the time while a person is dying, but he is also surrounded by many strangers, however compassionate and technically skilled they may be. Dying away from home is compounded by a noticeable and important medical trend: because medical technology has vastly improved, fewer people are dying from acute diseases and more from chronic diseases. Moreover, the usual duration of most chronic diseases has increased, so that terminal patients, in the aggregate, take longer to die than they used to. They may spend this time in the hospital, or return several times to the hospital while they are dying.

Dying away from home, and from a chronic disease, will become more common during the next decades, making the problem of "awareness" even more salient to everyone concerned. Hospitals are scientific establishments and staff members are expected to make competent judgments about what is wrong with patients and to assess their prospects for recovering—or not recovering. For this very reason more and more terminal patients will persist in asking questions, and in expecting explicit, detailed answers, about the nature of their illness, how long the hospitalization will last, and why, and in what shape they will leave for home. Inevitably, more of them will discover, or be told, the truth. (The widespread improvement in educational level will strengthen these trends.) And so it is predictable that the problem of awareness will become more and more central to

---

6. Robert Fulton, "Death and Self," *Journal of Religion and Health*, 3 (July 1964), p. 364.

what happens as people pass from life to death in American hospitals.

CLOSED AWARENESS

In American hospitals, frequently the patient does not recognize his impending death even though the hospital personnel have the information. This situation can be described as a "closed awareness" context. Providing the physician decides to keep the patient from realizing, or even seriously suspecting, what his true status is, the problem is to *maintain* the context as a closed one. With a genuinely comatose patient, the staff members naturally need not guard against disclosure of his terminal condition. As an interactant, the comatose person is what Goffman has called a "non-person."[7] Two nurses caring for him can speak in his presence without fear that, overhearing them, he will suspect or understand what they are saying about him. Neither they nor the physicians need to engage in tactics to protect him from any dread knowledge. And of course with terminal babies, no precautions against disclosure are needed either. But with conscious patients, care must be taken not to disclose the staff's secret.

CONTRIBUTING STRUCTURAL CONDITIONS

There are at least five important structural conditions which contribute to the existence and maintenance of the closed awareness context.[8] First, most patients are not especially experienced at recognizing the signs of impending death. Of course, a pa-

---

7. Erving Goffman, *The Presentation of Self in Everyday Life* (Edinburgh, Scotland: University of Edinburgh, 1956), pp. 95–96.

8. *Cf.* Barney Glaser and Anselm Strauss, "Awareness Contexts and Social Interaction," *American Sociological Review*, 29 (October, 1964), pp. 669–679.

tient who has been in an auto accident and is injured terribly, although still conscious, may recognize how close death is. He may also recognize it if he is himself a physician or a nurse, or if as a chronic hospitalized patient he has encountered fatal signs in dying comrades.[9] But most Americans have not had such opportunities to witness rehearsals for their own deaths.

A second structural condition is that American physicians ordinarily do not tell patients outright that death is probable or inevitable. As a number of studies have shown, physicians find medical justifications for not disclosing dying status to their patients.[10] For instance, Dr. Donald Oken has recently demonstrated that a chief reason offered is "clinical experience."[11] The physician states from "clinical experience," that when one announces terminality to a patient, he is likely to "go to pieces"; one must therefore carefully judge whether or not to tell after sizing up the individual patient. In actual fact, Oken notes, the clinical experience is not genuinely grounded experience, but a species of personal mythology. Generally the experience consists of one or two unfortunate incidents—or even incidents recounted by colleagues—and this effectively cuts off further clinical experimentation to discover the possible range of consequences of disclosure.

Among several articles of faith in professional ideology which support not disclosing terminality is the belief that pa-

---

9. Renée Fox, *Experiment Perilous* (New York: Free Press of Glencoe, 1959).

10. Herman Feifel, *op. cit.*, p. 17.

11. Donald Oken, "What to Tell Cancer Patients: A Study of Medical Attitudes," *Journal of the American Medical Association*, 175 (April 1, 1961), pp. 1120–28. See the bibliography cited in his paper for further studies on physicians' tendency not to announce terminality. See also the discussion of physicians' announcements in Barney G. Glaser and Anselm L. Strauss, *Awareness of Dying* (Chicago: Aldine Publishing Company, 1965), Chapter 8.

tients really do not wish to know whether they are dying. If they did, then they would find out anyhow, so there is no sense telling them directly. Presumably some patients do not wish to know their fates, but there is no really good evidence that *all* wish to remain in blissful ignorance or that these patients will find out while in the hospital. And there is some good evidence that they do wish to know.[12] Quite possibly also, physicians, like other Americans, shy away from the embarrassment and brutality of making direct reference to another person about his impending death. They also undoubtedly would rather avoid the scene that an announcement of impending death is likely to precipitate.

A third structural condition is that families also tend to guard the secret. Family members sometimes may reveal it, but in our own study we never witnessed deliberate disclosure by a family member. One psychiatrist told us, however, that he had disagreed with his father's physician about the wisdom of not telling his father, and so had made the disclosure himself. (Family members, of course, usually confirm what the physician has already announced.) An interesting contrast is the usual practice in Asian countries, where the extended kin gather around the hospital death bed, two or more days before death is expected, openly indicating to the patient that they are there to keep him company during his passage out of life.

A fourth structural condition is related both to the organization of hospitals and to the commitments of personnel who work within them. Our hospitals are admirably arranged, both by accident and by design, to hide medical information from patients. Records are kept out of reach. Staff is skilled at withholding in-

---

12. Eighty-two per cent of Feifel's sample of sixty patients wanted to be informed about their condition.

formation. Medical talk about patients generally occurs in far-removed places, and if it occurs nearby it is couched in medical jargon. Staff members are trained to discuss with patients only the surface aspects of their illnesses, and, as we shall see, they are accustomed to acting collusively around patients so as not to disclose medical secrets.

A fifth structural condition, perhaps somewhat less apparent, is that ordinarily the patient has no allies who reveal or help him discover the staff's knowledge of his impending death. Not only his family but other patients withhold that information, if they know. When a patient wants less distressing information, he may readily find allies among the other patients; but when he lies dying, the other patients follow ordinary rules of tact, keeping their knowledge to themselves or at least away from the doomed person. There may be exceptional incidents: the parents of a dying teenager told neighbors about his condition, and these neighbors told their son who in turn spilled out this information to the patient himself. Among adults, such failures of secrecy ordinarily do not occur.

While together these structural conditions contribute to the occurrence and maintenance of the closed awareness context, a change in any one condition may precipitate a change to another type of context. For example, the physician may decide to tell the patient—which leads to an "open awareness" context; or a patient begins to suspect something amiss because he begins to learn some of the indicators relevant to increasingly grave illness—which leads to a "suspicion awareness" context. Later we shall discuss how changing structural conditions may transform the closed awareness context.

THE PATIENT'S FICTIONAL BIOGRAPHY

A newly hospitalized patient has some basic questions about

his condition. He wants to know, if he does not know already, just how ill he is, and whether he is going to get better or worse, *how* much better or worse, and how quickly he will progress or retrogress. In short, he ordinarily is passionately concerned with his own sick status—he wishes to know what may usefully be referred to as his "future biography."

The patient who is dying but who has not yet discovered or been told of his terminality faces a peculiar problem in getting an accurate assessment of his condition from the medical and nursing personnel. Can he trust the doctor, can he trust the nurses and aides, to yield him a true account of his story?[13] Or will their account be tinged by deceit and perhaps thoroughly false? A false account is a real possibility, although the patient may not recognize it as such. So trust is important in his transactions with the staff members.

Developing trust is also basic in the staff's transactions with the patient. To keep the patient unaware of his terminality, the staff members must construct a *fictional* future biography for him, and they must sustain his belief in that biography by getting and keeping his trust.

What is involved in winning the patient's "trust"? First, consider a child who is old enough to know about death but still too young to doubt that his elders will properly care for him during his illness. The essence of his relations with adults is that he takes their actions at face value. What they are doing to him,

---

13. Research in hospitals where psychotherapy is practiced indicates the patients collectively develop a philosophy that one must have faith in one's doctor. *Cf.* William Caudill *et al.*, "Social Structure and the Interaction Process on a Psychiatric Ward," *American Journal of Psychiatry*, 22 (1952), pp. 314–334; also Anselm Strauss *et al.*, *Psychiatric Ideologies and Institutions* (New York: Free Press of Glencoe, 1964), pp. 271–273. But compare with the frequent distrust of doctors found in TB hospitals: Julius Roth, *Timetables* (Indianapolis: Bobbs-Merrill, 1963).

and what they make him do is, as they explain, to make him get better. With children of this age, hospital personnel need not be so concerned about betraying their own behind-the-scenes knowledge. Such suspicions as the child may have will be more "I don't trust them to help me" rather than "I don't trust them because they are not telling me the truth about my condition." Consequently, personnel on pediatric wards report no great danger of unwarily letting their younger patients know they are dying. Indeed, they report that less control of one's face in a child's presence is needed, as he is not so apt to draw conclusions from an expression.

With adults the matter of trust in physicians and nurses is rather more complicated. Trust does not arise automatically; it must either be part of the history of a particular relationship or it must be earned. Furthermore, once earned it must be maintained. The importance of keeping trust can be seen in the dilemma of an unaware patient who has long placed trust in a particular physician, but whose suspicions have now been aroused by some incident or remark. Can the man still be trusted in this new domain, trusted not only to "pull me through my illness" but "to tell me the worst"? In general, the physician and others must not arouse any suspicion by their words and actions that they are concealing knowledge about terminality. They must not even seem to fail in giving honest answers to any questions that might touch upon terminality. When staff members succeed in acting convincingly, the patient accepts their account of his future biography as accurate, or at least as accurate as they know how to make it.

ASSESSMENT MANAGEMENT

To sustain the unaware patient's belief in their version of his future biography, the staff members must control his assessments of those events and cues which might lead him to suspect or gain knowledge of his terminality. Their attempts at managing his assessments involve them in a silent game played to and around him, during which they project themselves to him as people who are trying to help him get better, or at least to keep him from getting worse. They must be sufficiently committed to this game, and sufficiently skilled at it, not to give it away. Their advantage is that they can collaborate as a team, sometimes a very experienced one, against an opponent who, as noted earlier, has ordinarily not much experience in discovering or correctly interpreting signs of impending death, and who is usually without allies.

Though the staff's explanations of his condition initially may seem convincing to the unaware patient, and though he may greatly trust the staff, he may begin to see and hear things that arouse his suspicions about his condition. Inevitably he wonders about, and requires explanation for, a host of events: Why is he given certain treatments or exposed to certain tests and procedures? Why is he moved from one room to another? Why has one more physician dropped into his room to examine him? Why is he not getting better more quickly? He wants answers to questions stimulated by various events even when he does not in the slightest suspect their true significance.

The staff members usually hasten to give him reasonable interpretations of those events. Frequently they even offer interpretations before he requests them, because they calculate he may otherwise secretly suspect the real meanings of those events. Their interpretations may be intentionally incorrect or only partly correct—if they feel that a correct one will potentially or actually reveal terminality to the patient. Thus, many of their interpretations are meant to mislead him. Of course a correct interpretation is offered when the staff member judges it will neither disclose nor arouse suspicions of terminality.

A patient near death, for instance, may be moved to a special space or room, but is informed that this move is only to permit more intensive care. A patient may even be sent home to die on request of his family, but his discharge from the hospital is explained in quite other terms. Occasionally the physician will give a patient an incorrect or incomplete diagnosis to explain his symptoms—as in one instance when a patient was discovered, through a diagnostic operation, to have incurable cancer of the pancreas but was sent home with a diagnosis of diabetes and given instructions in the use of insulin. If the patient believes that he has taken a turn for the worse, or at least is not improving, staff members are ready with reasonable answers that are meant to mislead him. At the very least, certain of his symptoms must be explained away, discounted, as signifying something much less alarming than they appear to him. Sometimes the physician warns him of anticipated symptoms, discounting them in advance. The physician and the nurses may also go out of their way continually to reassure him that things will turn out "all right," and indeed are "coming along fine." They will fabricate, hint at, or suggest favorable progress. Nurses especially compare the patient's condition, and his progress, with that of other patients they have known (including themselves), thus suggesting reasons for optimism. If the patient asks the nurses "Am I going to die?" as occasionally patients do without even real suspicion, they refer him to his physician for an answer ("Have you asked your physician?"), or change the subject without answering the question, or turn it aside with a stock answer (for instance, "We all have to go sometime"). When a patient asks the same question of the physician, the latter may simply lie.

The staff members also use tactics intended to encourage the patient to make his own interpretations inaccurately optimistic. They will comment favorably on his daily appearance, hoping he will interpret their comments optimistically. Some comments are downright misrepresentations and others are ambiguous enough to be misread easily. Staff members will attempt to establish a mood consonant less with terminality than with "things are not so bad even if not yet better." They also practice a sleight of hand, like magicians, drawing the patient's attention away from a dangerous cue by focusing his attention on an innocent one. They raise false scents, sometimes displaying elaborate interest in the symptoms he himself brings up for consideration. The physician may even put on diagnostic dramas for him, sending him for irrelevant tests. A certain amount of conversation with him about his imminent, or eventual, return home may occur; and his own reading of physical and temporal cues that represent progress to him may be supported. There is also what one might call a "sociability shield," or conversation that circumvents disclosure; during this conversation, personnel carry on as if the entire situation were quite normal. With such interactional devices, the staff simultaneously project their own trustworthy medical identities, conveying to the patient that he is not expected to die.

In addition to all these devices, other techniques reduce cues that might arouse the patient's suspicion. Space is carefully managed, so that talk about him occurs away from his presence. If a nurse believes her involvement with, or sadness about, the patient might give the secret away, she may move quickly outside his visual range. She may even request an assignment away from him. Possibly revealing cues are also reduced by decreasing the time spent with the patient. Personnel who fear that they may unwittingly disclose something may remain with the patient very little, or choose to work on his body rather than talk much with him. They may keep tabs on his physical condition by popping in and out of his room, but thereby keep conversation at a minimum. Sometimes, when the patient is extremely close to death but there is nothing much to be done for him, staff members tend to go no farther than the doorway. If the patient becomes genuinely comatose, nurses or aides can again circulate freely in the patient's room.

The disclosing cues are minimized most subtly by reducing the range of expression and topic. The face can be managed so as to minimize the dangerous cues it conveys; hence the conventionally bland or cheerful faces of nurse and physician. A less obvious mode of minimizing such cues is to censor and select conversational topics. Staff members, for instance, steer conversation away from potentially revealing subjects and toward safer ones. They may talk, especially, about the relatively straightforward meanings of procedures being used on the patient's body, providing those meanings are not revealing.

One aspect of talk that personnel are cautious about is its present-future orientation. When a patient is defined as certain to die within a few days, nurses tend to focus their conversation with him on the immediate present, discussing such matters as current doses of medication for pain relief or other topics relevant to his comfort. But if they do not anticipate death for some time, then they will extend the temporal range implied in their talk. One nurse thus said, before leaving for a weekend, "See you next week." Another told a patient that he would need another X ray in two weeks. Similarly, they talk about blood tests to be done next week, or about the family's impending visit. One young nurse told us that she used to chat with a young patient about his future dates and parties, but that after discovering his certain and imminent death, she unwittingly cut out all references to the distant future. It is not easy to carry on a future-oriented conversation without revealing one's knowledge that the conversation is, in some sense, fraudulent, especially if the speaker is relatively inexperienced.

Staff members, again especially if they are inexperienced, must also guard against displaying those of their private reactions to him and to his impending death as might rouse the patient's suspicions of his terminality. For instance, young nurses are sometimes affected by terminal patients of their own age whose deaths become standing reminders of their own potential death. ("I found . . . that the patients who concerned me most when they died were women of my own age. . . .") Identification of this kind is quite common, and makes more difficult the staff members' control of their behavioral cues.

Their reactions to the patient's "social loss"[14] can also be revealing. In our society, certain values are highly esteemed— among them youth, beauty, integrity, talent, and parental and marital responsibility—and when a terminal patient strikingly embodies such values, staff members tend to react to the potential or actual loss to his family or to society. But such reactions must not be allowed to intrude into the fictionalized future biography that is directly and indirectly proffered to the patient. Since personnel tend to share a common attribution of social value, that intrusion is quite possible unless they keep tight control over their reactions. Although the staff's control is not always fully conscious, it is no less real.

Finally, because the patient is usually in contact with many staff members during each day, his suspicions of terminality may be aroused if they do not give consistent answers to his questions or if their behavior yields him inconsistent cues. So they must

---

14. Barney G. Glaser and Anselm L. Strauss, "The Social Loss of Dying Patients," *American Journal of Nursing* (June 1964), pp. 119–121.

strive for consistency. But if he queries any inconsistency, then the staff members must offer him reasonable interpretations to explain away the "apparent" inconsistency.

FROM CLOSED TO OTHER AWARENESS CONTEXTS

Inherently, this closed awareness context tends toward instability, as the patient moves either to suspicion or full awareness of his terminality. The principal reasons for the instability of closed awareness require only brief notation, as they have already been adumbrated. First, any breakdown in the structural conditions that make for the closed awareness context may lead to its disappearance.[15] Those conditions include the physician's decision not to tell the patient, the family's supporting agreement, and the tactful silence of other patients. For example, such a break occurs repeatedly at one Veterans Administration hospital we studied, where patients who are eventually judged to be hopelessly terminal are sometimes asked whether they would care to become research subjects and receive medication that might prolong their lives.

Some unanticipated disclosures or tip-offs, stemming from organizational conditions, can also occur. The staff members who work in emergency rooms in hospitals need to be especially careful in controlling their facial surprises or immediately compassionate distress when suddenly confronted by obviously dying patients, often the battered victims of accidents caused by others' carelessness. Staff members' control in these instances is not always successful. On other hospital services, rotation of nursing

---

15. The Catholic practice of giving the sacrament requires calling in a priest prior to possible death, and this may function as an announcement to the dying patient. But non-Catholics probably need to be told that this is done only to insure that the patient does not die without the sacrament. If he recovers, whether to live for many years or merely days, then he may receive the sacrament once or perhaps several times again.

staff may bring the patient into contact with new persons who do not always know of his terminality or who have not been coached properly in the history of how the staff has conducted itself in the presence of this patient. Even the daily shift carries hidden dangers. For instance, the doctor may inform the day shift that his patient is dying, but unless specific measures are taken to transmit this information to the night shift, the patient may be cared for by personnel not sufficiently alert to the dangers of unwitting disclosure. This danger is especially grave when the patient is worried about certain new symptoms.

New symptoms understandably are likely to perplex and alarm the patient; and the longer his retrogressive course, the more difficult it becomes to give him plausible explanations, though a very complicated misrepresentational drama can be played for his benefit. Even so, it becomes somewhat more difficult to retain the patient's trust over a long time. When a patient's physical symptoms become compelling, sometimes he can force nurses into almost an open admission of the truth. Not to hint at, or tacitly admit to, the truth would be to risk losing his trust altogether. So it is not unknown for the staff to "snow a patient under" with drugs as he nears death, partly to reduce his suffering (and perhaps their own) and partly to reduce the likelihood that finally he will correctly read the fateful signs. Indeed, sometimes a race with time occurs, there being some question whether the patient will die, or at least become comatose, before he becomes suspicious or aware of his terminality.

Another threat to closed awareness, closely linked with retrogressive physical symptoms, is that some treatments make little sense to a patient who does not recognize that he is dying. Just as many polio patients will not take full advantage of rehabilitation programs because they do not anticipate being cured, so a terminal patient may refuse a medicine, a machine, an awkward position, or an inconvenient diet.[16] To accomplish her task, the nurse may have to hint at the extreme seriousness of her patient's condition, hoping that he will get the point just long enough for her to complete the procedure. But if this tactic works, it may then also stimulate an attempt by the patient to discover what is really happening to him. The staff then must redouble its assessment management. For instance, the nurse who alarmed him must immediately assure him that he has interpreted her words incorrectly—but she may not be wholly or at all successful. The physician can also have problems when explaining to his patient why he must undergo certain additional treatments, tests, and operations, or why he needs to return to the hospital "for a while."

At times, moreover, a patient may be unable to cope with his immensely deteriorating physical condition unless nurses interpret that condition and its symptoms to him. To do this, nurses may feel forced to talk of his dying. Not to disclose at this desperate point can torture and isolate the patient, which runs counter to a central value of nursing care, namely to make the patient as comfortable as possible. Similarly, the physician's inaccessibility may force nurses to disclose the truth in order to do something immediately for, or with, the patient.

The danger that staff members will give the show away by relaxing their usual tight control also increases as the patient nears death, especially when the dying takes place slowly. For instance, concerned personnel will continually pause at the patient's door, popping their heads into his room to see how he is —or if he is still alive. Sometimes a patient very close to death

---

16. *Cf.* Fred Davis, "Uncertainty in Medical Prognosis." *American Journal of Sociology,* 66 (July 1960), p. 45.

will be given more privileges because of simple compassion for him (like permitting him to eat previously denied favorite foods or to take an automobile ride or even to return home permanently); occasionally this can cue him into suspicion awareness. The staff will also sometimes relax their guard when they believe the patient is too far gone (physically dazed, comatose, or senile) to understand what would otherwise be revealing cues or downright disclosing conversations—but he may be sentient enough to understand.

This last set of conditions brings us to the question of whether, and how, personnel actually may engineer a change of the closed awareness context. For instance, a physician may drop hints to the patient that he is dying, giving the information gradually, and hoping that eventually the patient will comprehend the finality of his medical condition. Nurses have so often confided to us that they hoped certain patients were really aware of impending death that we can be sure they have signaled, however ambiguously, to such patients, especially when the latter are well beloved and the nurses can see no good reasons why they should not be prepared for death even though the physicians choose not to tell. The true situation can be deliberately conveyed to a patient by facial expression, by carefully oblique phrasing of words, or merely by failure to reassure him about his symptoms and prognosis. And of course the family members may occasionally signal or hint at the dreadful truth. Indeed, when the family actually knows the truth, the hazards to maintaining closed awareness probably are much increased, if only because kin are more strongly tempted to signal the truth.

CONSEQUENCES OF CLOSED AWARENESS

So many discrete consequences seem to flow from this closed awareness context that we must restrict our attention to a few of its consequences for the patient, his family, the hospital personnel, and the hospital itself.

We can approach the consequences of closed awareness by touching on a contrasting situation. In her book *Experiment Perilous*, Renée Fox has described a small research hospital whose patients recognized their own inevitable terminality because that was why they were research patients.[17] Death was an open and everyday occurrence. Patients could talk familiarly to each other about their respective fatal conditions, as well as to the staff members. Various consequences seemed to flow from this generally *open* situation, including the following: Patients could give each other support; and the staff could support patients. Patients could even raise the flagging spirits of the staff! From their deathbeds, they could thank the physicians for their unstinting efforts and wish them luck in solving their research problems in time to save other patients. They could close their lives with proper rituals, such as letter writing and praying. They could review their lives and plan realistically for their families' futures. All these various possibilities, available to aware patients in the open awareness situation, are of course not available to unaware patients in the closed awareness situation.

When patients are kept unaware of their terminality, then other consequences emerge. Since the unaware patient believes he will recover, he acts on that supposition. He may often be extremely cooperative with physicians and nurses because he believes faithful following of their orders will return him to good health. He talks and thinks as if his period of illness is only an interruption of normal life. Thus he may convert his sick room into a temporary workplace, writing his unfinished book, telephoning his business partners, and in other ways carrying on his

---

17. Renée Fox, *op. cit.*

work somewhat "as usual." He carries on his family life and friendship relations, also, with only the interruption necessitated by temporary illness. And of course, he can plan, if plans are called for, as if life stretched away before him. Since, in reality, it does not, other consequences may attend his acting as though it did. He may work less feverishly on his unfinished book than if he knew time was short, and so fail to finish it. He may set plans into operation that make little sense because he will soon be dead, and the plans will have to be undone after his death. Also, the unaware patient may unwittingly shorten his life because he does not realize that special care is necessary to extend it. Thus he may not understand the necessity for certain treatments and refuse them. Unaware cardiac patients, as another instance, may even destroy themselves by insisting upon undue activity.

A word or two should be said about the next of kin. It is commonly recognized that it is in some ways easier for the family to face a patient who does not know of his terminality, especially if he is the kind of person who is likely to die "gracelessly." And if an unaware person is suddenly stricken and dies, sometimes his family is grateful that "he died without knowing." On the other hand, when the kin must participate in the non-disclosure drama, especially if it lasts very long, the experience can be very painful. What is more, family members suffer sometimes because they cannot express their grief openly to the dying person; this is especially true of husbands and wives who are accustomed to sharing their private lives. Other consequences for the family of a patient who dies without awareness are poignantly suggested in the following anecdote: The dying man's wife had been informed by the doctor, and had shared this information with friends, whose daughter told the patient's young son. The son developed a strong distrust for the doctor, and felt in a way disinherited by his father since they had not discussed the responsibilities that would fall to him in the future (nor could they). The father, of course, could do nothing to ameliorate this situation because he did not know that he was going to die; and so, this closed awareness situation was, perhaps unnecessarily, made more painful and difficult for the family members.

We have already indicated in detail what difficulties the closed awareness context creates for the hospital staff, especially for the nurses. Nurses may sometimes actually be relieved when the patient talks openly about his demise and they no longer have to guard against disclosure. By contrast, the closed context instituted by the physician permits him to avoid the potentially distressing scene that may follow an announcement to his patient, but subjects nurses to strain, for they must spend the most time with the unaware patient, guarding constantly against disclosure. The attending physician visits the patient briefly and intermittently, sometimes rarely.

On the other hand, under certain conditions, nurses prefer the closed context. Some do not care to talk about death with a patient, especially a patient who does not accept it with fortitude. An unaware person is sometimes easier to handle anyway, for precisely the reason that he has not "given up," or is not taking death "badly" or "hard." (At one county hospital where we observed both nurses and interns, it was remarkable how little strain they experienced in their frequent contact with extremely ill, but unaware, terminal patients.) Nonetheless, the closed awareness situation prevents staff members from enjoying certain advantages that accompany a patient's resigned—or joyous —meeting with death.

As for the hospital itself, the important consequences of

closed awareness derive mainly from the consequences for the staff. Unaware patients who die quickly tend to do so without fuss, so the hospital's routine work is delayed less. On the other hand, as one can readily imagine, a patient who moves explosively and resentfully from an unaware to a highly suspicious or fully aware state is relatively disruptive. But these are only transitory consequences; the long-run consequences are most important.

The most crucial institutional consequence has already been mentioned: because American physicians choose not to tell most patients about terminality, the burden of dealing with unaware patients falls squarely and persistently upon the nursing personnel. Quite literally, if subtly, this considerable burden is built into the organization of the hospital services that deal with terminal patients. Another social structural condition intrinsic to the functioning of American hospitals also increases the nurses' burden. We refer to the nursing staff's commitment to work relatively closely with and around patients. Again, this structural condition can be better appreciated if one thinks of the contrast in Asian hospitals, where the family clusters thickly and persistently around the dying patient. A corollary of this familial clustering is that the nursing personnel can remain at a relatively great emotional distance from, and spend relatively little time with, the patient. The enormously high patient-to-personnel ratio increases the probability of great distance and little contact. Although American nurses are sometimes criticized for a propensity to anchor themselves at the nurses' station, they do spend more time with fewer patients, including those who are dying unaware.

Finally, we must ask about the consequences of closed awareness for continued interaction with the patient. Perhaps little need be said about this aspect of the closed awareness context. It should be abundantly clear that closed awareness can change smoothly and easily, or explosively and brutally, into another type of awareness context, depending on how the closed awareness was managed, and on the conditions under which the terminal patient discovered what the staff members were doing to or for him. At the most painful extreme, he can feel betrayed; the happiest outcome is that he feels grateful for their protection and genuine sensibility.

Selected Bibliography on Death and Dying

LEONARD PEARSON

THIS BIBLIOGRAPHY of books and articles on various aspects of dying, death, and bereavement has been organized on an empirical basis. Rather than deciding a priori what categories should be established and then classifying the literature accordingly, the material was classified according to a pattern that the material itself suggested.

A card was made for each entry and then grouped with others dealing with similar or related topics. After refining the piles, the final classification system was derived. Some of the resulting categories were not expected. The criticism and suggestions of the reader are invited.

For assistance in developing the system I am indebted to Michael Behrendt, M.A. For bibliographic assistance I am indebted to Mr. Behrendt, Mrs. Susan Maher, O.T.R., and a number of graduate students at Case Western Reserve University.

I also wish to acknowledge, with appreciation, the permission of Dr. Richard A. Kalish, Professor of Behavioral Sciences, School of Public Health, University of California, Los Angeles, to incorporate a number of annotated references previously published by him.

CLASSIFICATION OF LITERATURE ON DEATH AND DYING

   I.   Encyclopedia and General Sources
  II.   Philosophical and Literary Approaches
 III.   Cultural Patterns and Rituals

I. ENCYCLOPEDIA AND GENERAL SOURCES

1. Bartlett, J. *Familiar quotations.* Boston: Little, Brown, 1955.
    Four pages of index listings on death, dying, and bereavement in sources.
2. Dead; Death; Death rates. *Encyclopedia Britannica*, 1961, 7, 108 ff.
    General discussion of primitive funeral and burial procedures, legal and financial involvements with death, mortality rates, and biological aspects.
3. Death. *Encyclopedia Americana*, 1959, 8, 539–44.

A general discussion of death, emphasizing legal aspects and death customs and rites.

4. Death customs. *Encyclopedia of the social sciences*, 1931, *5*, 21–27.
   General discussion of funeral and burial rites, with emphasis upon preliterate groups.

5. Death customs and rites. *Colliers Encyclopedia*, 1968, 7, 757–65.
   General discussion of funeral and burial rites, with some comments on contemporary practices and trends.

6. Feifel, H. Death. In A. Deutsch (Ed.), *The encyclopedia of mental health*. Vol. 2. New York: Watts, 1963. Pp. 427–50.
   A general discussion of the entire field of death.

7. *Hastings Encyclopedia of Religion and Ethics*, 1911, 4.
   Several articles in this volume relate to the topics of death, bereavement, funerals, and so forth.

8. Portz, A. T. The psychological meaning of death: A review of the literature. California State College at Los Angeles, 1963. Mimeographed.
   This excellent literature review contains approximately 200 bibliographic items.

II. PHILOSOPHICAL AND LITERARY APPROACHES

1. Abrahamsson, H. The origin of death: Studies in African mythology. Unpublished doctoral dissertation, Princeton University, 1958.

2. Altman, L. L. "West" as a symbol of death. *Psychiat. Quart.*, 1959, *28*, 236–41.

3. Bacon, F. Of death. In S. H. Reynolds (Ed.), *Bacon's essays*. Oxford: Clarendon Press, 1890. Pp. 12–18.
   "He that dies in an earnest pursuit . . . doth avert the dolours of death" and two more pages of advice on death.

4. Banks, S. A. Dialogue on death: Freudian and Christian views. *Pastoral Psychol.*, 1963, *14*, 41–49.

5. Beauvoir, S. de. *A very easy death*. Trans. P. O'Brien. New York: Putnam, 1966.

"There is no such thing as a natural death: nothing that happens to a man is ever natural, since his presence calls the world into question. All men must die; but for every man his death is an accident, and even if he knows it and consents to it, it is an unjustifiable violation." *A Very Easy Death* is a novel of a mother who is medically kept alive past dignity's fine point and never told of her impending death.

6. Brill, A. A. Thoughts on life and death or Vidonian All Souls' Eve. *Psychiat. Quart.*, 1947, *21*, 199–211.

Paper read in memory of the Vidonians who died within the last 33 years; expresses author's philosophy of death; written in a sprightly manner.

7. Brown, N. *Life against death*. London: Kegan Paul, 1959.

8. Cain, A. C. The pre-superego "turning-inward" of aggression. *Psychoanal. Quart.*, 1961, *30*, 171–208.

Concepts of death instinct, from biopsychological to psychological. Death instinct in children developed as forms of autoaggression. This paper attempts to clarify the distinction between autoaggression and self-aggression, using field and experimental studies of animals and observational materials on early human development. It establishes the existence of the turning-inward of aggression, as a thing apart from or prior to significant superego development.

9. Caprio, F. S. Ethnological attitudes toward death: A psychoanalytic evaluation. *J. Clin. Exper. Psychopathol.*, 1946, 7, 737–52.

A discussion of the contemporary attitudes and superstitions concerning death as they reflect earlier traditions and primitive concepts.

10. Carmichael, B. The death wish in daily life. *Psychoanal. Rev.*, 1943, *30*, 59–66.

11. Caruse, I. A. A contribution to the study of Freud's concepts of the instincts for death and for aggression. *Bull. Psychologie*, 1965, *19*(1), 1–29.

The repetition compulsion demonstrates that some instincts return to an anterior state, toward the inorganic and death; but opposed to this return is an instinct, the libido, which tends toward the new, the organic. Freud's "psychic entropy" is related to the death instinct as its negentropy is related to the libido.

12. Choron, J. *Death and Western thought.* New York: Collier Books, 1963.

13. Choron, J. *Modern man and mortality.* New York: Macmillan, 1964.

   How to cope with the acute awareness of mortality: an "old-fashioned" approach to the question of what death means and "does" to the individual.

14. Cleveland, F. P. The dance of death. Editorial in *J.A.M.A.*, 1961, *176*(2), 142–43.

   The Dance of Death idea is as old as the life of the race, but each new period of human thought expresses it in new forms to correspond with its predominant philosophy. Not until World War I was the physician dissociated from the Dance.

15. Cochrane, A. L. Elie Metschnikoff and his theory of an *instinct de la mort. Int. J. Psychoanal.*, 1934, *15*, 265–70.

   Metschnikoff, a contemporary of Freud's, felt that man carried with him a collection of physical and psychic "dishar-monies" which were the chief cause of human unhappiness. He considered fear of death the greatest disharmony. He also attacked the concept of the immortality of the soul and of life after death, feeling that only science could solve the problem of human happiness and human death.

16. Feifel, H., *The meaning of death.* New York: McGraw-Hill, 1959.
   A collection of 19 articles covering death from numerous points of view, including art, music, literature, psychology, philosophy, theology, and medicine.

17. Feifel, H. The problem of death. Paper presented at the meeting of the American Psychological Association, Los Angeles, 1964.

18. Feifel, H. The taboo on death. *Amer. Behav. Sci.*, 1963, *6*, 66–67.
   A discussion of the contemporary situation in which death is a taboo topic for conversation and investigation.

19. Fenichel, O. A critique of the death instinct. In *Collected papers of Otto Fenichel: First series.* New York: Norton, 1953. Pp. 363–72.
   A general discussion of the death instinct.

20. Fiedler, L. A. *Love and death in the American novel.* New York: Criterion Books, 1960.

    A study of American literature from 1789 to 1960, finding "a literature almost pathologically incapable of dealing with adult sexuality and driven towards an obsession with death."

21. Flugel, J. C. Death instinct, homeostasis and allied concepts. *Int. J. Psychoanal.* [Suppl.], 1953, *34*, 43–74. Also in *Studies in feeling and desire.* London: Duckworth, 1955. Pp. 96–154.

22. Fodor, N. Jung's sermons to the dead. *Psychoanal. Rev.*, 1964, *51*(1), 74–78.

    A result of Jung's break with Freud; if Jung could not teach the living, he would teach the dead, for the dead only know what they have knowledge of at the moment of death.

23. Foxe, A. N. Critique of Freud's concept of a death instinct. *Psychoanal. Rev.*, 1943, *30*, 417–27.

    The life instinct (libidinal instinct and erotic instinct); the life and death instincts (pleasure principle and reality principle); the death instinct (stability tendency and Nirvana principle) discussed as terminology. The author finds confusion created by Freud's lack of consistency in interpretation.

24. Frankl, V. E. *From death camp to existentialism: A psychiatrist's path to new therapy.* Boston: Beacon Press, 1959.

    Stimulation of the will to meaning (logotherapy) in the face of death.

25. Frankl, V. E. Psychiatry and man's quest for meaning. *J. Religion Health*, 1962, *1*, 93–103.

26. Freud, S. The theme of the three caskets. In *Collected papers.* Vol. 4. New York: Basic Books, 1959. Pp. 244–56.

    A discussion of death as conceptually reversed in literature, dreams, and myth to signify the choosing of a fair lover (life).

27. Freud, S. Thoughts for the times on war and death. In *Complete psychological works of Sigmund Freud.* Vol. 14. London: Hogarth, 1957. Pp. 275–300.

    War forces us to recognize the "primal man" in each of us.

28. Fulton, R. *Death and identity.* New York: Wiley, 1965.

    A collection of readings on death and bereavement with extensive editorial commentary by the author, a sociologist.

29. Fulton, R., & Faunce, W. A. The sociology of death: A neglected area of research. *Soc. Forces,* 1958, *36,* 205–9.

    American sociologists have overlooked the area of death. The paper suggests a number of research possibilities. Death is viewed "as the nucleus of a particular culture complex involving a group of interrelated cultural traits which function together in a more or less consistent and meaningful way."

30. Galdston, I. Eros and thanatos: A critique and elaboration of Freud's death wish. *Amer. J. Psychoanal.,* 1955, *15,* 123–34.

31. Gorer, G. The pornography of death. In W. Phillips & P. Rahv (Eds.), *Modern writing.* New York: Berkeley Press, 1956. Pp. 56–62.

    Death, rather than sex, is the pornographic theme of the twentieth century.

32. Gottlieb, C. Modern art and death. In H. Feifel (Ed.), *The meaning of death.* New York: McGraw-Hill, 1959. Pp. 157–88.

    An article which traces death in art through history, concluding that modern art makes death anonymous, for the most part.

33. Greenson, R. R. Sleep, dreams and death. Transcript of radio broadcast on Station KPFK, Los Angeles, November 16, 1961. Mimeographed. Pp. 12.

34. Heuscher, J. E. Death in the fairy-tale. *Dis. Nerv. Syst.,* 1967, *28,* 462–67.

    Inevitable growth, the encountering of new patterns of life and their substitution for the familiar old ones, is seen as initiating an existential crisis in the individual. Death can be viewed as a new, if completely unknown, pattern of life. But from birth, each growth or new step includes a crisis that carries with it some of the connotations of death. Viewed in the context of the fairy-tale, each stage of growth plays the part of another in the series of developmental crises in which, simultaneously, no doubt is allowed of eventual success.

35. Hocking, W. E. *The meaning of immortality in human experience.* New York: Harper, 1957.

> A discussion of some of the needless obstacles to a just judgment of what one thinks about death, the immortality of man, or the total sense of human life.

36. Hoffman, F. J. Grace, violence, and self. *Virginia Quart. Rev.,* 1958, *34,* 439–54.

> An article on death and modern literature, showing how each of the terms—grace, violence, self—relates to the ways in which death as an event is vested in image and metaphor; the pattern of life-death-immortality is distinct in each case.

37. Hoffman, F. J. *The mortal no: Death and the modern imagination.* Princeton, N. J.: Princeton University Press, 1964.

38. Hoffman, F. J. Mortality and modern literature. In H. Feifel (Ed.), *The meaning of death.* New York: McGraw-Hill, 1959. Pp. 133–56.

> A discussion of the place of death in contemporary literature.

39. Jones, W. T. *Metaphysics of life and death.* New York: George H. Doran, 1924.

40. Kalish, R. A. A continuum of subjectively perceived death. *Gerontologist,* 1966, *6,* 73–76.

> Subjectively perceived death need not coincide with biological death; a variety of conditions can be interpreted as social death, psychological death, or social immortality. A majority of college student respondents seemed able to accept these types of nonbiological deaths as valid and meaningful.

41. Kastenbaum, R. Cognitive and personal futurity in later life. *J. Individ. Psychol.,* 1963, *19,* 216–22.

> The ability to utilize futurity as an abstract category for organizing experience is differentially available to the young and to the elderly.

42. Levin, A. J. The fiction of the death instinct. *Psychiat. Quart.,* 1951, *25,* 257–81.

> Attacks Freud's theory of the "death instinct" in an exploration of the theory of the literature of psychotherapy, showing the many ways in which culture has immobilized human func-

tions. Attention is paid to individual reactions to external dangers rather than to internal instincts. Thus, fear of death is caused by actual and single situations, not by one main cause.

43. Luza, S. La muerte en filisofia y en psicologia (Death in philosophy and psychology). *Revta. Psicol.* (Lima), 1960, pp. 279–91.

In contrast to the negative concepts of death found in philosophy, especially with existentialists, psychology offers a more positive vision. The fatalistic view of existence is held only by mentally sick people of the depressive and hypochondriac type. The majority of normal people look forward to all developmental stages of life. "Psychologists look at death in a positive way, taking it as a phenomenon of a distinct quality, as a new and decisive fact, representing thus a biological disturbance of equilibrium that got hold of the being."

44. Malinowski, B. *Magic, science, and religion, and other essays.* Boston: Beacon Press, 1948.

The myths of death and the bereavement rituals of the Melanese Island natives are described.

45. Marcuse, H. The ideology of death. In H. Feifel (Ed.), *The meaning of death.* New York: McGraw-Hill, 1959. Pp. 64–76.

The meaning of death is often couched either in philosophic terms as a natural phenomenon or in religious terms as the beginning of a new life.

46. Menninger, K. *Man against himself.* New York: Harcourt, Brace, 1938.

47. Moore, W. E. Time—the ultimate scarcity. *Amer. Behav. Sci.,* 1963, 6, 58–60.

Control of time indicates control of "fate," but only partially, since death is inevitable.

48. Myers, F. W. H. *Human personality and its survival of bodily death.* London: Longmans, Green, 1919.

Ample evidence exists for life after death; the author discusses such matters as trances, hypnotism, and hysteria.

49. Needleman, J. Imagining absence, non-existence and death: A sketch. *Rev. Exist. Psychol. Psychiat.,* 1966, 6(3), 230–36.

Speculations on the cognitive possibilities of imagining death (state) and nonpresence (relationship): refers to Freud's thesis that a man cannot imagine his own nonpresence.

50. Ostow, M. The death instinct—a contribution to the study of instincts. *Int. J. Psychoanal.*, 1958, *39*, 5–16.

A discussion of the interrelation of regression, the death instinct, and various other instincts.

51. Pratt, J. S. Epilegomena to the study of Freudian instinct theory. *Int. J. Psychoanal.*, 1958, *39*, 17–24.

In part a discussion of Freud's death instinct theory as influenced by 19th-century biology.

52. Rheingold, J. C. *The mother anxiety and death: The catastrophic death complex.* Boston: Little, Brown, 1967.

The psychology of death, the meaning of basic anxiety, and the character of the mother-infant relationship are seen not only to be interrelated, but mutually determined by maternal destructiveness.

53. Sachs, H. *Beauty, life and death. Amer. Imago*, 1940, *1*, 81–133.

Both life and death are needed for the creation of beauty.

54. Searles, H. F. *The nonhuman environment.* New York: International Universities Press, 1960.

Kinship exists between man and his nonhuman environment; man's destiny is for his body to become a part of this environment at death.

55. Shaler, N. S. *The individual: A study of life and death.* New York: D. Appleton, 1901.

A naturalist of 1900 attempts to view the phenomenon of human death in context with that of other life forms. Defines immortality as the passing of wisdom and knowledge from generation to generation.

56. Shor, R. E. A survey of representative literature on Freud's death-instinct hypothesis. *J. Humanistic Psychol.*, 1961, *1*, 73–83.

57. Spark, M. *Memento mori.* New York: Avon Books, 1959.

"Remember, you must die"; a novel of old age and death, centering on a group of friends who strut, fret, fuss, and remember.

58. Sulzberger, C. *My brother death.* New York: Harper, 1961.

Defines death and its relationship to man; discusses how to meet its approach; speculates what may lie beyond. Draws heavily from the history of human thought and experience, from all principal religions of East and West, from the philosophers, saints, kings, and heroes. Documents the panorama of ways in which men die: by acts attributed to the God of disaster, pestilence, famine, and illness; by man's own hand in murder, war, cannibalism, capital punishment, and religious persecution.

59. Tillich, P. The eternal now. In H. Feifel (Ed.), *The meaning of death.* New York: McGraw-Hill, 1959. Pp. 30–38.

Man places great emphasis upon anticipation of the end of his life.

III. CULTURAL PATTERNS AND RITUALS

1. Becker, R. J. Funeral—memorial or burial? *Pastoral Psychol.,* 1964, *15,* 50–53.

The article makes a plea for a religious funeral practice that avoids commercialism.

2. Bendann, E. *Death customs: An analytical study of burial rites.* New York: Knopf, 1930. Pp. 40–65.

Burial rites and related concepts in Melanesia, Australia, Northeast Siberia, and India come under intense investigation.

3. Borkenau, F. The concept of death. *Twentieth Century,* 1955, *157,* 313–29.

Attitudes toward death are vital in shaping human history, and changes in these attitudes mark epochs of historical evolution.

4. Bossard, J. H. S., & Boll, E. S. *Ritual in family living.* Philadelphia: University of Pennsylvania Press, 1950. Pp. 14–30.

Rituals regarding death in the family are undergoing extensive change, reflecting a secular trend.

5. Bowman, L. *The American funeral.* Washington, D.C.: Public Affairs Press, 1959.

A thorough evaluation and discussion of American funerals, including descriptions of various services as prescribed by the different major religious groupings.

6. Brooks, J. Ways of death. *Consumer Reports*, 1964, *29*, 40–43.

    A review comparing the three recent books dealing with funerals by authors Bowman, Mitford, and Harmer.

7. Carpenter, E. S. Eternal life and self-definition among the Aivilik Eskimos. *Amer. J. Psychiat.*, 1954, *110*, 840–43.

    According to the Aiviliks, death is not an end but the beginning of a new life, the soul leaving one "home" and eventually entering another.

8. Devereux, G. Primitive psychiatry, funeral suicide and the Mohave social structure. *Bull. Hist. Med.*, 1942, *11*, 522–42.

    A description of Mohave funeral customs, including the cultural motivations for funeral suicide.

9. Devos, G., & Wagatsuma, H. Psycho-cultural significance of concern over death and illness among rural Japanese. *Int. J. Soc. Psychiat.*, 1959, *5*, 5–19.

10. Eaton, J. W. The art of aging and dying. *Gerontologist*, 1964, *4*, 94–100.

    A discussion of how the way of life of the Hutterite religious sect enables them to deal with the six universal problems of aging: economic insecurity, the inactivity of retirement, prestige loss, social isolation, loss of health, and death. Gives emphasis to the theory that old-age adjustment begins when people are young.

11. Evans-Pritchard, E. E. *Witchcraft, oracles, and magic among the Azande.* New York: Oxford University Press, 1937.

12. Feifel, H. Scientific research in taboo areas—death. *Amer. Behav. Sci.*, 1962, *5*, 28–30.

13. Forest, J. D. The major emphasis of the funeral. *Pastoral Psychol.*, 1963, *14*, 19–24.

14. Frazer, J. G. *The fear of the dead in primitive religion.* London: Macmillan, 1933. 3 vols.

    Examples from all over the world of reactions to immortality of the human soul.

15. Fulton, R. L. The clergyman and the funeral director: A study in role conflict. *Soc. Forces*, 1961, *39*, 317–23.

Report of a survey of attitudes of clergymen regarding funerals. Protestant ministers are more critical of funerals and of the role of the morticians than are Catholic priests.

16. Fulton, R. L. *The sacred and the secular: Attitudes of the American public toward death.* Milwaukee: Bulfin Printers, 1963. Pp. 23.

A large sample of the general public responded to mailed questionnaires concerning their feelings about funerals and funeral directors.

17. Gealy, F. D. The biblical understanding of death. *Pastoral Psychol.*, 1963, *14*, 33–40.

18. Geertz, C. Ritual and social change: A Japanese example. *Amer. Anthrop.*, 1958, *59*, 32–54.

19. Geis, G., & Fulton, R. Death and social values. *Int. J. Soc. Res.*, 1962, *3*, 7–14.

Attitudes toward death reflect the values prevailing within a particular society. In America, secularization of death has led to opening the subject for social scientific study.

20. Giesey, R. E. The royal funeral ceremony in Renaissance France. Unpublished doctoral dissertation, University of California (Berkeley), 1954.

21. Glidden, T. The American funeral. *Pastoral Psychol.*, 1963, *14*, 9–18.

22. Goody, J. *Death, property and the ancestors: A study of the mortuary customs of the Lo Dagaa of West Africa.* Palo Alto: Stanford University Press, 1962.

23. Gorer, G. *Death, grief, and mourning in contemporary Britain.* London: Cresset, 1965.

24. Gough, E. K. Cults of the dead among the Nayars. *J. Amer. Folklore*, 1958, *71*, 446–78.

25. Grotjahn, M. About the representation of death in the art of antiquity and in the unconscious of modern man. In G. B. Wilbur & W. Muenstergerger (Eds.), *Psychoanalysis and culture.* New York: International Universities Press, 1951. Pp. 410–24.

A Freudian approach to death symbols in ancient art and in contemporary customs.

26. Habenstein, R. W., & Lamers, W. M. *Funeral customs the world over.* Milwaukee: Bulfin Printers, 1961.
Description of death, funerals, and bereavement throughout the world (excluding the United States).

27. Habenstein, R. W., & Lamers, W. M. *The history of American funeral directing.* Milwaukee: Bulfin Printers, 1955.
The history of funerals in the United States, published under the auspices of the National Funeral Directors Association.

28. Hallowell, A. I. Aggression in Salteaux society. *Psychiatry*, 1940, 3, 395–407.
In this preliterate culture, death is attributed to sorcery.

29. Harmer, R. M. *The high cost of dying.* New York: Crowell-Collier, 1963.
A book directed at the popular market which attacks business methods utilized by funeral directors. A brief history of funerals is presented.

30. Havighurst, R. The career of the funeral director. Unpublished doctoral dissertation, University of Chicago, 1954.

31. Hickerson, H. The feast of the dead among the seventeenth century Algonkians of the upper Great Lakes. *Amer. Anthrop.*, 1960, 62, 81–107.

32. Howard, A., & Scott, R. A. Cultural values and attitudes toward death. *J. Exist.*, 1965–66, 6, 161–74.
Attitudes toward death, like so many other aspects of a people's "world view," are strongly influenced by dominant cultural themes. The authors analyze some of the cultural values that appear to affect American attitudes toward death, and explore their social consequences. The American patterns are then contrasted with those of a Polynesian people, the Rotumans.

33. Irion, P. E. *The funeral and the mourners.* New York: Abingdon Press, 1954.

34. Jackson, E. N. *For the living.* New York: Channel Press, 1963.
Answers to questions that are frequently asked regarding death, bereavement, and funerals.

35. Jakobovits, I. The dying and their treatment in Jewish law. *Hebrew Med. J.*, 1961, 2, 242–51.

36. Kalish, R. A., & Wolf, D. Semantic differential measurements of funeral directors, life insurance salesmen, and comparable vocations. University of California at Los Angeles, 1965. Mimeographed.

37. Kelly, W. H. Cocopa attitudes and practices with respect to death and mourning. *Southwest. J. Anthrop.*, 1949, 5, 151–64.
    This paper discusses the Cocopa Indians of Southwestern United States and adjacent areas of Mexico between 1870–90.

38. Kennard, E. A. Hopi reactions to death. *Amer. Anthrop.*, 1937, 29, 491–94.
    The spirits of the dead are very important in Hopi religious ceremonies.

39. Kephart, W. M. Status after death. *Amer. Sociol. Rev.*, 1950, 15, 635–43.
    Social-class differences in funeral and burial customs in the Philadelphia area are described.

40. Kidorf, I. W. Jewish tradition and the Freudian theory of mourning. *J. Religion Health.*, 1963, 2, 248–52.

41. Krupp, G. R., & Kligfeld, B. The bereavement reaction: A cross-cultural evaluation. *J. Religion Health*, 1962, 1, 222–46.
    A discussion of bereavement, comparing reactions in different regions of the world and different time periods.

42. Lamm, M., & Eskreis, N. Viewing the remains: A new American custom. *J. Religion Health*, 1966, 5(2), 137–43.
    Questions the validity of the custom of viewing the corpse from both theological and psychological viewpoints.

43. Lear, G. S. Embalming and cremating. *Practitioner*, 1948, 161, 94–100.
    Discussion of practices in Great Britain.

44. Lee, R. P. *Burial customs, ancient and modern.* Minneapolis: The Arya Co., 1929.

45. Mandelbaum, D. G. Social uses of funeral rites. In H. Feifel (Ed.), *The meaning of death.* New York: McGraw-Hill, 1959. Pp. 189–217.
    Description of funeral ceremonies of several diverse cultures.

46. Matz, M. Judaism and bereavement. *J. Religion Health*, 1964, *3*, 345–52.

47. Melikian, L. H. The use of selected T.A.T. cards among Arab university students: A cross-cultural study. *J. Soc. Psychol.*, 1964, *62*, 3–19.
    > The illness or death of a parent or central character is more frequent in stories by Arabs than by Americans: an indication of a suppressed revolt against figures of authority, or against culture and its adult surrogates.

48. Mitford, J. *The American way of death.* New York: Simon and Schuster, 1963.
    > Written for the popular market, this widely discussed book was aimed at exposing alleged malpractices of funeral directors.

49. Mitra, D. N. Mourning customs and modern life in Bengal. *Amer. J. Sociol.*, 1947, *52*, 309-11.

50. Morgan, E. *A manual of simple burial.* Burnsville, N.C.: Celo Press, 1966.
    > A standard reference work of memorial societies, including discussions of the philosophy and practice of simplicity in funeral arrangements.

51. Murdock, G. *Social structure.* New York: Macmillan, 1949.
    > This book includes several references to such social patterns as funeral behavior, remarriage following bereavement, inheritance, and so forth.

52. Murgoci, A. Customs connected with death and burial among the Roumanians. *Folklore*, 1919, *30*, 89–102.
    > Discussion of the very elaborate death rites of the Roumanians at the turn of the century, along with comments on their attitudes toward death.

53. Noon, J. A. A preliminary examination of the death concepts of the Ibo. *Amer. Anthrop.*, 1942, *44*, 638–54.

54. Opler, M. E. The Lipan Apache death complex and its extensions. *Southwest. J. Anthrop.*, 1945, *1*, 122–41.

55. Opler, M. E. Reactions to death among the Mescalero Apache. *Southwest. J. Anthrop.*, 1946, *2*, 454–67.

56. Opler, M. E., & Bittle, W. E. The death practices and eschatology of the Kiowa Apache. *Southwest. J. Anthrop.*, 1961, *17*, 383–94.

57. Paton, L. B. *Spiritism and the cult of the dead in antiquity.* New York: Macmillan, 1921.

58. Paz, O. The day of the dead. In *Labyrinth of solitude: Life and thought in Mexico.* Trans. Lysander Kemp. New York: Grove Press, 1961. Pp. 47–64.

59. Puckle, B. *Funeral customs.* London: T. W. Laurie, 1926.
    A full discussion of funeral customs throughout the world prior to 1926.

60. Rivers, W. H. R. *Psychology and ethnology.* London: Kegan Paul, 1926. Pp. 36–50.
    Primitive people in many instances do not regard the demarcation between the living and the dead as being distinct in the same way that "modern" societies do.

61. Rush, A. C. *Death and burial in Christian antiquity.* Washington, D.C.: The Catholic University of America Press, 1941.

62. Simmons, L. W. *The role of the aged in primitive society.* New Haven: Yale University Press, 1945. Pp. 217–244.
    An anthropological approach to comparative cultural treatment of the aged in preliterate societies.

63. Slater, P. E. Cultural attitudes toward the aged. *Geriatrics*, 1963, *18*, 308–14.
    Our attitudes toward the aged are ambivalent, because they are based on two conflicting traditions: that age is a misfortune (Greek) and that age is the pinnacle of life (Middle East).

64. Spiro, J. D. The Jewish way of death. *Amer. Judaism*, 1964, *27*, 16–19.
    Jews should not succumb to the social pressures for status-seeking in the selection of funeral services and coffins, but should maintain simplicity in death rituals.

65. Sterba, R. On Halloween. *Amer. Imago*, 1948, *5*, 213–24.
    The limitations on the celebration of Halloween are another indication of death denial in America.

66. Stewart, D., & Ass. *Analysis of attitudes toward funeral directors.* Milwaukee: National Funeral Directors Association, 1948.

67. Wahl, C. W. The fear of death. In H. Feifel (Ed.), *The meaning of death.* New York: McGraw-Hill, 1959. Pp. 16–29.

    Contemporary man uses all sorts of magic to protect himself from death, including the rituals involved with the death industry and acceptance of beliefs which claim that death is just a transition, not a termination.

68. Warner, W. L. *The living and the dead.* New Haven: Yale University Press, 1959. Pp. 280–320.

    Discusses the cemetery as an important part of life in "Yankee City" and the problem of the sacred and secular aspects of the graveyard.

69. Warthin, A. S. The physician of the Dance of Death. *Ann. Med. Hist.*, New Series. Part 1: The period of great wall paintings, 1930, *2*, 351–71. Part 2: The pre-Holbein manuscripts, block books, and incunabula, 1930, *2*, 453–69. Part 3: Holbein—the great Dance of Death of the Renaissance, 1930, *2*, 697–710. Part 4: The imitators of Holbein, 1931, *3*, 75–109. Part 5: The period of caricature, 1931, *3*, 134–65.

    A study of the role of the physician in artistic representations of the Dance of Death, which in its variants has great significance in the cultural evolution of modern society.

70. Waugh, E. Death in Hollywood. *Life Magazine, 23* (September 29, 1947), 73–74.

    A satirical description of Forest Lawn, nonfictional.

71. Wolf, A. W. M. *Helping your child to understand death.* New York: Child Study Association, 1958.

    Suggests methods of answering children's questions about death. Discusses major religious attitudes and ceremonies in the United States.

IV.   CAUSES OF DEATH

A.   ILLNESS

1. Adelson, L., & Kinney, E. R. Sudden and unexpected death in in-

fancy and childhood. *Pediatrics*, 1956, *17*, 663–97.
Description of various diseases causing death in infancy and childhood.

2. Beecher, H. K. Nonspecific forces surrounding disease and the treatment of disease. *J.A.M.A.*, 1962, *179*, 437–40.
Presents evidence that fear can kill.

3. Beigler, J. S. Anxiety as an aid in the prognostication of impending death. *Arch. Neurol. Psychiat.*, 1957, 77, 171–77.
A somatic illness can sometimes be detected for the first time by its psychiatric manifestations.

4. Carrington, J., & Meader, C. *Death, its causes and phenomena.* New York: Dodd, Mead, 1911.
Discusses the moment of death, the signs of death, the physical causes (or circumstances) of death, and oddities such as premature burial, vampires, and cellular death.

5. Fax, J. *The chronically ill.* New York: Philosophical Library, 1957.
The effects of chronic sickness on the individual, on those charged with his care, and on society illustrate that illness is a public health problem. The number of persons affected, definitions of chronic illness, and techniques for helping the patient to lead a satisfying life are reviewed.

6. Gengerelli, J. A., & Kirkner, F. J. (Eds.) *The psychological variables of human cancer: A symposium.* Berkeley: University of California Press, 1954. (See lecture by E. M. Blumberg, p. 30.)

7. Greene, W. A., & Miller, G. Psychological factors and reticuloendothelial disease. *Psychosom. Med.*, 1958, *20*, 124–44.
Report includes observations on 33 children and adolescents below the age of 20 with diagnosis of leukemia. Formulations for comprehending some of the multiple conditions determining occurrence of leukemia in an individual child were presented.

8. Horder, L. Signs and symptoms of impending death. *Practitioner*, 1948, *161*, 73–75.
Signs and symptoms of *impending* death are extremely unreliable when one rules out the incurable diseases and extreme degrees of enfeeblement. The greater experience the physician has, the more caution he displays.

9. LeShan, L., & Gassmann, M. L. Some observations on psychotherapy with patients suffering from neoplastic disease. *Amer. J. Psychother.*, 1958, *12*, 723–34.

10. Lindemann, E. Modifications in the course of ulcerative colitis in relationship to changes in life situations and reaction patterns. In H. G. Wolff (Ed.), *Life stress and bodily disease.* Baltimore: Williams & Wilkins, 1950. Pp. 706–23.

    Discusses the relationship between grief and the onset of an organic disease.

11. Lindemann, E. Symptomatology and management of acute grief. *Amer. J. Psychiat.*, 1944, *101*, 141–48.

    Delineation of bereavement and morbid grief indices.

12. McCully, R. S. Fantasy productions of children with a progressively crippling and fatal illness. *J. Genet. Psychol.*, 1963, *102*, 203–16.

13. Means, M. H. Fears of one thousand college women. *J. Abnorm. Soc. Psychol.*, 1936, *31*, 291–311.

    Fear stimuli for 1,000 women were elicited and rated on an intensity scale. Cancer and bereavement were the most fear-provoking.

14. Monsour, K. J. Asthma and the fear of death. *Psychoanal. Quart.*, 1960, *29*, 56–71.

    Asthma may be an expression of anxiety which later appears as death phobia.

15. Morrissey, J. R. Children's adaptation to fatal illness. *Soc. Work,* 1963, *8*, 81–88.

16. Rezek, P. R. Dying and death. *J. Forensic Sci.*, 1963, *8*, 200–208.

    A discussion of death and dying as related to anabolism and catabolism, with a survey of some problems of metabolism linked with certain morphological aspects and autopsy findings.

17. Rohrod, M. G. The meaning of "cause of death." *J. Forensic Sci.*, 1963, *8*, 15–21.

    Three principal purposes for wanting to know cause of death are (1) scientific, (2) statistical, (3) legal. Indexing systems in the future must consider the multiplicity of factors which cause death.

18. Ryle, J. A. *Angor animi,* or the sense of dying. *Guy Hosp. Rep.,* 1950, *99,* 230–35.

    An awareness of dying is reported to be associated with certain somatic conditions. The author suggests the possibility that it may be a "protective" medullary storm.

19. Schmale, A. H. Relationship of separation and depression to disease. *Psychosom. Med.,* 1958, *20,* 259–77.

20. Stearns, S. Self-destructive behavior in young patients with diabetes mellitus. *Diabetes,* 1959, *8,* 379–82.

21. Wardwell, W. I., Bahnson, C. B., & Caron, H. S. Social and psychological factors in coronary heart disease. *J. Health Hum. Behav.,* 1963, *4,* 154–65.

    Several personality and social characteristics were found to be closely associated with coronary heart disease.

22. Wardwell, W. I., Hyman, M., & Bahnson, C. B. Stress and coronary heart disease in three field studies. *J. Chronic Dis.,* 1964, *17,* 73–84.

    This paper supports the hypothesis that sociological and social factors play a role in the etiology of coronary artery disease.

B. AGING

1. Bellin, S. S., & Hardt, R. H. Marital status and mental disorders among the aged. *Amer. Sociol. Rev.,* 1958, *23,* 155–62.

2. Birren, J. *The psychology of aging.* Englewood Cliffs, N. J.: Prentice-Hall, 1964.

3. Group for the Advancement of Psychiatry. *Psychiatry and the aged.* (Report 59.) New York: GAP, 1965.

4. Jarvik, L. F., & Falek, A. Intellectual stability and survival: Data on aged twins relating intellectual decrement and survival. *J. Geront.,* 1963, *18,* 173–76.

5. Kastenbaum, R. The mental life of dying geriatric patients. *Proc. 7th Int. Congr. Geront.,* 1966, pp. 153–59.

    Psychological findings for 61 geriatric patients failed to support the conventional assumption that most aged persons are in poor mental contact as they are dying. Positive death references were heard more frequently than negative references.

Mental contact was positively related to "social viability" in the geriatric hospital.

6. Kastenbaum, R. The realm of death: An emerging area in psychological research. *J. Hum. Rel.*, 1965, *13*, 538–52.

Reliabilities of longevity estimates by physicians are fairly high when evaluating patients in a hospital for the aged. The article also includes a discussion of the theoretical background of the problem.

7. Kastenbaum, R. The reluctant therapist. *Geriatrics*, 1963, *18*, 296–301.

Psychotherapists are reluctant to work with elderly people because of certain stereotypes and because of concern that the potential of the client is not sufficient to reward the emotional investment.

8. Kastenbaum, R., & Aisenberg, R. *The psychology of death.* New York: Springer, in press.

As nearly as can be determined, this is the first book to be written on this topic from a social scientific point of view. It discusses death in the context of aging.

9. Kastenbaum, R. (Ed.) *Contributions to the psycho-biology of aging.* New York: Springer, 1965.

10. Kastenbaum, R. (Ed.) *New thoughts on old age.* New York: Springer, 1964.

11. Kay, D. W. K., Norris, V., & Post, F. Prognosis in psychiatric disorders of the elderly: An attempt to define indicators of early death and early recovery. *J. Ment. Sci.*, 1956, *102*, 129–40.

The authors were successfully able to predict the death, or discharge from care, of 75% of a group of patients admitted for observation to a mental care unit.

12. Levin, S. Depression in the aged: A study of the salient external factors. *Geriatrics*, 1963, *18*, 302–7.

Depression in the aged may be caused by loss, attack, or restraint, or threats of any of these, and occurs more frequently than in younger people.

13. Lieberman, M. A. Psychological correlates of impending death. Paper presented at the meeting of the Gerontological Society, Boston, April 1963. Mimeographed.

Measurable psychological changes preceding death in an aged

population are demonstrated: Bender-Gestalt and figure-drawing measures are considered.

14. Platt, R. Reflections on aging and death. *Lancet*, January-June 1963, *1*, 1–6.

15. Rhudick, P. J., & Dibner, A. S. Age, personality, and health correlates of death concerns in normal aged individuals. *J. Geront.*, 1961, *16*, 44–49.

    Although demographic variables were not essentially related to death concerns among a population of elderly, certain personality test scores were related.

16. Riegel, K. F., Riegel, R. M., & Meyer, G. A study of the dropout rates in longitudinal research on aging and the prediction of death. *J. Personality Soc. Psychol.*, 1967, *5*, 342–48.

    Intelligence, verbal abilities, attitudes, interests, and social conditions of 380 subjects above 55 years were measured, with all available subjects retested after five years. In numbers increasing with age, some subjects had died, or were too sick to be tested. Those unavailable because of refusal to be retested bore no relationship to age. It was concluded that previous studies have underestimated the amount of attrition, leaving developmental trends based on increasingly biased samples. Various implications of this are finally presented with respect to studying determinants of death.

17. Roth, M. The natural history of mental disorder in old age. *J. Ment. Sci.*, 1955, *101*, 281–301.

18. Scheinfeld, A. The mortality of men and women. *Sci. Amer.*, 1958, *198*, 22–27.

    Studies of males and females in other countries continue to reveal tendency of women to live longer than men. The study of the differences in death rates of the two sexes may hold clues to the prevention and treatment of many diseases.

19. Simmons, L. W. *The role of the aged in primitive society*. New Haven: Yale University Press, 1945. Pp. 217–44.

    An anthropological approach to comparative cultural treatment of the aged in preliterate societies.

20. Slater, P. E. Cultural attitudes toward the aged. *Geriatrics*, 1963, *18*, 308–14.

    Our attitudes toward the aged are ambivalent, because they are based on two conflicting traditions: that age is a misfortune (Greek) and that age is the pinnacle of life (Middle East).

21. Slater, P. E. Prolegomena to a psychoanalytic theory of aging and death. In R. Kastenbaum (Ed.), *New thoughts on old age*. New York: Springer, 1964. Chap. 2.

22. Swenson, W. M. The many faces of aging. *Geriatrics.*, 1962, *17*, 659–63.

    Several major social psychological problems of aging in the United States are identified, e.g., lack of respect for the aged, rapid increase in percentage of elderly in population, uncertainty concerning abilities of aged.

23. Swenson, W. M. The psychology of aging: Its significance in the practice of geriatric medicine. *Postgrad. Med.*, 1963, *34*, 89–93.

    The author presents several suggestions for dealing with the aged, emphasizing the idea that senescence is a psychological as well as a biological process, and that the elderly need to be treated as individuals who still have some life ahead.

24. Weinberg, J. Aging of groups. In *VA prospectus: Research in aging*. Washington, D. C.: U.S. Veterans Administration, 1959. Pp. 107–16.

C. PSYCHIC CAUSES

1. Aldrich, C. K. Personality factors and mortality in the relocation of the aged. *Gerontologist*, 1964, *4*, 92–93.

    A study of the relation of mortality and personality factors in the relocation of residents of a home which closes for administrative reasons. Observations give added weight to the conclusion that among aged people psychological patterns of adaptation and specific types of emotional response to stress situations are significant determinants of survival.

2. Barber, T. X. Death by suggestion: A critical note. *Psychosom. Med.*, 1961, *23*, 153–55.

    A criticism of other reports providing biological bases for

"voodoo death." The author claims that poison, starvation, and organic disease, not biochemical responses to fear, have been the cause.

3. Cannon, W. B. "Voodoo death." *Amer. Anthrop.*, 1942, *44*, 169–73. See also *Psychosom. Med.*, 1957, *19*, 182–90.
   The author presents a psychosomatic basis for "voodoo deaths."

4. Ellison, D. L. Alienation and the will to live of retired steelworkers. *Proc. 7th Int. Congr. Geront.*, 1966, pp. 167–70.
   The "will to live" is proposed as a relevant concept for study of changes occurring prior to death. A scale was designed and administered to 108 retired steelworkers. Low will to live was correlated with poor (perceived) health, normlessness, and loss of functional roles.

5. Engel, G. L. *Psychological development in health and disease.* Philadelphia: Saunders, 1962. Chap. 26.

6. Ewing, L. S. Fighting and death from stress in a cockroach. *Science*, 1967, *155*, 1035–36.
   Illustrates the sequence of events involved in the fighting behavior between pairs of male cockroaches, in which deaths occur independent of external damage. Stable dominant-subordinate relationships are established, with subsequent deaths seen as resulting from stress.

7. Feifel, H. Death—relevant variable in psychology. In R. May (Ed.), *Existential psychology.* New York: Random House, 1961.

8. Fulton, R. L. Death and the self. *J. Religion Health*, 1964, *3*(4), 359–68.
   Discusses previous studies on the relationship between grief and death, psychosomatic responses, present trends in coping with death in the U.S., and some psychological implications of these trends.

9. Glaser, B. G., & Strauss, A. L. Expecting patients to die: Temporal aspects of status passage. San Francisco: University of California Medical Center, 1963. Mimeographed. Pp. 22.

10. Horder, L., Signs and symptoms of impending death. *Practitioner*, 1948, *161*, 73–75.

    Signs and symptoms of *impending* death are extremely unreliable when one rules out the incurable diseases and extreme degrees of enfeeblement. The greater experience the physician has, the more caution he displays.

11. Jelliffe, S. E. The death instinct in somatic and psychopathology. *Psychoanal. Rev.*, 1933, *20*, 121–31.

    Procedures used to treat emotionally disturbed patients with organic problems may ameliorate both the functional and the organic difficulties.

12. Kraus, A. S., & Lilienfeld, A. M. Some epidemiological aspects of the high mortality rate in the young widowed group. *J. Chronic Dis.*, 1959, *10*, 207–17.

13. Menninger von Lerchenthal, E. Death from psychic causes. *Bull. Menninger Clin.*, 1948, *12*, 31–36.

    Psychic deaths occur from both hysteria and suggestion.

14. Milici, P. S. The involutional death reaction. *Psychiat. Quart.*, 1950, *24*, 775–81.

    A case description of a clear-cut preinvolutional melancholic personality make-up reacting to internal and external dissatisfactions in a pathologically regressive manner; a disease resulting in a psychologically "protective" but annihilating death reaction.

15. Richmond, J. B., & Waisman, H. A. Psychologic aspects of management of children with malignant diseases. *J. Dis. Child.*, 1955, *89*, 42–47.

    A discussion of the treatment of children with malignant diseases, including the suggestion that parents be allowed to assist more with the physical care.

16. Richter, C. P. On the phenomenon of sudden death in animals and man. *Psychosom. Med.*, 1957, *19*, 191–98. See also in H. Feifel (Ed.), *The meaning of death.* New York: McGraw-Hill, 1959. Pp. 302–13.

A physiological explanation of the sudden death of rats as the result of excessive stimulation of the parasympathetic system, with the possibility this explanation could be extended to humans.

17. Rioch, D., Herbert, C. C., Mead, M. E., Goldstein, M. S., & Weinstein, E. A. The psychophysiology of death. In A. Simon (Ed.), *The physiology of emotions.* Springfield, Ill.: Charles C Thomas, 1961. Pp. 77–225.

18. Stern, K., Williams, G. M., & Prados, M. Grief reactions in later life. *Amer. J. Psychiat.*, 1951, *108*, 289–94.
    Tendencies toward somatic illness in elderly bereaved subjects are evaluated.

19. Szasz, T. S. A contribution to the psychology of bodily feelings. *Psychoanal. Quart.*, 1957, *26*, 25–49.
    A philosophical discussion of psychoanalytical theory and bodily feelings. Case illustrations are given.

20. Walters, M. J. Psychic death: Report of a possible case. *Arch. Neurol. Psychiat.*, 1944, *52*, 84–85.
    A middle-aged woman died at almost exactly the same age as her mother, with whom she strongly identified. No physical causes for the death were found.

21. Wardwell, W. L., Bahnson, C. B., & Caron, H. S. Social and psychological factors in coronary heart disease. *J. Health Hum. Behav.*, 1963, *4*, 154–65.
    Several personality and social characteristics were found to be closely associated with coronary heart disease.

22. Wardwell, W. I., Hyman, M., & Bahnson, C. S. Stress and coronary heart disease in three field studies. *J. Chronic Dis.*, 1964, *17*, 73–84.
    This paper supports the hypothesis that sociological factors play a role in the etiology of coronary artery disease.

23. Weisman, A. D., & Hackett, T. P. Predilection to death: Death and dying as a psychiatric problem. *Psychosom. Med.*, 1961, *23*, 232–56.

> A discussion and evaluation of five surgical patients who appeared to be predilected to death at the time of their arrival at the hospital; all died shortly after surgery.

24. Weiss, S. Instantaneous "physiologic" death. *New Eng. J. Med.*, 1940, *223*, 793–97.

> A medical discussion of the causes of sudden, usually unexpected, death.

25. Young, M., Benjamin, B., & Wallis, C. The mortality of widowers. *Lancet*, July-December 1963, *2*, 454–56.

D. SUICIDE

1. Bender, L. Psychiatric mechanisms with child murderers. *J. Nerv. Ment. Dis.*, 1934, *80*, 32–47.

> Child murder by parents is a suicidal act resulting from identification processes.

2. Bender, L., & Schilder, P. Suicidal preoccupations and attempts in children. *Amer. J. Orthopsychiat.*, 1937, 7, 225–34.

> A study of several case histories suggests that children's suicide is primarily the result of obvious conscious motives.

3. Cleveland, F. P. "Masquerades": Homicide, suicide, accident or natural death. *J. Indiana Med. Ass.*, 1960, *53*, 2181–84.

> An article written principally for investigating coroners. Many forms of "natural" death may appear to have been produced by violence.

4. Farberow, N. L. Personality patterns of suicidal mental hospital patients. *Genet. Psychol. Mono.*, 1950, *42*, 3–79.

> A description of personality characteristics of suicidal hospital patients through the use of tests.

5. Farberow, N. L., & Shneidman, E. S. *The cry for help.* New York: McGraw-Hill, 1961.

> A collection of articles dealing with evaluation and treatment of suicide, as well as its relationship to personality. A lengthy bibliography is included.

6. Feifel, H. Some aspects of the meaning of death. In E. S. Shneidman & N. L. Farberow (Eds.), *Clues to suicide.* New York: McGraw-Hill, 1957.

7. Friedlander, K. On the "longing to die." *Int. J. Psychoanal.*, 1940, *21*, 416–26.
    A discussion of suicide, with emphasis on one case in which the suicide wishes to be saved by his loving mother.

8. Jameison, G. R. Suicide and mental disease. *Arch. Neurol. Psychiat.*, 1936, *36*, 1–12.
    A review of 100 hospitalized patients who subsequently committed suicide.

9. Jones, E. Dying together. In *Essays in applied psycho-analysis*. London: Hogarth Press, 1951. Pp. 9–15.
    The neurotic may view death as a region where all hopes that are denied in this life may be realized.

10. Jones, E. An unusual case of dying together. In *Essays in applied psycho-analysis*. London: Hogarth Press, 1951. Pp. 16–21.
    In dangerous situations, persons may "freeze" or otherwise obstruct their normal efforts to save themselves. A duality motivation may result in a suicide.

11. Jones, F., & Laskowitz, D. Rorschach study of adolescent addicts who die of an overdose: A sign approach. *Psychiat. Dig.*, 1964, *25*, 21–30.
    Rorschach sign approach to compare death-by-overdose (DOD) and control group with regard to four basic areas of functioning: reality contact, energy level, feelings, and control. Findings were essentially negative; DOD subjects may be more inclined toward premature closure from review of previous psychological records.

12. Lindemann, E., & Greer, I. M. A study of grief: Emotional responses to suicide. *Pastoral Psychol.*, 1953, *4*, 9–13.

13. Litman, R. E. When patients suicide. Paper presented at the meeting of the American Psychological Association, Los Angeles, August 1964.
    Discusses the impact of suicide of a patient in therapy upon the therapist.

14. Moss, L. M., & Hamilton, D. M. The psychotherapy of the suicidal patient. *Amer. J. Psychiat.*, 1956, *112*, 814–20.
    Bereavement was the precipitating factor in a large proportion of mental illnesses involving suicide attempts.

15. Rosen, A., Hales, W. M., & Simon, W. Classification of "suicidal" patients. *J. Consult. Psychol.*, 1954, *18*, 359–62.

    MMPI records of patients classified as "Suicide Thought" showed more disturbance that those classified as "Suicide Attempt" or controls.

16. Shneidman, E. S. Suicide, sleep, and death: Some possible interrelations among cessation, interruption, and continuation phenomena. *J. Consult. Psychol.*, 1964, *28*, 95–106.

17. Shneidman, E. S., & Farberow, N. L. Suicide and death. In H. Feifel (Ed.), *The meaning of death.* New York: McGraw-Hill, 1959. Pp. 284–301.

    A description of a series of studies investigating the social and psychological nature of suicide.

18. Tabachnick, N., & Klugman, D. Suicide research and the death instinct. *Yale Scientific Magazine*, March 1967, pp. 12–15.

    A discussion of Freud's death instinct and its exhibition in suicide. The authors point out that there are many reasons behind suicide other than the wish to die, but they find the ultimate question as to the existence of the death instinct unanswered by research to date.

19. Weiss, J. M. A. The gamble with death in attempted suicide. *Psychiatry*, 1957, *20*, 17–25.

    Suicide attempts serve to discharge aggressive tendencies; once an unsuccessful attempt has been made, the outlook of the individual on other individuals and on society as a whole changes.

20. Williams, M. Changing attitudes to death: A survey of contributions in *Psychological Abstracts* over a thirty-year period. *Hum. Rel.*, 1966, *19*(4), 405–23.

    A qualitative comparison of contributions in 1931 and in 1961 on death, murder, and suicide, classified by field of interest—psychoanalytic, psychiatric, sociological, parapsychological.

21. Wolfgang, M. E. Suicide by means of victim-precipitated homicide. *J. Clin. Exper. Psychopathol.*, 1959, *20*, 335–49.

    Individuals who provoke others to kill them may be seeking

to destroy themselves through unconscious guilt; the slayer is usually a close friend or family member who may function as a parent image and dispenser of punishment.

22. Zilboorg, G. Differential diagnostic types of suicide. *Arch. Neurol. Psychiat.*, 1936, *35*, 270–91.

23. Zilboorg, G. Suicide among civilized and primitive races. *Amer. J. Psychiat.*, 1936, *92*, 1347–69.

Discusses occurrence of suicide among primitive and civilized persons, suicide as caused by mental disease, and suicide as a substitute for murder, and concludes that suicide is probably as old as murder, and almost as old as natural death.

E.   EUTHANASIA AND CAPITAL PUNISHMENT

1. Banks, A. L. Euthanasia. *Practitioner*, 1948, *161*, 101–7.

A revolutionary change in the minds of the profession and of the public at large is needed before the doctor is recognized in law as an executioner.

2. Bedau, H. A. A social philosopher looks at the death penalty. *Amer. J. Psychiat.*, 1967, *123*, 1361–70.

The right of life as a human right is explored in the context of the death penalty, with constitutional, penological, equalitarian, and ethical arguments against that punishment included. To discuss the killing of our fellow man as punishment through coercive state action makes necessary the clarification and elucidation of such doctrines as the sanctity of life and the right of life.

3. Catholic theologian defends man's right to die. *J.A.M.A.*, 1962, *180*, 23–24.

"A man is obliged to take reasonable means to preserve life and health. But he is not obliged to accept means involving excessive hardship to himself or others. . . ."

4. Deutsch, F. Euthanasia: A clinical study. *Psychoanal. Quart.*, 1936, *5*, 347–68.

5. Eliot, T. D. Attitudes toward euthanasia. *Res. Studies, St. Coll. Wash.*, 1947, *15*, 131–34.

   Statistics regarding responses to a questionnaire on legalizing euthanasia.

6. Jones, T. T. Dignity in death: The application and withholding of interventive measures. *J. Louisiana Med. Soc.*, 1961, *113*(5), 180–83.

   Plea for agathanasia (a good death, a death with dignity). Two case studies reported; more early instruction is needed by the physician in the art of attending the dying, in a ministry of medicine as a terminal service.

7. Kalish, R. A. The aged and the dying process: The inevitable decisions. *J. Soc. Issues*, 1965, *21*(4), 87–96.

   Deals with the questions: who is allowed to live, who to die; where death occurs, how and why it takes place; who is to be with the dying and how the patient is to learn of his imminent dying.

8. Koupernik, C. A drama of our times: Euthanasia. *Concours Med.* (Paris), 1962, *84*, 4687–88.

9. Letourneau, C. U. A soliloquy on death. *Hosp. Manage.*, 1963, *96*, 58.

   A British doctor discusses a case of illegally "allowed" death. He poses the question: when is a person medically *or* legally dead—what are the criteria of death?

10. Mengert, W. F. Terminal care. *Illinois Med. J.*, 1957, *112*(3), 99–104.

    There is a tendency, with young practitioners, for the *science* of medicine to outweigh the *art* of medicine when a terminal prognosis is given.

11. Nahum, L. H. Dealing with the last chapter of life. *Conn. Med.*, 1966, *30*, 170-74.

    Examines the role of the physician in the treatment of terminal cases ("Do physicians have the obligation always to prolong life with every means at [their] disposal?"), and in the grieving and regrouping of the family after death.

V. PSYCHOTHERAPY WITH THE DYING; MANAGING DEATH

A. GENERAL CONSIDERATIONS; ADULTS

1. Aldrich, C. K. The dying patient's grief. *J.A.M.A.*, 1963, *184*, 329–31.
2. Allen, C. L. *When you lose a loved one.* Westwood, N. J.: Fleming H. Revell, 1959.
   Intended to help the bereaved during the days when they are struggling to comprehend and accept the emptiness in their lives and hearts.
3. Alvarez, W. C. Care of the dying. *J.A.M.A.*, 1952, *150*, 86–91.
4. Angrist, A. A. A pathologist's experience with attitudes toward death. *Rhode Island Med. J.*, 1960, *43*, 693–97.
   Widespread denial of reality of death can be overcome to some extent by adequate preparation for death and by education in the proper procedures for the care of the dead human body.
5. Aronson, G. J. Treatment of the dying person. In H. Feifel (Ed.), *The meaning of death.* New York: McGraw-Hill, 1959. Pp. 251–58.
   To help the patient remain an individual human being, the physician should mobilize all resources to outweigh the isolation of death.
6. Autton, N. A study of bereavement. *Nurs. Times*, 1962, *58*, 1551–52.
   One can prepare adequately for grief and bereavement only by preparing adequately for death and by avoiding the "conspiracy of silence."
7. Baker, J. M., & Sorensen, K. C. A patient's concern with death. *Amer. J. Nurs.*, 1963, *63*(7), 90–92.
8. Bakke, J. L. Managing the fatal illness. *Northwest. Med.*, 1960, *59*, 901–4.
9. Barber, H. The art of dying. *Practitioner*, 1948, *161*, 76–79.

The nature of the last illness, the doctor and the patient, and the doctor and the patient's relatives all interact.

10. Bean, W. B. On death. *Arch. Intern. Med.*, 1958, *101*, 199–202.

    The author, a physician, discusses the physician and death: "The great terror of death is fear, and fear can be defeated."

11. Beatty, D. C. Shall we talk about death? *Pastoral Psychol.*, 1955, 6, 11–14.

    It is better that the dying be allowed to discuss their imminent death than to enter into the conspiracy of silence with medical personnel and relatives.

12. Benda, C. E. Bereavement and grief work. *J. Pastoral Care*, 1962, *16*, 1–13.

13. Bowers, M. K., Jackson, E. N., Knight, J. A., & LeShan, L. *Counseling the dying.* New York: Nelson, 1964.

    A psychoanalyst, a professor of psychiatry, a clinical psychologist, and a minister draw from their years of work in this field to give the reader the benefit of their observations and experience.

14. Brewster, H. H. Separation reaction in psychosomatic disease and neurosis. *Psychosom. Med.*, 1952, *14*, 154–60.

    Three patients with psychosomatic illnesses responded more severely to separation from their therapist than did three patients with neurosis.

15. Bulger, R. The dying patient and his doctor. *Harvard Med. Alumni Bull.*, 1960, *34*, 23.

16. Burkhart, R. A. The clergyman's role in death and bereavement. *Pastoral Psychol.*, 1950, *1*(5), 22–27.

    A discussion of the Protestant minister's role in the management of the funeral and his responsibility to the bereaved.

17. Buxbaum, R. E. A study of the emotional needs of the dying and the responses of physicians, nurses, and Protestant clergymen evaluated in the light of the interprofessional images of these professional groups. Unpublished master's thesis, Wesley Theological Seminary, Washington, D. C., 1966.

    This study attempts to identify the major emotional needs of hospitalized dying persons and the ways in which physicians, nurses, and Protestant clergymen evaluate and respond to them. Attention is also given to the images that each of these professional groups holds of the others in their work with the dying. It examines the traditional methods employed in the pastoral care of the dying and their reported effectiveness in meeting the dying person's emotional needs.

18. Cappon, D. The dying. _Psychiat. Quart._, 1959, _33_, 466–89.

    This article discusses the results of interviews with dying hospital patients, with the aim of improving communication with the dying.

19. Chodoff, P. A psychiatric approach to the dying patient. _Cancer_, 1960, _10_, 29–32.

20. Christ, A. E. Attitudes toward death among a group of acute geriatric psychiatric patients. _J. Geront._, 1961, _16_, 56–59.

    It was found "patients were fearful of death, but as a whole were willing, and in some cases were relieved, to discuss it." Denial of death appears to be a frequent symptom and "it becomes incumbent on the physician to broach the topic with his patient, and not wait for the patient to raise the question of his approaching death."

21. Christenson, L. The physicians' role in terminal illness and death. _Minn. Med._, 1963, _46_, 881–83.

22. Curphey, T. J. The role of the forensic pathologist in the multidisciplinary approach to death. Paper presented at the meeting of the American Psychological Association, Los Angeles, August 1964.

23. Custer, H. R. Nursing care of the dying. _Hosp. Programs_, 1961, _42_, 68.

24. Dickinson, A. R. Nurses' perceptions of their care of patients dying with cancer. Unpublished doctoral dissertation, Columbia University, 1966.

    Data collected from registered nurses were analyzed for dominant characteristics of care situations defined as adequate or inadequate, as well as for clues to possible relationships between respondents' backgrounds and their perceptions. Among the conclusions reached was an indication of insufficient preparation of nurses to meet the religious needs of dying patients and the needs of the families of these patients.

25. Eissler, K. R. *The psychiatrist and the dying patient.* New York: International Universities Press, 1955.

26. Fairbanks, R. J. Ministering to the dying. *J. Pastoral Care.*, 1948, 2, 6–14.

    An article suggesting ways to minister to the dying.

27. Farrell, J. J. The right of the patient to die. *J. S. Carolina Med. Ass.*, 1958, 7, 231–33.

    Surgery is a philosophy of medicine and is concerned with myriad facets of life and death. There is a need for a balance between the science and the art of medicine.

28. Feifel, H., Hanson, S., Jones, R., & Edwards, L. Physicians consider death. *Proc. 75th Annual Conv. Amer. Psychol. Ass.*, 1967, 2, 201–2.

29. Folck, M. M., & Nie, P. J. Nursing students learn to face death. *Nurs. Outlook*, 1959, 7, 510–13.

30. Foster, L. E., Lindemann, E., & Fairbanks, R. J. Grief. *Pastoral Psychol.*, 1950, 1(5), 28–30.

    Counseling the bereaved; differentiating between "healthy" and "unhealthy" expressions of grief. The morbidity of refusing to deal with the real occurence is discussed.

31. Fox, J. E. Reflections on cancer nursing. *Amer. J. Nurs.*, 1966, 66, 1317–19.

    The nurse caring for the patient in the terminal stages of cancer has one primary and all-encompassing goal: to guide the patient, with love and understanding, to a peaceful death. This is not a morbid task if the nurse believes that it is man's nature always to try, despite adversity, to reach the full potential of his being.

32. Fulton, R. Death and self. *J. Religion Health*, 1964, 3, 359–68.

    Defiance of death, the belief in immortality, is at the core of Christian thought. Death-defying and death-denying are seen as two paths, one leading to healthy grief, the other to a costly concept of the self.

33. Gerle, B., Tunden, C., & Sanblom, P. The patient with inoperable

cancer from the psychiatric and social standpoints: A study of 101 cases. *Cancer*, 1960, *13*, 1206–17.

34. Gibson, P. C. The dying patient. *Practitioner*, 1961, *186*, 85–91.

35. Ginzberg, R. Should the elderly cancer patient be told? *Geriatrics*, 1949, *4*, 101–7.

36. Glaser, B. G. Disclosure of terminal illness. *J. Health Hum. Behav.*, 1966, *7*(2), 83–91.

    Presents a descriptive process for understanding disclosure of terminal illness which combines both the stages typically present in the response stimulated by such disclosures, and the characteristic forms of interaction between the patient and hospital staff at each stage of the process.

37. Glaser, B. G., & Strauss, A. L. Expecting patients to die: Temporal aspects of status passage. San Francisco: University of California Medical Center, 1963. Mimeographed. Pp. 22.

38. Glaser, B. G., & Strauss, A. L. The social loss of dying patients. *Amer. J. Nurs.*, 1964, *64*, 119–21.

    Inevitably, a social value is placed on a patient, and that value has much to do with the impact of his dying on the nurse and frequently affects the kind of care he receives. This is what the authors have discovered in a study that they, with a nurse faculty member, Jeanne Quint, are making of hospital personnel, nursing care, and dying patients at the University of California Medical Center. A clear recognition by the nurse of the evaluating she does can help buffer the impact and make it easier for her to determine nursing needs objectively.

39. Glaser, B. G. & Strauss, A. L. *Time for dying.* Chicago: Aldine, 1967.

40. Goldfarb, A. I. The psychiatric aspects of integrated services for the terminally ill patient and his family. Symposium on terminal illness held by the National Cancer Institute, Detroit, June 1956.

41. Graham, J. B. Acceptance of death—beginning of life. *N. Carolina Med. J.*, 1963, *24*, 317–19.

    Author reflects on what medical treatment might be if the physician were to face up to his ultimate and personal death.

42. Grant, I. Care of the dying. *Brit. Med. J.*, 1957, *2*, 1539–40.

General practitioner discusses the role of the physician in patient relationships, hospital care, and the medical program of
the dying patient.

43. Greenberger, E. S. Fantasies of women confronting death: A study
of critically ill patients. Unpublished doctoral dissertation, Rad-
cliffe College, 1961.

44. Greer, I. M. Grief must be faced. *Christian Century*, 1945, *62*,
269–71.

45. Group for the Advancement of Psychiatry. *Death and dying: Attitudes of patient and doctor.* New York: GAP, 1965.
This report is based on a symposium presented at a meeting of
GAP in 1963. Among the participants are Goldfarb, Dovenmuehle, Feder, Greenberg, Feifel, Brosin, Weinberg, Aldrich, Wheelwright, Wedge, Mendell, and Bartemeier.

46. Hackett, T. P., & Weisman, A. D. The dying patient. Paper presented at Forest Hospital, Des Plaines, Ill., 1961.
A discussion of how to help the dying patient.

47. Hackett, T. P., & Weisman, A. D. The treatment of the dying.
Curr. Psychiat. Ther., 1962, *2*, 121–26.
The degree of fear of dying varies from patient to patient, but
the relationship between terminally ill and physician is a sen-
sitive one in any case.

48. Hebb, F. Care of the dying. *Canad. Med. Ass. J.*, 1951, *65*, 261–63.
Care of the dying should focus on the need to avoid harming
the patient. Belated attempts at remedial treatment and prag-
matic surgery of little practical value are to be avoided. The
case for narcotics in the final stages of a painful death is presented.

49. Hinton, J. M. *Dying.* Baltimore: Penguin Books, 1967.
The rational and irrational emotions associated with death are
discussed by a psychiatrist who has long been concerned with
patients suffering from incurable illnesses. He attempts to
take from the contemplation of death some of its more
"frightening magnetism." Chapters include fear of death and
dying, physical distress in the terminal illness, speaking of

death with the dying, prolonging life and hastening death, reactions to bereavement.

50. Hinton, J. M. The physical and mental distress of the dying. *Quart. J. Med.*, 1963, *32*, 1–21.

51. Hinton, J. M. Problems in the care of the dying. *J. Chronic Dis.*, 1964, *17*, 201–5.

An interesting résumé of several studies often ignored by American authors. The studies cited suggest that what Glaser and Strauss call the "open awareness context" is more effective than its alternatives. The author feels that physicians should let good research provide them with some guidance.

52. Ingles, T. Death on a ward. *Nurs. Outlook*, 1964, *12*, 28.

53. Jackson, E. N. *You and your grief*. New York: Channel Press, 1964.

A brief statement by a minister to the mourner on dealing with his own grief and that of his children.

54. Jensen, G. D., & Wallace, J. G. Family mourning process. *Family Process*, 1967, *6*, 56–66.

Two family cases are presented as illustrations of the role of therapeutic management as a family process. Bereavements seemingly the preoccupation of a surviving single child are observed under family therapy to be a function of the interpersonal reactions of the entire remaining family. Healthy, mutually need-satisfying relationships blocked by the mourning process were restored by therapeutic intervention.

55. Jones, T. T. Dignity in death: The application and withholding of interventive measures. *J. Louisiana Med. Soc.*, 1961, *113*(5), 180–83.

Plea for agathanasia (a good death, a death with dignity). Two case studies reported; more early instruction is needed by the physician in the art of attending the dying, in a ministry of medicine as a terminal service.

56. Joseph, F. Transference and counter-transference in the case of a dying patient. *Psychoanal. & Psychoanal. Rev.*, 1962, *49*(4), 21–34.

The analyst can bring comfort to a postanalytic dying patient because of the years of intimate communication between them.

57. Kalish, R. A. Dealing with the grieving family. *R.N.*, 1963, *26*, 81–84.
   Suggestions to the nurse regarding the handling of bereaved relatives in the hospital situation.

58. Kalsey, V. As life ebbs. *Amer. J. Nurs.*, 1948, *48*, 170–73.

59. Kasper, A. M. The doctor and death. In H. Feifel (Ed.), *The meaning of death*. New York: McGraw-Hill, 1959. Pp. 259–70.
   Much is expected of doctors in their coping with death, but medical school training makes no allowance for this.

60. Kastenbaum, R. The mental life of dying geriatric patients. *Proc. 7th Int. Congr. Geront.*, 1966, pp. 153–59.
   The findings refute the assumption that massive cognitive impairment is the typical status of the aged dying person.

61. Kelly, W. D., & Friesen, S. R. Do cancer patients want to be told? *Surgery*, 1950, *27*, 822–26.

62. Kennedy, N. Untitled article on the social worker's role. In *Helping the dying patient and his family*. Section 3. New York: National Association of Social Workers, 1960.

63. Kevorkian, J. The eye in death. *Ciba Clin. Symposia*, 1961, *13*, 51–62.
   "Eyegrounds may provide more accurate information on the exact time of death than can be obtained by any other means."

64. Kostrubala, T. Therapy of the terminally ill patient. *Illinois Med. J.*, 1963, *124*, 545–47.

65. Langston, A. D. B. Tudor books of consolation. Unpublished doctoral dissertation, University of North Carolina, 1940.
   A history of advice to the bereaved during the Tudor period.

66. Leak, W. N. The care of the dying. *Practitioner*, 1948, *161*, 80–87.
   The patient should always be considered as a person, with a minimum of medical and nursing procedures to discomfort him. The role of the physician, nursing care, and medical treatment should reflect a human approach based on experience.

67. LeShan, L., & LeShan, E. Psychotherapy and the patient with a limited life span. *Psychiatry*, 1961, *24*(4), 318–23.
    Therapy with patients dying of cancer, and the reluctance of therapists to treat such patients, are discussed.

68. Leslie, R. C. Untitled article on the minister's role. In *Helping the dying patient and his family*. Section 1. New York: National Association of Social Workers, 1960.

69. Litin, E. M. Should the cancer patient be told? *Postgrad. Med.*, 1960, *28*, 470–75.

70. Litman, R. E. When patients suicide. Paper presented at the meeting of the American Psychological Association, Los Angeles, August 1964. Mimeographed.
    Discusses the impact on the therapist of the suicide of a patient in therapy.

71. Love, E. F. "Do all hands help ease sting of death by tact and kindliness." *Hospitals*, 1944, *18*, 47–48.

72. Magazu, P., Golner, J., & Arsenian, J. Reactions of a group of chronic psychotic patients to the departure of the group therapist. *Psychiat. Quart.*, 1964, *34*, 292–303.
    The departure of a therapist creates some of the same responses as does the death of a therapist.

73. McVay, L. An interaction study involving a patient with a guarded prognosis. *Amer. J. Nurs.*, 1966, *66*, 1071–73.
    From analyzing the verbatim data in a series of "purposeful" conversations, this author learned a great deal about a woman patient's feelings about her illness and also increased her own perceptions.

74. Mengert, W. F. Terminal care. *Illinois Med. J.*, 1957, *112*(3), 99–104.
    There is a tendency, with young practitioners, for the *science* of medicine to outweigh the *art* of medicine when a terminal prognosis is given.

75. Middaugh, B. L. The ministry of bereavement. *Pastoral Psychol.*, 1950, *1*.

76. Murphy, B. J. Psychological management of the patient with incurable cancer. *Geriatrics*, 1953, *8*, 130–34.

77. Norton, J. Treatment of a dying patient. *Psychoanal. Stud. Child*, 1963, *18*, 541–60.

     A depressed dying woman who had contemplated suicide received psychiatric treatment for the last few months of her life and obtained protection against much physical and emotional pain. Object loss, both actual and threatened, is a major psychological problem of the dying patient.

78. O'Connor, Sister M. C. *The art of dying well—the development of* ars moriendi. New York: Columbia University Press, 1942.

79. Ogilvie, H. Journey's end. *Practitioner*, 1957, *179*, 584–91.

     An English surgeon discusses his attitude toward death and his approach to it with his patients.

80. Oken, D. What to tell cancer patients. *J.A.M.A.*, 1961, *175*, 1120–28.

     Doctors need to overcome their reluctance to inform their patients when they have cancer.

81. Pack, G. T. Counseling the cancer patient: Surgeon's counsel. Symposium on the physician and the total care of the cancer patient presented at the Scientific Session of the American Cancer Society, New York, January 1961.

82. Park, R. Thanatology. *J.A.M.A.*, 1912, *58*, 1243–46.

     Thanatology is defined as a department of science for the study of death, its nature and its causes. Among the questions investigated: when does death occur; what are the possibilities of the dead body affording viable products for transplants into the living body?

83. Pattison, E. M. The experience of dying. *Amer. J. Psychother.*, 1967, *21*, 32–43.

     Death is a crisis event and can be understood in the clinical terms of crisis-intervention therapy. The question facing the clinician is more than whether or not, or how, to tell a patient he is dying. The problem is how one faces death and goes about the process of dying. Although we cannot deal with the ultimate problem of death, we can help the person to deal with the various parts of the experience of dying: fear of the unknown, fear of loneliness, fear of loss of family and friends, fear of loss of body, fear of loss of self-control, fear of loss of identity, and fear of regression. The clinician can use specific measures to help the patient with each of these aspects of the experience so that an appropriate death can occur.

84. Paul, N. L., & Grosser, G. H. Operational mourning and its role in conjoint family therapy. *Community Ment. Health J.*, 1965, *1*(4), 339–45.

A derivative of incompleted mourning is a pervasive defense against further losses and disappointment. This reaction is often transmitted unwittingly to other family members, especially offspring. The resulting interaction promotes a family equilibrium that is fixated at a maladaptive level. The technique of operational mourning is designed to involve the family in a belated mourning experience with extensive grief reactions. This shared affective experience can provide for empathy and understanding of the origin of current relational difficulties. The effect is a weakening of the maladaptive family equilibrium, with a gradual emergence of individuation and sense of personal identity. A case illustration is furnished.

85. Peniston, D. H. The importance of death education in family life. *Family Life Coordinator*, 1962, *11*, 15–18.

86. Quint, J. C. *The nurse and the dying patient*. New York: Macmillan, 1967.

87. Quint, J. C. Obstacles to helping the dying. *Amer. J. Nurs.*, 1966, *66*, 1568–71.

Most nurses are ill at ease with dying patients. This discomfort increases if the patient has not been informed of his prognosis. Ramifications of this and related situations for the patient-nurse relationship are explored.

88. Quint, J. C. When patients die: Some nursing problems. *Canad. Nurse*, 1967, *63*(12), 1–4.

Presents determinants of interactional difficulties between the nurse and the dying patient, where medical technology has forced emphasis to be placed on both recovery and comfort. Problems arise where personal and professional threats are present: personal to the extent that familial concern, limitations of conversational ability, and the length and intensity of the dying process all can add personal reactions to regular work requirements; professional to the extent that demands for comfort conflict with demands for recovery. Although more demands of both kinds are made today, the profession still retains its priority on control and recovery.

89. Quint, J. C., & Strauss, A. L. Nursing students, assignments, and dying patients. *Nurs. Outlook*, 1964, *12*, 24–27.

Very little if any nurses' training equips the RN to cope with death and dying.

90. Regan, P. F. The dying patient and his family. *J.A.M.A.*, 1965, *192*, 666–67.

Recognizing that death is a crisis for the physician as well as for the patient and his family, the physician can direct the crisis toward a satisfactory outcome for family and patient.

91. Renneker, R. E. Countertransference reaction to cancer. *Psychosom. Med.*, 1957, *19*, 409–18.

Describes countertransference reactions of seven analysts investigating psychosomatic correlations in the psychological treatment of women with cancer of the breast, with the therapists' reactions to the threat of death.

92. Rhoads, P. S. Management of the patient with terminal illness. *J.A.M.A.*, 1965, *192*, 661–65.

Honesty tempered with optimistic uncertainty is the formula for this physician. The role of the doctor, along with the clergyman, is to provide spiritual support. His ability to do this will be determined by his own philosophy of life (and death).

93. Riggins, H. M. Man, medicine and the ministry—a symposium. *Bull. N. Y. Acad. Med.*, 1961, *37*(8), 551–79.

Five papers discussing ways that ministry and medicine can work together positively and cooperatively in patient relationships.

94. Ristus, R. The loneliness of death. *Amer. J. Nurs.*, 1958, *58*, 1283–84.

95. Rogers, W. F. Needs of the bereaved. _Pastoral Psychol._, 1950, _1_, 17–21.

96. Rogers, W. F. _Ye shall be comforted._ Philadelphia: Westminster Press, 1950.

97. Rosenthal, H. R. Psychotherapy for the dying. _Amer. J. Psychother._, 1957, _11_, 626–33.
    Psychotherapy for the terminally ill patient, whether or not he is aware of his condition, is extremely helpful.

98. Rosenthal, P. The death of the leader in group psychotherapy. _Amer. J. Orthopsychiat._, 1947, _17_, 266–77.
    A discussion of the reactions of group-therapy patients to the death of Dr. Paul Schilder, himself active in research on reactions to death.

99. Rothenberg, A. Psychological problems in terminal cancer management. _Cancer_, 1961, _14_, 1063–73.

100. Ruff, F. Have we the right to prolong dying? _Med. Economics_, 1960, _37_, 39–44.

101. Saunders, C. The last stages of life. _Amer. J. Nurs._, 1965, _3_, 70.
    A description of the work at St. Joseph's Hospice, London. The author maintains that an atmosphere of trust, a positive approach, and men and women who care are needed to bring terminal patients to a comfortable and peaceful end.

102. Saunders, C. The need for institutional care for the patient with advanced cancer. _Cancer Inst. Anniversary Vol._, 1964, pp. 18–24.

103. Saunders, C. The treatment of intractable pain in terminal cancer. _Proc. Royal Soc. Med._, 1963, _56_(3), 191–97.

104. Schneck, J. M. Hypoanalytic elucidation of the hypnosis-death concept. _Psychiat. Quart._ [Suppl.], 1950, _24_, 286–89.

105. Schwartz, A. M. Parameters in the psychoanalytic treatment of a dying patient. Paper presented at the meeting of the Association for Psychoanalytic Medicine, New York, December 1961.

106. Scott, W. C. Mania and mourning. _Int. J. Psychoanal._, 1964, _45_(2–3), 373–77.
    During treatment of mania, both the depression against which it is a defense and the hopeful mourning of which it is a

pathological expression should be sought and brought into consciousness. Fear and aggression may thereby be mitigated and love enhanced with an increase in reparative tendencies and a lessening of guilt.

107. Shepherd, J. B. Ministering to the person. *Pastoral Counselor*, 1966, *4*(2), 15–22.

108. Sheps, J. Management of fear of death in chronic disease. *J. Amer. Geriat. Soc.*, 1957, *5*, 793–97.

109. Smith, H. C. Care of the dying patient: A comparison of institutional plans. *Dissertation Abstracts*, 1966, *27*(2–8), 526.

110. Staff, C. Death is no outsider. *Psychoanalysis*, 1953, *2*, 56–70.

111. Standard, S., & Nathan, H. *Should the patient know the truth?* New York: Springer, 1955.

112. Stevens, A. C. Facing death. *Nurs. Times*, 1962, *58*, 777–78.

113. Strauss, A. L., Glaser, B. G., & Quint, J. C. The nonaccountability of terminal care. *Hospitals*, 1964, *38*, 73–87.
Exact procedures in dealing with the terminally ill are unknown but may reflect the difficulty of medical personnel in coping with death.

114. Sudnow, D. *Passing on: The social organization of dying.* Englewood Cliffs, N.J.: Prentice-Hall, 1967.
This book explores dying and death as they concern the staff members of two large municipal hospitals, one private and the other a charity institution. The author observed the activities in these hospitals as they related to the dying process. Topics include the care of the dying, the techniques of breaking bad news, the processing of dead bodies, social-class differences in care and in handling of the dying and the dead, and the activities of the hospital personnel.

115. Sutherland, A. M., & Orbach, C. E. Psychological impact of cancer and cancer surgery: Depressive reactions associated with surgery for cancer. *Cancer*, 1953, *6*, 958–62.
A discussion of patients with emotional problems involving self-destructiveness who become vulnerable to acute preoperative anxiety about death or mutilation in surgery.

116. Toch, R., *et al.* Management of the child with a fatal disease. *Clin. Pediat.*, 1964, *3*, 418–27.

A physician discusses his personal views on how to handle information in cases of fatal childhood diseases, especially leukemia. Deals largely with caring for the family of the dying child. The article is followed by comments by Protestant, Catholic, and Jewish chaplains at Massachusetts General Hospital.

117. Ulanoz, B. *Death—a book of preparation and consolation.* New York: Sheed & Ward, 1959.

118. Ulman, M. *The psychiatrist and the stroke patient.* Toronto: University of Toronto Press, 1962.

119. Wahl, C. W. The physician's management of the dying patient. *Curr. Psychiat. Ther.,* 1962, *2,* 127–36.

120. Wahl, C. W. Untitled article on the psychiatrist's role. In *Helping the dying patient and his family.* Section 2. New York: National Association of Social Workers, 1960.

121. Waxenberg, S. D. The importance of the communication of feelings about cancer. *Ann. N.Y. Acad. Sci.,* 1966, *125,* 1000–1005.
Professional opinions differ as to what the terminally ill cancer patient should be told. "From various samplings, it appears that the large majority of physicians do not tell their patients they have cancer, while the large majority of the afflicted and the members of their families say they wish to be told." The advantages of open communication are discussed.

122. Weisman, A. D., & Hackett, T. P. The dying patient. *Forest Hosp. Pub.* (Des Plaines, Ill.), 1962, *1,* 16–21.

123. Westberg, G. *Minister and doctor meet.* New York: Harper, 1961. Chap. 12.

124. Wodinsky, A. Psychiatric consultation with nurses on a leukemia service. *Ment. Hyg.,* 1964, *48,* 282–87.
Discussion of the results of a series of meetings with nurses working with leukemia patients. Reactions to the terminally ill.

125. Worcester, A. *The care of the aged, the dying, and the dead.* (2nd ed.) Springfield, Ill.: Charles C Thomas, 1940.
The book is addressed to the general practitioner and others who deal with elderly patients.

126. Wylie, H. W., Lazaroff, P., & Lowy, F. A dying patient in a psychotherapy group. *Int. J. Group Psychother.*, 1964, *14*(4), 482–91.

Presentation of the data is based on Thomas Tranch's theory of local conflict. A group of four men and two women met once a week for group therapy. After initial distrust of group-therapy methods the group came to accept this treatment. After seven months, one of the women told the group she was suffering from a fatal illness. The group attempted to deny the problem at first, expressing guilt and anger at one another, withdrawing from the stricken woman. The therapists were forced to recognize their own fears of death. They then were able to help the whole group face the conflict which the fact of fatal illness presented.

127. Young, W. H., Jr. Death of a patient during psychotherapy. *Psychiatry*, 1960, *23*(1), 103–8.

Discussion of a case where patient and therapist shifted back and forth between a patient's morbid fantasies and fears of death and her concern with death as a real and imminent prospect. Diagnosis of terminal cancer reported after patient had entered therapy.

128. Zeligs, R. Death is a part of life. *Calif. Parent-Teacher*, 1959, *36*, 7.

129. Zilboorg, G. Fear of death. *Psychoanal. Quart.*, 1943, *12*, 465–75.

Fundamental psychological issue involved in the problem of morale is reduced to the problem of how one reacts to the fear of death—a basic fear. In war, fear of death is mobilized into aggression, a hatred of the enemy, and a readiness to make sacrifices.

130. Zinker, J. C., & Fink, S. L. The possibility for psychological growth in a dying person. *J. Gen. Psychol.*, 1966, *74*, 185–99.

A study to investigate the possibility of positive aspects of human experience in an uneducated Southern Negro woman dying of metastatic cancer. Utilizing the Q-sort statistic, aspects of decline, growth, and stability of the patient's needs (physiological, safety, belongingness and love, esteem, self-actualization) during the last six months of life were discovered.

B. CHILDREN

1. Arnstein, H. S. *What to tell your child about birth, death, divorce, illness, and other family crises.* New York: Bobbs-Merrill, 1962.
2. Becker, D., & Margolin, F. How surviving parents handled their young children's adaptation to the crisis of loss. *Amer. J. Orthopsychiat.*, 1967, *37*, 753–57.

   Study of nine children under seven years old who had experienced the death of a parent. Observations were made of how and when the surviving parent informed the child of the death; the handling of the child's reactive questions; and the handling of the loss feelings of the child by the parent thereafter. The interaction between parent and child regarding the crisis and the child's behavior and adjustment were emphasized. Intervention for therapeutic purposes was occasioned only when the parent had unusual difficulty in his grief, and the child's behavior was thereby hampered. Conclusions were that the young child is aware of death; circumstances, preparations, and all experiences radiating from the death should be disclosed to facilitate the normal process of mourning.
3. Best, P. An experience in interpreting death to children. *J. Pastoral Care*, 1948, *2*, 29–34.
4. Birk, A. The bereaved child. *Ment. Health*, 1966, *25* (4), 9–11.

   Parental reactions to a child's expression of bereavement, whether it be in terms of aggressiveness, withdrawal, guilt, or inward mourning, is determinative of the effect on the child of the loss suffered. If the parent is overwhelmed with grief himself, teachers, uncle figures, or a child-guidance clinic is needed. Above all, the child must not be made to feel rejected, and thus the emphasis here is on dealing with bereavement rather than with the death itself.
5. Carpenter, K. M., & Stewart, J. M. Nursing in a parent participa-

tion program. *Mono. Amer. Nurs. Conv.*, 1962, pp. 28–35.
Description of facilities and services in a unit for terminally
ill children at City of Hope Medical Center.

6. Carpenter, K. M., & Stewart, J. M. Parents take heart at City of
   Hope. *Amer. J. Nurs.*, 1962, *62*, 82–85.
   Description of services at the City of Hope Medical Center,
   in a unit of children with leukemia and malignant tumors.
   Stresses innovations such as parental visits to bathe and dress
   children, parent planning of activities, etc.

7. Cohen, R. K. *A boy's quiet voice.* New York: Greenberg, 1957.

8. Hamovitch, M. B. *The parent and the fatally ill child.* Duarte, Cal.:
   City of Hope Medical Center, 1964.
   Discussion of interviews with parents of terminally ill children; the results show that the opportunity to discuss their
   feelings is valuable.

9. Hamovitch, M. B. Research interviewing in terminal illness. *Soc.
   Work*, 1963, *8*, 4–9.
   Interviews in a hospital unit for terminally ill children were
   conducted with both parents and involved medical personnel.

10. Jackson, E. N. *Telling a child about death.* New York: Channel
    Press, 1965.
    How and what to tell your child when a death occurs.

11. Knudson, A. G., Jr., & Natterson, J. M. Participation of parents in
    the hospital care of fatally ill children. *Pediatrics*, 1960, *26*,
    482–90.
    Description of the effects of a special care program for termi-
    nally ill children upon different age groupings.

12. Lourie, R. S. The pediatrician and the handling of terminal illness.
    Pediatrics, 1963, *32*, 477–79.

13. Morrissey, J. R. A note on interviews with children facing immi-
    nent death. *Soc. Casework*, 1963, *44*, 343–45.
    A pilot study of eight terminally ill children showed that
    they had considerable concern and anxiety about their illness,
    and that they welcomed the opportunity to discuss their feel-
    ings and experiences.

14. Natterson, J. M., & Knudson, A. G., Jr. Observations concerning

fear of death in fatally ill children and their mothers. *Psycho-som. Med.*, 1960, 22, 456–65.

Thirty-three children, ages 0–13, were followed over a two-year period. In terms of "full development" of the fear, separation fear was earliest; mutilation fear and then death fear predominated as the children grew older. The mothers reacted to the death threat with initial denial; later there was calm acceptance of the death of the child, with improved integration and increased sublimation. The hospital staff, on the other hand, were least well integrated during the terminal phase.

15. Plank, E. N. *Working with children in hospitals.* Cleveland: The Press of Western Reserve University, 1962. See Chap. 5.

16. Solnit, A. J. The dying child. *Develop. Med. Child Neurol.*, 1965, 7, 693–95.

This article deals with the responsibilities faced by the physician in treating the dying child's bodily and psychological pain, stressing the need for familiarizing the patient with his own resources and the benefits he can expect from medical resources. The question of knowledge of the extent of illness must be answered individually with each patient.

17. Solnit, A. J., & Green, M. The pediatric management of the dying child: The child's reaction to the fear of dying. *Mod. Perspect. Child Develop.*, 1963, 8, 217–28.

Major considerations in the reactions of children to dying: Am I safe? Will there be a trusted person to help me? Will you make me feel all right?

18. Solnit, A. J., & Green, M. Psychologic considerations in the management of deaths on pediatric hospital services: The doctor and the child's family. *Pediatrics*, 1959, 24, 106–12.

Practical guides from the author's experiences in aiding the families of terminally ill children.

19. Zeligs, R. Children's attitudes toward death. *Ment. Hyg.*, 1967, 51, 393–96.

When a parent is overwhelmed by the death of his spouse or child, his living child may absorb his anxiety. If the parent is afraid to talk about the death, his child may repress his own fears, guilt, and confusion, and become seriously disturbed. He may think he caused the sibling's death by his own death wishes. The child must be told the truth: i.e., the real cause of death, and that death is final. He should not be sent away during the funeral or mourning period and should be allowed to attend the funeral if he wants to.

20. Zeligs, R. Judy learns about death. *Calif. Parent-Teacher*, 1964, *41*, 6–7.

VI. THE EXPERIENCE OF DEATH

1. Carnes, P. C. The fact of death. *Register-Leader* (a Unitarian-Universal publication), October 1966, pp. 10–11.

   Reflections on the quality of death and its influence on our lives are offered by a minister who three years earlier was told that he had an incurable form of cancer. "A candid confrontation of the fact of our having to die can do much to rub down the rough edges with which we abrasively meet life. It is the beginning of our mastery over life's terrors."

2. Fodor, N. Jung's sermons to the dead. *Psychoanal. Rev.*, 1964, *51*(1), 74–78.

   A result of Jung's break with Freud: if Jung could not teach the living, he would teach the dead, for the dead only know what they have knowledge of at moment of death.

3. Frankl, V. E. *From death camp to existentialism: A psychiatrist's path to new therapy.* Boston: Beacon Press, 1959.

   The will to meaning (logotherapy) in the face of death.

4. Hart, H. Scientific survival research. *Int. J. Parapsychol.*, 1967, *9*, 43–52.

   Describes scientific research, based on evidentially supported cases reinforced by experimental findings, on the hypothesis that survival consists in the permanent projection of the psychic body from the biological body. Speculation on the early stages of life after death focuses on the experience of persons who have felt themselves temporarily projected out-of-body.

5. Langsley, D. G. Psychology of a doomed family. *Amer. J. Psychother.*, 1961, *15*, 531–38.

   This paper discusses the psychologic defenses with which a family, both as a unit (consisting of ten siblings) and as individuals, dealt with the threat of premature death from an inherited renal disorder. Only the eldest was able to handle the imminence of his own death in a mature manner; denial and repression characterized three other encounters with death.

6. Leviton, A. Time, death, and the ego-chill. *J. Exist.*, 1965, *6*(21), 69–80.

   The ego-chill ("a shudder which comes from the sudden awareness that our non-existence is entirely possible") is described in the case history of a woman who sought to avoid thoughts of her own death by frantic activity, drugs, sex, and alcohol.

7. Lifton, R. J. Psychological effects of the atomic bomb in Hiroshima: The theme of death. *Daedalus*, 1963, *92*, 462–97.

   A discussion of interviews with 75 atomic bomb survivors, emphasizing the sudden and overwhelming encounter with death.

8. Moritz, A. R., & Zamcheck, N. Sudden and unexpected death of young soldiers. *Arch. Path.*, 1946, *42*, 479–94.

   Medical description of sudden, unexpected death.

9. Ryle, J. A. The sense of dying—a postscript. *Guy Hosp. Rep.*, 1950, *99*, 204–9.

   A noted author on death reports symptoms encountered during a fatal illness involving six years of slow failure. He postulates that such symptoms are protective measures, false signals usually, to warn of impending problems.

10. Saul, L. J. Reactions of a man to natural death. *Psychoanal. Quart.*, 1959, *28*, 383–86.

    Case history covering six months in the life of a physician with carcinoma of the stomach; reveals his delusional views of reality together with his sound attitudes and judgment; the will to live produced wish-fulfilling delusions.

11. Schneck, J. M. Unconscious relationship between hypnosis and death. *Psychoanal. Rev.*, 1951, *38*, 271–75.

12. Thurmond, C. J. Last thoughts before drowning. *J. Abnorm. Soc. Psychol.*, 1943, *38*, 165–84.

Transcription of the actual words of a 19-year-old boy during a period of delirium after narrowly escaping death by drowning.

13. Walkenstein, E. The death experience in insulin coma treatment. *Amer. J. Psychiat.*, 1956, *112*, 985–90.

VII. ATTITUDES TOWARD DEATH

A. CONCEPTUALIZATION

1. Alexander, I. E., & Alderstein, A. M. Studies in the psychology of death. In H. P. David & J. C. Brenglemann (Eds.), *Perspectives in personality research*. New York: Springer, 1960. Pp. 65–92.

2. Anthony, S. *The child's discovery of death*. New York: Harcourt, Brace, 1940.

Death ideas occur readily in children's fantasy-thinking. In giving up his belief in magical powers a child may no longer attach absolute finality to death and may also cast off a load of responsibility in respect to the deaths of others.

3. Bender, L. *Aggression, hostility, and anxiety in children*. Springfield, Ill.: Charles C Thomas, 1953. Pp. 40–65.

A discussion of the literature involving children's perceptions of death and dying.

4. Brodsky, B. The self-representation, anality, and the fear of dying. *J. Amer. Psychoanal. Ass.*, 1959, *7*, 95–108.

Utilization of three cases to support the idea that during the anal stage, feces and the dead body are equated.

5. Burton, A. Death as a countertransference. *Psychoanal. Rev.*, 1962, *49*, 3–20.

The author disagrees with Freud's implication that the unconscious does not know of death.

6. Caprio, F. S. A psycho-social study of primitive conceptions of death. *J. Crim. Psychopathol.*, 1943, *5*, 303–17.

7. Caprio, F. S. A study of some psychological reactions during pre-pubescence to the idea of death. *Psychiat. Quart.*, 1950, *24*, 495–505.

   Free associations of 100 unclassified adults to their preadoles-cent reactions to death.

8. Cobalt, N. K. The meaning of religion to older people. *Geriatrics*, 1960, *15*, 658–64.

   The author states: "I can find no evidence of increased re-ligious yearnings in older people who have been patients." He notes the communication void between the "treating" phy-sician and the "visiting" minister.

9. Cousinet, R. L'idee de la mort chez les enfants. *J. Psychol. Norm. Path.*, 1939, *36*, 65–76. (Obtained from *Psychol. Abstracts.*)

   Cousinet presents a developmental statement concerning in-creasing awareness of death as a function of age in children.

10. Crown, B., O'Donovan, D., & Thompson, T. G. Attitudes toward attitudes toward death. *Psychol. Rep.*, 1967, *20*, 1181–82.

    Individual attitudes were studied, with the social desirability of statements with respect to both positive/negative scales and anxiety-denying / anxiety-acknowledging scales emphasized. Forty-five male graduate students were asked to rate 17 state-ments concerning attitudes toward death. The statements were included on the basis of their obsessive/hysterical qualities and their sensitivity/insensitivity qualities. Positive sensitivity was preferred over negative sensitivity.

11. Diggory, J. C. Death and self-evaluation. In *Self-evaluation.* New York: Wiley, 1966. Pp. 381–415.

    An excellent chapter on death and self-evaluation, including the personal notes of several doctors and statistical tabulations on death attitudes.

12. Fast, I., & Cain, A. C. Fears of death in bereaved children and adults. Paper presented at the meeting of the American Ortho-psychiatric Association, Chicago, March 1964. Pp. 16.

    Several beliefs maintained by children regarding a deceased person are discussed.

13. Federn, P. The reality of the death instinct. *Psychoanal. Rev.*, 1932, *19*, 129–50.

     The death instinct is most readily observable in severe melancholia, because the person perceives no remaining possibility of pleasure.

14. Feifel, H. Older persons look at death. *Geriatrics*, 1956, *11*, 127–30.

     The results of questionnaire data obtained from a sample of elderly.

15. Foxe, A. N. Critique of Freud's concept of a death instinct. *Psychoanal. Rev.*, 1943, *30*, 417–27.

     The life instinct (libidinal instinct and erotic instinct); the life and death instincts (pleasure principle and reality principle); the death instinct (stability tendency and Nirvana principle) discussed as terminology. The author finds confusion created by Freud's lack of consistency in interpretation.

16. Fulton, R. L., & Langton, P. Attitudes toward death: An emerging mental health problem. *Nurs. Forum*, 1964, *3*, 104–12.

     Discusses the dilemma inherent in the nurse's role with regard to the dying patient, and the need to end the cowardice and hypocrisy of avoiding the subject of death or of using euphemisms to deal with it.

17. Gerenczi, S. The problems of acceptance of unpleasant ideas: Advances in knowledge of the sense of reality. *Int. J. Psychoanal.*, 1926, *7*, 312–23.

     Psychoanalytic discussion of the acceptance of unpleasant ideas, which occurs in two steps: (1) conscious denial followed by (2) recognition of the unpleasant idea.

18. Greenberger, E. Flirting with death: Fantasies of a critically ill woman. *J. Project. Techn.*, 1966, *30*(2), 197–204.

     The TAT stories of a woman hospitalized for cancer are analyzed with particular attention to material suggesting that the fantasy of death as a lover, dating back to antiquity, continues to live in the unconscious. The *Liebestod* motif in this unmarried woman follows upon a theme of disappointment in men, especially the father. It is suggested that as the patient faces the possible termination of life, she personifies death and libidinizes their encounter.

19. Grinberg, L. Two kinds of guilt: Their relations with normal and pathological aspects of mourning. *Int. J. Psychoanal.*, 1964, 45(2–3), 366–71.

In addition to that guilt (described by Klein) which is under the influence of the depressive position, there is a kind of guilt that appears in the earlier paranoid-schizoid phase. The earlier persecutory guilt is related to the death instinct; the depressive guilt, to normal mourning from depressive guilt.

20. Haider, I. Attitudes toward death of psychiatric patients. *Int. J. Neuropsychiat.*, 1967, 3, 10–14.

Fifty psychiatric patients over 50 years of age were examined for their attitudes toward death by means of a direct questionnaire. Patients who were alone (single, widowed, divorced, separated), who came from institutions or old peoples' homes, who were physically ill, or who were not religious, more frequently looked forward to death.

21. Hinton, J. M. Facing death. *J. Psychosom. Res.*, 1966, 10, 22–28.

The first part of this paper discusses the opinions expressed by people about their wish to be told if they have a potentially fatal disease, and compares these views with the willingness of doctors to tell. The second part is concerned with the reported reactions of patients on being told that they probably have a fatal illness, and with the proportion of fatally ill people who become aware that they may be dying. The third part of this paper reports the attitudes toward death shown by a group of patients dying in the hospital.

22. Hopper, T., & Spilka, B. Some meanings and correlates of future time and death among college students. University of Denver, 1964. Mimeographed.

23. Ilg, F. L., & Ames, L. B. *Child behavior*. New York: Dell, 1955. Pp. 332–38.

Statement of the interest and understanding children have regarding death, at different age levels.

24. Jackson, E. N. Grief and religion. In H. Feifel (Ed.), *The meaning of death*. New York: McGraw-Hill, 1959. Pp. 218–33.

The religious function in bereavement is to work against destructive fantasy and illusions, and toward a framework of reality.

25. Jacques, E. Death and the mid-life crisis. *Int. J. Psychoanal.*, 1965, *46*, 506–12.

Association of change in the levels of creativity with the "mid-life" crisis, using examples from the lives of the masters of art and literature. This "crisis" is defined as the mid-life encounter with the reality of one's own eventual death. How one reacts is influenced by the infantile unconscious relation to death.

26. Jeffers, F. C., Nichols, C. R., & Eisdoifer, C. Attitudes of older persons toward death: A preliminary study. *J. Geront.*, 1961, *16*, 53–56.

With Ss 60 years and older, "the factors associated with no fear of death include a tendency to read the Bible oftener, [a greater] belief in a future life, higher scores on full scale and performance I.Q., and more responses to the Rorshach."

27. Kalish, R. A. An approach to the study of death attitudes. *Amer. Behav. Sci.*, 1963, *6*, 68–70.

A questionnaire consisting of items measuring attitudes toward death, dying, and related variables is factor analyzed; factors are subsequently related to demographic data.

28. Kalish, R. A. A continuum of subjectively perceived death. *Gerontologist*, 1966, *6*, 73–76.

Subjectively perceived death need not coincide with biological death; a variety of conditions can be interpreted as social death, psychological death, or social immortality. A majority of college student respondents seemed able to accept these types of nonbiological deaths as valid and meaningful.

29. Kalish, R. A. Social distance and the dying. *Community Ment. Health J.*, 1966, *2*(2), 1952–55.

To determine the relative degree of avoidance elicited by the dying, a sample of 203 college students responded to a social-distance scale evaluating 14 ethnic and nonethnic groups. Males indicated basically less avoidance than females, and ethnic groups (e.g., Negro, Mexican-American) were less avoided than the nonethnic groups (e.g. drug addicts, dying persons, alcoholics). Problems of mental health workers in their own dealings with the dying are presented.

30. Kalish, R. A. Some variables in death attitudes. *J. Soc. Psychol.*, 1963, *59*(7), 137–45.

 Questionnaires administered to 210 adult college students indicate no correlations between fear of death and religious affiliation; attitudes regarding birth control, euthanasia, abortion, and capital punishment are included.

31. Kastenbaum, R. Time and death in adolescence. In H. Feifel (Ed.), *The meaning of death.* New York: McGraw-Hill, 1959. Pp. 99–113.

 The adolescent, having difficulty stabilizing his perception of time, is limited in his perceptions of death.

32. Klingberg, G. The distinction between living and not living among 7- to 10-year-old children, with some remarks concerning the so-called animism controversy. *J. Genet. Psychol.*, 1957, *90*, 227–38.

 Children were found to differentiate meanings in the expressions "Is it alive?" and "Has it life?" Animistic thinking appears to be involved.

33. Klopfer, W. G. Attitudes toward death in the aged. Unpublished doctoral dissertation, College of the City of New York, 1947.

34. Knapp, R. H. A study of the metaphor. *J. Proj. Techn.*, 1960, *24*, 389–95.

 Scales dealing with time, love, success, death, conscience, and self-image were administered to 223 Ss: interscale correlations found love, success, conscience, and self-image significantly related to each other.

35. Krupp, G. R. How children feel about death. *Parents' Magazine*, April 1967, pp. 54–55.

 This brief article addressed to a general audience emphasizes the importance of giving children the chance to express their fears and worries openly. The author declares that "most of us can take care to help our children achieve 'a separation tolerance.' " Several ways of developing a separation tolerance are suggested.

36. Lowry, R. J. Male-female differences in attitudes toward death. Unpublished doctoral dissertation, Brandeis University, 1965.

 Results of this study suggest that the two sexes do indeed

tend to have different concerns about death. Violence and mutilation were dominant themes in TAT stories given by male undergraduates, while loss was the most dominant theme for female undergraduates. Responses to the projective materials were in marked contrast to the bland expressions of "indifference" toward death obtained from them through direct questioning.

37. MacDonald, A. Death psychology of historical personages. *Amer. J. Psychol.*, 1921, *32*, 552–56.

Discussion of the age, manner of death, and mood of final communication of historical figures.

38. Mahler, M. S. Helping children to accept death. *Child Study*, 1950, *27*, 98–99, 119–20.

39. Maurer, A. Adolescent attitudes toward death. *J. Genet. Psychol.*, 1964, *105*, 75–90.

An evaluation of 172 compositions on death by high school seniors.

40. Maurer, A. The child's knowledge of non-existence. *J. Exist. Psychiat.*, 1961, *2*, 193–212.

Discussion of infant response to nonexistence as revealed in such commonplace activities as playing peek-a-boo, having nails clipped or hair cut, and so forth.

41. Maurer, A. Did Little Hans really want to marry his mother? *J. Humanistic Psychol.*, 1964, *4*, 8–19.

Emphasis upon death, rather than sex, in causing phobia.

42. Maurer, A. The game of peek-a-boo. *Dis. Nerv. Syst.*, 1967, *28*, 118–21.

Peek-a-boo, one of the earliest of human interpersonal relationships, is seen as allaying primordial anxiety in its concern with life, death, and survival. From an etymological point of view, both "peek" and "boo" have in the past connoted, respectively, "life" and "death." That the game seeks to reconcile, in secure surroundings, the child's first preconceptual problem—that of being and nonbeing—is supported by the fact that adult recollections always involve the concept of fright. The baby, with face covered, meets a "brush of death," endured because the subsequent relief is ecstatic, with familiar surroundings and all the concomitants of life restored.

43. Middleton, W. C. Some reactions toward death among college students. *J. Abnorm. Soc. Psychol.*, 1936, *31*, 165–73.

A questionnaire was administered to 825 college students regarding death, dying, funerals, and afterlife.

44. Mitchell, M. E. *The child's attitude to death.* New York: Schocken Books, 1967.

An outline of some of the religious, scientific, and sociological influences surrounding the British child today, including the role of myth in determining attitudes to death. Observations on fear of death, separation, bereavement, killing, and war are explored, giving adequate description of the literature in each field, together with reference to the appropriate orthodox psychological theories. The author concludes with a plea to rid educational facilities of death mythology, which should be replaced with ideas which emphasize the scientific community's new and forthcoming insights into the mysteries of life.

45. Moellenhoff, F. Ideas of children about death. *Bull. Menninger Clin.*, 1939, *3*, 148–56.

46. Nagy, Maria H. The child's theories concerning death. *J. Genet. Psychol.*, 1948, *73*, 3–27. Reprinted in H. Feifel (Ed.), The meaning of death. New York: McGraw-Hill, 1959. Pp. 79–98.

Written compositions, drawings, and interviews were analyzed to determine developmental stages in death conceptualization.

47. Natterson, J. M., & Knudson, A. G., Jr. Observations concerning fear of death in fatally ill children and their mothers. *Psychosom. Med.*, 1960, *22*, 456–65.

48. Needleman, J. Imagining absence, non-existence, and death: A sketch. *Rev. Exist. Psychol. Psychiat.*, 1966, *6*(3), 230–36.

An analysis of Freud's stated impossibility: "Our own death is indeed unimaginable." The question posed is whether the unimaginable is death itself, or ourselves dying. In exploring the differences between imagining nonexistence, death, and human death, on the one hand, and our own death, on the other, the latter is characterized as being possible only in proportion to the extent of self-knowledge.

49. Papageorgis, D. On the ambivalence of death: The case of the missing harlequin. *Psychol. Rep.*, 1966, *19*(1), 325–26.

Various descriptions of death were rated in terms of appropriateness by 30 male and 45 female undergraduate students. The results failed to support McClelland's Harlequin hypothesis but did provide some suggestive evidence consistent with the more traditional punishment/mutilation approach to death.

50. Parkhurst, H. *Exploring the child's world*. New York: Appleton-Century-Crofts, 1951. Pp. 184–207.

A child's idea of death is explained; central theme is a big storm which comes and "kills the world."

51. Peck, R. The development of the concept of death in selected male children. *Dissertation Abstracts*, 1966, *27*(4-B), 1294.

"An experimental investigation of the development of the concept of death in selected children from the point of no concept to the point where a fully developed concept is attained with an investigation of some factors which may affect the course of concept development."

52. Piaget, J. *The language and thought of the child*. (3rd ed.) London: Routledge & Kegan Paul, 1959.

53. Portz, A. The meaning of death to children. *Dissertation Abstracts*, 1965, *25* (12, Pt. 1), 7383.

54. Ries, H. An unwelcome child and her death instinct. *Int. J. Psychoanal.*, 1945, *26*, 153–61.

55. Rothstein, S. H. Aging awareness and personalization of death in the young and middle adult years. Unpublished doctoral dissertation, University of Chicago, 1967.

A theory of aging awareness is proposed and tested in a pair of investigations. "In our society, as a consequence of usual experiences with death, the individual changes from feeling unconcerned, to feeling shocked, to feeling resigned. It is this process that has been called the personalization of death." Personalization of death occurred more frequently among older than among younger respondents.

56. Russell, B. Your child and the fear of death. *Forum*, 1929, *81*, 174–78.

Knowledge of death and sorrow should be communicated to children truthfully and unemotionally, except for death in the family, which should be discussed with appropriate sorrow.

57. Schilder, P. The attitude of murderers toward death. *J. Abnorm. Soc. Psychol.*, 1936, *31*, 348–63.

Questionnaires administered to 33 murderers indicated three groupings of personality and attitudinal types.

58. Schilder, P., & Wechsler, D. The attitudes of children toward death. *J. Genet. Psychol.*, 1934, *45*, 406–51.

A presentation of the results of research on children's feelings regarding death, as determined through interviews and projective techniques.

59. Sendak, M. *Higglety, pigglety, pop!* Harper & Row, 1967.

The child and his acceptance of dying.

60. Sherrill, L. J., & Sherrill, H. H. Interpreting death to children. *Int. J. Relig. Educ.*, 1951, *28*, 4–6.

Parents should be aware of mental health considerations in the child's knowing about death, much as they are in his knowing about birth and sex.

61. Shneidman, E. S. Orientations toward death: A vital aspect of the study of lives. *Int. J. Psychiat.*, 1966, *2*, 167–90. Also in R. W. White (Ed.), *The study of lives.* New York: Atherton Press, 1963. Pp. 201–27.

Discussions by A. D. Weisman, K. Menninger, J. Sato, R. E. Litman; reply by Shneidman. Assuming that the concept of death is a semantic confusion, more useful concepts and their relation to experience are proposed: cessation, termination, interruption, and continuation. A discussion of four subcategories (intentioned, subintentioned, unintentioned, contra-intentioned) relating to the role of the individual in his own demise follows.

62. Soddy, K. *Identity: Mental health and value systems.* Chicago: Quadrangle Books, 1962.

   A cross-cultural study in mental health by the World Federation of Mental Health, with brief reference to children and death and the different attitudes toward death.

63. Stacey, C. L., & Markin, K. The attitudes of college students and penitentiary inmates toward death and a future life. *Psychiat. Quart.* [Suppl.], 1952, *26*, 27–32.

   Comparison of attitudes toward death of prison inmates and students majoring in engineering, forestry, and law.

64. Steiner, G. L. Children's concepts of life and death: A developmental study. Unpublished doctoral dissertation, Columbia University, 1965.

   This study focuses on the different ideas regarding death held by children as they pertain to the self and to different forms of life, as well as the differentiations between living and dead objects. The author aims to determine whether the child's ideas follow the sequence of cognitive development as hypothesized by Piaget; the results are generally consistent with this hypothesis.

65. Steinzor, B. Death and the construction of reality. In J. G. Peatman & E. L. Hartley (Eds.), *Festschrift for Gardner Murphy.* New York: Harper, 1960. Pp. 358–75.

   The author integrates much research and thinking concerning the development of children's ideas about death.

66. Swenson, W. M. Attitudes toward death in an aged population. *J. Geront.*, 1961, *16*, 49–52.

   Attitudes toward death can be measured by a structured psychometric device, are not often admitted when negative, are regulated to religious involvement, and are different for people living in homes for the aged than for community residents.

67. VonHug-Hellmuth, H. The child's concept of death. *Psychoanal. Quart.*, 1965, *34* (4), 499–516.

68. Williams, M. Changing attitudes to death: A survey of contributions in *Psychological Abstracts* over a thirty-year period. *Hum. Rel.*, 1966, *19*(4), 405–23.

A qualitative comparison of contributions in 1931 and in 1961 on death, murder, and suicide, classified by field of interest—psychoanalytic, psychiatric, sociological, parapsychological.

69. Wolf, A. W. M. Helping your child to understand death. New York: Child Study Association, 1958.

Suggests methods of answering children's questions about death. Discusses major religious attitudes and ceremonies in the United States.

70. Wolff, K. Personality type and reaction toward aging and death: A clinical study. *Geriatrics*, 1966, *21* (8), 189–92.

Attitudes toward aging and death of 90 patients in nine psychopathological groups were studied. The lifelong adjustment patterns are predictive of these attitudes. In facing problems of aging the elderly person shows an accentuation of lifelong personality defenses.

71. Zeligs, R. Judy learns about death. *Calif. Parent-Teacher*, 1964, *41*, 6–7.

72. Zinker, J. C. *Rosa Lee: Motivation and the crisis of dying.* Painesville, Ohio: The Lake Erie College Press, 1966.

A study of a woman dying of cancer, her needs and growth during her last days.

B. PERSONAL ANXIETY; FEAR OF DEATH

1. Alexander, I. E., & Adlerstein, A. M. Affective responses to the concept of death in a population of children and early adolescents. *J. Genet. Psychol.*, 1958, *93*, 167–77.

Galvanic skin responses to death words indicated affective reactions from three age groups: 5–8, 9–12, and 13–16. The 9–12 group showed the least reactivity.

2. Alexander, I. E., Colley, R. S., & Adlerstein, A. M. Is death a matter of indifference? *J. Psychol.*, 1957, *43*, 277–83.

University students, in spite of indicating little verbal affect to death, showed considerable galvanic skin-response change and time-latency increase to death words.

3. Angrist, A. A. A pathologist's experience with attitudes toward death. *Rhode Island Med. J.*, 1960, *43*, 693–97.

Widespread denial of reality of death can be overcome to some extent by adequate preparation for death and by education in the proper procedures for the care of the dead human body.

4. Bahnson, C. R. Emotional reactions to internally and externally derived threat of annihilation. Paper presented at the meeting of the American Association for the Advancement of Science, Washington, D.C., August 1962.

5. Baker, J. M., & Sorensen, K. C. A patient's concern with death. *Amer. J. Nurs.*, 1963, *63*(7), 90–92.

6. Bataille, G. *Death and sensuality: A study of eroticism and the taboo.* New York: Walker, 1962.

7. Bluestone, H., & McGahee, C. C. Reaction to extreme stress: Impending death by execution. *Amer. J. Psychiat.*, 1962, *119*, 393–96.

8. Brodsky, B. Liebestod fantasies in a patient faced with a mental illness. *Int. J. Psychoanal.*, 1959, *40*, 13–16.

The case history of a young woman with a fatal illness who fantasizes joining her brother, who was killed in the war.

9. Bromberg, W., & Schilder, P. The attitudes of psychoneurotics toward death. *Psychoanal. Rev.*, 1936, *23*, 1–25.

Anxiety and hysteria cases are primarily concerned with object loss in death, but depressives are more disturbed by the thought of eternal destruction.

10. Carnell, E. J. Fear of death. *Christian Century*, 1963, *80*, 136–37.

11. Chadwick, M. Notes upon the fear of death. *Int. J. Psychoanal.*, 1929, *10*, 321–34.

Certain forms of psychological anxiety are caused by fear of death, even during the adolescent period.

12. Christ, A. E. Attitudes toward death among a group of acute geriatric psychiatric patients. *J. Geront.*, 1961, *16*, 56–59.

The Ss described in the title were basically willing to give responses to the questions; their attitudes showed fear and marked denial.

13. Cochrane, A. L. Elie Metschnikoff and his theory of an *instinct de la mort*. *Int. J. Psychoanal.*, 1934, *15*, 265–70.

   Metschnikoff, a contemporary of Freud's, felt that man carried with him a collection of physical and psychic "disharmonies" which were the chief cause of human unhappiness. He considered fear of death the greatest disharmony. He attacked the idea of the immortality of the soul and of life after death, feeling that only science could solve problem of human happiness and human death.

14. Corey, L. G. An analogue of resistance to death awareness. *J. Geront.*, 1961, *16*, 59–60.

   Young Ss coped with death more frequently by acceptance and neutralization, while an older sample more frequently showed avoidance.

15. Dickstein, L. S., & Blatt, S. J. Death concern, futurity and anticipation. *J. Consult. Psychol.*, 1966, *30*(1) 11–17.

   The relationship between death concern and future-time perspective was investigated. Undergraduate male Ss selected from the upper and lower quartiles of a death-concern questionnaire were compared on a measure of future-time perspective and on the picture arrangement and vocabulary subtests of the WAIS. Ss with low death concern significantly showed extension into the future and obtained significantly higher scores on the picture-arrangement subtest than did Ss with high death concern.

16. Diggory, J. C. Death and self-esteem. Paper presented at the meeting of the American Psychological Association, New York, August 1962.

   The author discusses various reactions to death from a variety of sources, both contemporary and less recent; he then summarizes research by himself and D. Z. Rothman regarding the effects of success and failure on TAT death imagery.

17. Diggory, J. C., & Rothman, D. Z. Values destroyed by death. *J. Abnorm. Soc. Psychol.*, 1961, *63*, 205–10.

It is hypothesized that people fear death because it eliminates all opportunity to pursue self-building goals. A questionnaire was presented to 563 Ss to test the hypothesis.

18. Ekman, P., Cohen, L., Moos, R., Raine, W., Schlesinger, M., & Stone, G. Divergent reactions to the threat of war. *Science*, 1963, *139*, 88–94.

    Two types of responses to the possibility of death from atomic attack are examined: the movement toward fallout shelters and the movement toward action for peace. Members of each group are interviewed and tested.

19. Eliot, T. D. —of the shadow of death. *Ann. Amer. Acad. Pol. Soc. Sci.*, 1943, *229*, 87–99.

    Comparision of death attitudes during World War I and World War II.

20. Fast, I., & Cain, A. C. Fears of death in bereaved children and adults. Paper presented at the meeting of the American Orthopsychiatric Association, Chicago, March 1964. Pp. 16.

    Several beliefs maintained by children regarding a deceased person are discussed.

21. Feifel, H. Attitudes of mentally ill patients toward death. *J. Nerv. Ment. Dis.*, 1955, *122*, 375–80.

    A direct investigation of the death attitudes of mentally ill patients, using the questionnaire approach.

22. Feifel, H. Attitudes toward death in some normal and mentally ill populations. In H. Feifel (Ed.), *The meaning of death*. New York: McGraw-Hill, 1959. Pp. 114–30.

    Presentation and discussion of research findings on death attitudes of elderly and mentally ill, including factors in ability to cope with death.

23. Feifel, H. Death. In N. L. Farberow (Ed.), *Taboo topics*. New York: Atherton Press, 1963. Pp. 8–21.

24. Feifel, H. Psychiatric patients look at old age: Level of adjustment and attitudes toward aging. *Amer. J. Psychiat.*, 1954, *111*, 459–65.

    Both open-ward and closed-ward hospitalized patients view old age gloomily, degree of disturbance apparently having little effect on this attitude.

25. Feldman, M. J., & Hersen, M. Attitudes toward death in nightmare subjects. *J. Abnorm. Psychol.*, 1967, *72*, 421–25.

> This study investigated whether or not subjects manifested greater conscious concerns about death in proportion to their frequency of nightmares. On a 10-item Death Scale a marked relationship between scores on the scale and nightmare frequency was found. There was also a suggestion that both nightmare behavior and/or attitudes toward death might be rooted in concrete experiences. The more frequent nightmare Ss had a history of greater frequency of deaths of relatives and close friends, especially when Ss were under 10 years of age.

26. Friedman, D. B. Death anxiety and the primal scene. *Psychoanal. & Psychoanal. Rev.*, 1961, *48*, 108–19.

27. Glaser, B. G., & Strauss, A. L. *Awareness of dying*. Chicago: Aldine, 1965.

28. Golding, S. L., Atwood, G. E., & Goodman, R. A. Anxiety and two cognitive forms of resistance to the idea of death. *Psychol. Rep.*, 1966, *18*(2), 359–64.

> A relationship between affective orientation to death and two cognitive forms of resistance to the idea of death was hypothesized. Affect was measured by the Samoff Fear of Death Scale.

29. Greenberg, I. M., & Alexander, I. E. Some correlates of thoughts and feelings concerning death. *Hillside Hosp. J.*, 1962, *2*, 120–26.

30. Greene, W. A. Role of a vicarious object in the adaptation of object loss. *Psychosom. Med.*, 1958, *20*, 344–50.

> A sample of terminal patients is studied to determine their adapting mechanisms.

31. Grotjahn, M. Ego identity and the fear of death and dying. *Hillside Hosp. J.*, 1960, *9*, 147–55.

> The ego develops two defense systems: one to protect against the outer world where death exists, and the other to protect against the inner world's death instincts.

32. Group for the Advancement of Psychiatry. *Death and dying: Attitudes of patient and doctor*. New York: GAP, 1965.

This report is based on a symposium presented at a meeting of GAP in 1963. Among the participants are Goldfarb, Dovenmuehle, Feder, Greenberg, Feifel, Brosin, Weinberg, Aldrich, Wheelwright, Wedge, Mendell, and Bartemeier.

33. Hall, G. S. A study of fears. *Amer. J. Psychol.*, 1897, 8, 147–249.
   Out of 6,500 reported fears, death was mentioned fourth most frequently.

34. Hall, G. S. Thanatophobia and immortality. *Amer. J. Psychol.*, 1915, *26*, 550–613.
   A summary of Hall's ideas, along with responses to nearly 300 questionnaires he had administered.

35. Harnik, J. One component of the fear of death in early infancy. *Int. J. Psychoanal.*, 1930, *11*, 485–91.
   The author contends that fear of death evolves from narcissism and fear of suffocation.

36. Hoffman, F. H., & Brody, M. W. The symptom: Fear of death. *Psychoanal. Rev.*, 1957, *44*, 433–38.
   A case history of a woman whose major symptom is fear of death.

37. Howard, J. D. Fear of death. *J. Indiana Med. Ass.*, 1961, *54*, 1773–79.

38. Hutschnecker, A. A. Personality factors in dying. In H. Feifel (Ed.), *The meaning of death.* New York: McGraw-Hill, 1959. Pp. 237–50.
   Although terminal illness is often entered with a feeling of depression, personality changes in dying are not extensive.

39. Jacobs, H. L. Spiritual resources for the aged in facing the problem of death. *Bull. Inst. Geront.*, 1959, *6*(Suppl. 3), 3–8.

40. Jung, C. G. The soul and death. In H. Feifel (Ed.), *The meaning of death.* New York: McGraw-Hill, 1959. Pp. 3–15.
   A discussion of the importance of death and the reality of death fears.

41. Kalish, R. A., & Simpson, W. C. Perceptual defense to death-related words. Unpublished.

Students with high death fears appeared to take longer to perceive death words flashed tachistoscopically than Ss with lower death fear. Significance levels, however, were between .05 and .10.

42. Kastenbaum, R. As the clock runs out. *Ment. Hyg.*, 1966, *50*, 332–36.

Observations and experiences with aged institutionalized men and women suggest that the meaning of death is intimately related to the meaning of time: that time is less fascinating and precious, and death less formidable and devastating, for many aged people than for younger people.

43. Kastenbaum, R., & Goldsmith, C. E. The funeral director and the meaning of death. *Amer. Funeral Dir.*, 1963, April, pp. 35–37; May, pp. 47–48; June, pp. 45–46.

Because of the anxiety aroused in individuals regarding death, the funeral director becomes the target for displaced hostilities and anxieties.

44. Kaufmann, W. Existentialism and death. In H. Feifel (Ed.), *The meaning of death*. New York: McGraw-Hill, 1959. Pp. 39–63.

A person who has made something of his life can face death without anxiety.

45. Keyes, E. L. The fear of death. *Harper's Magazine*, 1909, *99*, 208–12.

Death should be considered as a natural occurrence: pain and suffering have usually ceased before actual death.

46. Lester, D. Experimental and correlation studies of the fear of death. *Psychol. Bull.*, 1967, *67*, 27–36.

Incisive review of psychological research literature.

47. Lester, D. Inconsistency in the fear of death of individuals. *Psychol. Rep.*, 1967, *20*, 1084.

Using 85 undergraduate students, the author administered a questionnaire regarding fear of death. Those Ss whose responses were least consistent also indicated significantly more death fear than Ss with the most consistent responses.

48. Leviton, A. Time, death and the ego-chill. *J. Exist.*, 1965, 6(21), 69–80.

    Erickson's term of ego-chill ("a shudder which comes from the sudden awareness that our non-existence . . . is entirely possible") is described in detail in the case history of a woman who used frantic activity, drugs, sex, and alcohol to avoid thoughts of her own death. It is suggested that the therapist look beneath symptoms and interpretations and consider issues that are related to the meaningfulness of life if he is to help his patient.

49. Lieberman, M. A. Psychological correlates of impending death. Paper presented at the meeting of the Gerontological Society, Boston, November 1963. Mimeographed.

    Measurable psychological changes preceding death in an aged population are demonstrated; Bender Gestalt and figure-drawing measures are considered.

50. Loeser, L., & Bry, T. The role of death fears in the etiology of phobic anxiety as revealed in group psychotherapy. *Int. J. Group Psychother*, 1960, *10*, 287–97.

51. McClelland, D. C. The Harlequin complex. In R. W. White (Ed.), *The study of lives*. New York: Atherton Press, 1963. Pp. 94–119.

    ". . . a historical study of the mythical Harlequin and an experimental study of the fantasies of women approaching death. . . ."

52. McCully, R. S. Fantasy productions of children with a progressively crippling and fatal illness. *J. Genet. Psychol.*, 1963, *102*, 203–16.

53. Means, M. H. Fears of one thousand college women. *J. Abnorm. Soc. Psychol.*, 1936, *31*, 291–311.

    Fear stimuli for 1,000 women were elicited and rated on an intensity scale. Cancer and bereavement were the most fear-provoking.

54. Meissner, W. W. Affective responses to psychoanalytic death symbols. *J. Abnorm. Soc. Psychol.*, 1958, *56*, 295–99.

    Galvanic skin responses to death words were greater than to neutral words.

55. Mira y Lopez, E. Psychopathology of anger and fear reactions in wartime. *Amer. Clinician*, 1943, *5*, 98 ff.

56. Monsour, K. J. Asthma and the fear of death. *Psychoanal. Quart.*, 1960, *29*, 56–71.

    Asthma may be an expression of anxiety which later appears as death phobia.

57. Morrissey, J. R. Children's adaptation to fatal illness. *Soc. Work*, 1963, *8*, 81–88.

58. Morrissey, J. R. A note on interviews with children facing imminent death. *Soc. Casework*, 1963, *44*, 343–45.

    A pilot study of eight terminally ill children showed that they had considerable concern and anxiety about their illness, and that they welcomed the opportunity to discuss their feelings and experiences.

59. Muensterberger, W. Vom Ursprung des Todes. *Psyche*, 1963, *17*, 169–84.

    The dying person goes into a state of regression and separation anxiety modeled after early infantile experiences. The author considers this a possibility neglected by investigators and practitioners.

60. Natterson, J. M., & Knudson, A. G., Jr. Observations concerning fear of death in fatally ill children and their mothers. *Psychosom. Med.*, 1960, *22*, 456–65.

    Thirty-three children, ages 0–13, were followed over a two-year period. In terms of "full development" of the fear, separation fear was earliest; mutilation fear, and then death fear, predominated as the children grew older. The mothers reacted to the death threat with initial denial; later there was calm acceptance of the death of the child, with improved integration and increased sublimation. The hospital staff, on the other hand, were least well integrated during the terminal phase.

61. Opitz, E. Psychotherapie im hoheren Lebensalter (Psychotherapy at advanced age). *Psychol. Rdsch.*, 1963, *13*(4), 241–55.

    Specific techniques of treating neurotic difficulties usually centered around apprehension of death are discussed. Death anxiety is seen as masked greed for life; firm guidance of the therapist is advocated to direct the patient in a critical analysis of his thinking and behavior patterns in order to resolve this anxiety.

62. Orlansky, H. Reactions to the death of President Roosevelt. *J. Soc. Psychol.*, 1947, *26*, 235–66.

An evaluation of the social-psychological phenomena displayed following the death of President Franklin D. Roosevelt, suggesting that people are simultaneously afraid of and deny death.

63. Osipov, N. Strach ze smrti (Fear of death). *Rev. Neurol. Psychiat.* (Praha), 1935, *32*, 17–25. (Obtained from *Psychol. Abstracts.*)

A discussion of the reactions of children and adults to death, with some emphasis upon the etiology of fear.

64. Paris, J., & Goodstein, L. D. Responses to death and sex stimulus materials as a function of repression-sensitization. *Psychol. Rep.*, 1966, *18*, 1283–91.

From a large subject pool, 36 male and 30 female repressers and an equal number of male and female sensitizers were given a selection of literature to read before and after self-ratings on six different five-point rating scales were obtained. In a random fashion, one third were given highly erotic reading material, one third neutral, and one-third death-related reading material; "sexually aroused," "disgusted," "emotionally upset," "anxious," "bored," and "angry" were the feelings rated. Neither of the two hypotheses presented were supported: that sensitizers would express more anxiety to sex and death-related materials, and more anxiety would be verbalized to both of the experimental materials than to the control materials.

65. Parsons, T. Death in American society—a brief working paper. *Amer. Behav. Sci.*, 1963, *6*, 61–65.

The author disagrees that denial is the major mode of coping with death and suggests some alternatives.

66. Plutchik, R. *The emotions.* New York: Random House, 1962. Pp. 91–95.

67. Renneker, R. E. Countertransference reactions to cancer. *Psychosom. Med.*, 1957, *19*, 409–18.

Paper describes countertransference reactions of seven analysts investigating psychosomatic correlations in the psychological treatment of women with cancer of the breast, with the therapists' reactions to the threat of death.

68. Rhudick, P. J., & Dibner, A. S. Age, personality, and health correlates of death concerns in normal aged individuals. *J. Geront.*, 1961, *16*, 44–49.

   Death concerns were not related to demographic variables but were associated with test scores indicative of neurotic tendencies.

69. Roberts, W. W. The death instinct in morbid anxiety. *J. Royal Army Med. Corps*, 1943, *81*, 61–73.

70. Rosenthal, H. The fear of death as an indispensable factor in psychotherapy. *Amer. J. Psychother.*, 1963, *17*, 619–30.

71. Ross, R. P. Separation fear and the fear of death in children. *Dissertation Abstracts*, 1967, *27*(4), 2878B–79B.

   Posits that the relationship between separation fear and fear of death is specific and dynamic, rather than that both are simply manifestations of general fearfulness. In exploring children's responses to upset from separation, pursued by arousing separation fear on social-affiliation behavior, it was shown that fear responses take on different properties when the context changes from one of habitual to one of aroused separation fear. In this way, the special significance of the child's fear of death was highlighted.

72. Sarnoff, I., & Corwin, S. M. Castration anxiety and the fear of death. *J. Personality*, 1959, *27*, 374–85.

   Ss with high castration anxiety were found to have greater fear of death after the arousal of their sexual feelings than Ss with low castration anxiety.

73. Schaffer, H. R., & Callender, W. M. Psychological effects of hospitalization in infancy. *Pediatrics*, 1959, *24*, 528–39.

   Seventy-six infants under 12 months of age were studied; 7 months was determined as a critical age for the infant to be affected by maternal deprivation.

74. Schilder, P. *Goals and desires of man.* New York: Columbia University Press, 1942. Pp. 61–110.

   A general discussion of the author's psychiatric experiences and research relating to death attitudes of children and adults.

75. Schneider, F., & Gullans, C. *Last letters from Stalingrad.* New York: New American Library, 1965.

76. Scott, C. A. Old age and death. *Amer. J. Psychol.*, 1896, 8, 67–122.
    A questionnaire administered to 226 Ss indicated that death is an important element in the consciousness of men.

77. Searles, H. F. Schizophrenia and the inevitability of death. *Psychiat. Quart.*, 1961, *35*, 631–65.
    It is hypothesized that schizophrenia results from the anxiety caused by the effort to ward off or deny death. This view does not deny that the earliest roots of schizophrenia may antedate the time in the future schizophrenic's life when he is confronted by the inevitability of death.

78. Segal, H. Fear of death: Notes on the analysis of an old man. *Int. J. Psychoanal.*, 1958, *39*, 178–81.

79. Seigman, A. W. On the use of Rorschach in cross-cultural research. Paper presented at the meeting of the Southeastern Psychological Association, Nashville, February 1957.
    The fact that religious Ss indicate more death themes in Rorschach responses is brought out in this paper.

80. Sevenson, W. M. Attitudes toward death among the aged: Their significance in the practice of geriatric medicine. *Minn. Med.*, 1959, *42*, 399–402.

81. Sevenson, W. M. Attitudes toward death in an aged population. *J. Geront.*, 1961, *16*, 49–52.

82. Sheps, J. Management of fear of death in chronic disease. *J. Amer. Geriat. Soc.*, 1957, *5*, 793–97.

83. Shontz, F. C., & Fink, S. L. A psychobiological analysis of discomfort, pain and death. *J. Gen. Psychol.*, 1959, *60*, 275–87.
    The authors discuss four possible orientations to discomfort, pain, and death: positive, negative, oscillating, and integrating.

84. Shrut, S. D. Attitudes toward old age and death. *Ment. Hyg.*, 1958, *42*, 259–66.
    Elderly Ss living in apartments showed less fear of death than those living in institutional environments.

85. Simmel, E. Self-preservation and the death instinct. *Psychoanal. Quart.*, 1944, *13*, 160–85.

Fear of death results from the perception that there is a hostile object stronger than the ego.

86. Solnit, A. J., & Provence, S. A. (Eds.) *Modern perspectives in child development.* New York: International Universities Press, 1963. Pp. 217–28.

The pediatric management of the dying child and the child's reaction to the fear of dying.

87. Stacey, C. L., & Reichen, M. L. Attitudes toward death and future life among normal and subnormal adolescent girls. *Exceptional Child*, 1954, *20*, 259–62.

Subnormal adolescent girls appear to be more emotional and fearful regarding death in general, while normals think more frequently of their own death.

88. Sutherland, A. M., & Orbach, C. E. Psychological impact of cancer and cancer surgery: Depressive reactions associated with surgery for cancer. *Cancer*, 1953, *6*, 958–62.

A discussion of patients with emotional problems involving self-destructiveness who become vulnerable to acute preoperative anxiety about death or mutilation in surgery.

89. Swenson, W. M. Attitudes toward death among the aged. *Minn. Med.*, 1959, *42*, 399–402.

Responses of elderly Ss to a death-attitude check list indicated three groups: death-avoiding, death-fearing, and death-accepting or death-desiring.

90. Swenson, W. M. Attitudes toward death in an aged population. *J. Geront.*, 1961, *16*, 49–52.

Attitudes toward death can be measured objectively. Such a measure has indicated that religious Ss are less likely to fear death than nonreligious.

91. Teicher, J. D. "Combat fatigue" or death anxiety neurosis. *J. Nerv. Ment. Dis.*, 1953, *117*, 234–43.

What is commonly called combat exhaustion is really a neurosis caused by the fear of death, resulting partly from guilt of the fantasized oedipal killing of the father.

92. Vernick, J., & Myron, K. Who's afraid of death on a leukemia ward? *Amer. J. Dis. Child.*, 1965, *109*, 393–97.

The answer to the title question is "Everyone," and resolving the fear is also everyone's problem. The "life-space" interview approach is followed with 51 children of ages 9–20. The program was based on the assumption that the most meaningful way that adults can help meet the emotional needs of the fatally ill child is to let him express his fears and receive an honest answer to any question.

93. Vispo, R. H. Pre-morbid personality in the functional psychoses of the senium: A comparison of ex-patients with healthy controls. *J. Ment. Sci.*, 1962, *108*, 790–800.

Clinical study of 25 ex-patients and 25 controls indicates sharp differences in personality in earlier years, but not sufficient to allow prediction of breakdown from specific personality attributes. The approach of death presents a final challenge which the neurotic may be unable to meet.

94. Vitanza, A. A. Toward a theory of crying. *Psychoanal. & Psychoanal. Rev.*, 1960, *47*(4), 65–79.

Implications for a relationship between crying and death or dying.

95. Wahl, C. W. The fear of death. *Bull. Menninger Clin.*, 1958, *2*, 214–23.

Since the fact of death does not yield to science or to rationality, men resort to magic and to irrationality. The fear of death, or specific anxiety about it, has almost no description in the psychiatric literature. If we are to understand death and the fear of death, "we must understand the mind of the child, which is the place where the fear of death first manifests itself."

96. Wittgenstein, B. Fear of dying and of death as a requirement of the maturation process in man. *Hippokrates*, 1960, *31*, 765–69.

97. Wolff, K. Helping elderly patients face the fear of death. *Hosp. Community Psychiat.*, 1967, *18*, 142–44.

The nature, frequency, and significance of death fears among the elderly are explored, including the relationships of such fears to the individual's total attitude-personality complex. Such information is essential in any therapeutic approach to the geriatric patient, in which the patient's positive feelings toward death, if any, must be emphasized. If the image of aging can be improved both in the elderly themselves and among the whole society, undue fear of death can be replaced by self-esteem, realism, and a continuing hope of achievement.

98. Zilboorg, G. Fear of death. *Psychoanal. Quart.*, 1943, *12*, 465–75.
Fundamental psychological issue involved in the problem of morale is reduced to the problem of how one reacts to the fear of death—a basic fear. In war, fear of death is mobilized into aggression, a hatred of the enemy, and a readiness to make sacrifices.

VIII.   REACTIONS TO THE DEATH OF ANOTHER

A.   NORMAL RESPONSES

1. Adlerstein, A. M. The relationship between religious belief and death affect. Unpublished doctoral dissertation, Princeton University, 1958.

2. Alexander, I. E., & Adlerstein, A. M. Death and religion. In H. Feifel (Ed.), *The meaning of death.* New York: McGraw-Hill, 1959. Pp. 271–83.
An elucidation and description of how the concept of death affects a population of young people. Reports of experimental research are included.

3. Anderson, C. Aspects of pathological grief and mourning. *Int. J. Psychoanal.*, 1949, *30*, 48–55.

4. Becker, H. Some forms of sympathy. *J. Abnorm. Soc. Psychol.*, 1931, *26*, 58–68.

5. Becker, H. The sorrow of bereavement. *J. Abnorm. Soc. Psychol.*, 1933, *27*, 391–410.
Four types of bereavement response are outlined and discussed, with illustrative case material.

6. Becker, H., & Bruner, D. K. Attitudes toward death and the dead, and some possible causes of ghost fear. *Ment. Hyg.*, 1931, *15*, 828–37.
This article traces explanations of preliterate attitudes toward

death, the dead, and ghosts. It also compares "civilized"
groups with preliterates.

7. Bellin, S. S., & Hardt, R. H. Marital status and mental disorders
among the aged. *Amer. Sociol. Rev.*, 1958, *23*, 155–62.

8. Bowlby, J. Childhood mourning and its implications for psychiatry.
Amer. J. Psychiat., 1961, *118*, 481–98.
This article traces the psychological processes that commonly
result from the loss of the mother (and, to a lesser extent, the
father) in infancy and early childhood.

9. Bowlby, J. Grief and mourning in infancy and early childhood.
Psychoanal. Stud. Child, 1960, *15*, 9–52.
This paper makes two major points: that grief is intimately
related to separation anxiety, and that the importance of
weaning may be exaggerated.

10. Bowlby, J. The nature of the child's tie to his mother. *Int. J. Psychoanal.*, 1958, *39*, 350–73.
Not directly related to death, dying, or bereavement, this article discusses the relationship of the child and his mother, setting the stage for the author's work on separation anxiety.

11. Bowlby, J. Processes of mourning. *Int. J. Psychoanal.*, 1961, *42*,
317–40.
The basic psychological processes of mourning divide into
three parts: urge to recover the lost object, disorganization,
and reorganization.

12. Bowlby, J. Separation anxiety. *Int. J. Psychoanal.*, 1940, *41*, 89–
113.
Separation anxiety, grief, and mourning are closely related,
because they all result from the loss of the mother figure.

13. Bozeman, M. F., Orbach, C. E., & Sutherland, A. M. Psychological
impact of cancer and its treatment: The adaptation of mothers
to the threatened loss of their children through leukemia. *Cancer,* 1955, *8*, 1–19.

14. Brewster, H. H. Grief: A disrupted human relationship. *Hum.
Org.*, 1950, *9*, 19–22.
A case history is described to show the need for the bereaved
to release the emotional tie to the deceased.

15. Buxbaum, R. E. Grief begins not with death, but with knowing it
is near. *Texas Med.*, 1966, *62*, 44–45.

The process of grief frequently begins before death, and can include the dying patient, his friends and relatives, *and* the professionals who seek to deal with the process of dying. Much consideration and study has been given to postmortem grief, but we need to know more about the interpersonal and intrapersonal process which is premortem grief. Professional groups often have difficulty in communicating their real feelings in this area.

16. Cain, A. C., & Cain, B. S. On replacing a child. *J. Amer. Acad. Child Psychiat.*, 1964, *3*, 443–56.

17. Cain, A. C., Fast, I., & Erickson, M. E. Children's disturbed reactions to the death of a sibling. *Amer. J. Orthopsychiat.*, 1964, *34*, 741–52.

Guilt feelings and other reactions are commonly found in children when a sibling dies.

18. Carstairs, G. M. Attitudes to death and suicide in an Indian cultural setting, *Int. J. Soc. Psychiat.*, 1955, *1*, 33–41.

19. Chodoff, P., *et al.* Stress, defenses and coping behavior: Observations in parents of children with malignant disease. *Amer. J. Psychiat.*, 1964, *120*, 743.

20. Cobb, B. Psychological impact of long illness and death of a child on the family circle. *J. Pediat.*, 1956, *49*, 746–51.

Four major categories of family reactions to lengthy illness and death of a child are discussed.

21. Creegan, R. F. A symbolic action during bereavement. *J. Abnorm. Soc. Psychol.*, 1942, *37*, 403–5.

22. Deutsch, H. A two-year-old boy's first love comes to grief. In L. Jessner & E. Pavenstedt (Eds.), *Dynamic psychopathology in childhood*. New York: Grune & Stratton, 1959. Pp. 1–5.

A two-year-old boy's mourning for his deceased nurse is described.

23. Eliot, T. D. The adjustive behavior of bereaved families: A new field for research. *Soc. Forces*, 1930, *8*, 543–49.

There is a great need to overcome the taboos surrounding death, just as the sex taboos have been overcome. (This: in 1930!)

24. Eliot, T. D. The bereaved family. *Ann. Amer. Acad. Pol. Soc. Sci.*, 1932, *160*, 184–90.

A discussion of the reactions of the family to bereavement, including typical behavior patterns and changes in family roles.

25. Eliot, T. D. Bereavement as a field of social research. *Bull. Society Soc. Res.*, 1938, *17*, 4.

    A shift in focus from the dead to the survivors may be necessary to promote research on bereavement.

26. Eliot, T. D. Bereavement as a problem for family research and technique. *Family*, 1930, *2*, 114–15.

    The author suggests research that will lead to a mental hygiene of grief.

27. Eliot, T. D. Bereavement: Inevitable but not unsurmountable. In H. Becker & R. Hill (Eds.), *Family, marriage, and parenthood.* Boston: Heath, 1955. Pp. 641–68.

    A discussion of bereavement, with case histories.

28. Eliot, T. D. A step toward the social psychology of bereavement. *J. Abnorm. Soc. Psychol.*, 1933, *27*, 380–90.

    An outline for approaching research into the problems of bereavement.

29. Eliot, T. D. War bereavements and their recovery. *Marr. Fam. Liv.*, 1946, *8*, 1–6.

    Compares bereavement from wartime killing with the usual causes of bereavement.

30. Engel, G. L. Grief and grieving. *Amer. J. Nurs.*, 1964, *64*, 93–98.

31. Engel, G. L. Is grief a disease? *Psychosom. Med.*, 1961, *23*, 18–22.

    The author feels that grief can best be approached by medical scientists when it is considered as a disease.

32. Feifel, H., & Fulton, R. L. Evaluation of ability of students in medicine, nursing, and mortuary science to cope with death and dying. Los Angeles: Veterans Administration Regional Office, 1966. Mimeographed.

33. Fleming, J., & Altschul, S. Activation of mourning and growth by psychoanalysis. *Int. J. Psychoanal.*, 1963, *44*, 419–31.

    An analysis of a 29-year-old woman, illustrating a variety of pathological mourning. This woman, who lost her parents at age 15 when she left them behind in fleeing Germany, at first refused to believe that they had died, and for years was unable to express any grief at their death. Her treatment enabled her to confront the painful emotions associated with the recognition of this loss, and to complete the work of mourning.

34. Freud, A. Discussion of Dr. John Bowlby's paper. *Psychoanal. Stud. Child*, 1960, *15*, 53–62.
   The author presents differences between Bowlby's statements on grief and mourning in infants, and her own.

35. Freud, S. Dreams of the death of persons of whom the dreamer is fond. In *Complete psychological works of Sigmund Freud*. Vol. 4. London: Hogarth, 1953. Pp. 248–71.
   Dreams of the death of individuals often represent death wishes toward these people; children during the oedipal period have such dreams.

36. Friedman, J., & Zaris, D. Paradoxical response to death of a spouse. *Dis. Nerv. Syst.*, 1964, *25*, 480–83.

37. Friedman, S. B., *et al.* Behavioral observations of parents anticipating the death of a child. *Pediatrics*, 1963, *32*, 610–25.

38. Fritz, M. A. A study of widowhood. *Sociol. & Soc. Res.*, 1930, *14*, 553–59.

39. Fulcomer, D. M. The adjustive behavior of some recently bereaved spouses. Unpublished doctoral dissertation, Northwestern University, 1942.

40. Gauthier, Y. The mourning reaction of a ten-year-old boy. *Canad. Psychiat. Ass. J.* [Suppl.], 1966, *11*, S 307–8.
   Hypothesizes that the complicated process used by a 10-year-old boy to communicate and identify with his deceased father, and to work through his ambivalence toward him, constituted the mourning process and prevented the appearance of a clinical depressive reaction.

41. Goldfarb, W. Emotional and intellectual consequences of psychological deprivation in infancy: A re-evaluation. In P. Hoch & J. Zubin (Eds.), *Psychopathology of childhood*. New York: Grune & Stratton, 1955.

42. Granville-Grossman, K. L. Early bereavement and schizophrenia. *Brit. J. Psychiat.*, 1966, *112*, 1027–34.
   Schizophrenics have been compared with their nonschizo-

phrenic sibs with respect to their ages at the death of their parents, using a standardization procedure designed to eliminate any effect of number of sibs. No significant difference was found between schizophrenics and nonschizophrenics, suggesting that bereavement of a parent is not of importance in the etiology of schizophrenia.

43. Greenberg, N. H., Loesh, J. G., & Laskin, M. Life situations associated with the onset of pregnancy. *Psychosom. Med.*, 1959, *21*, 296–311.

    Cites cases in which object loss or threatened object loss appeared to be related to conceiving out of wedlock, preceding conception by one to three months.

44. Grotjahn, M. Ego identity and the fear of death and dying. *Hillside Hosp. J.*, 1960, *9*, 147–55.

    The ego develops two defense systems: one to protect against the outer world where death exists, and the other to protect against the inner world's death instincts.

45. Hamovitch, M. B. *The parent and the fatally ill child.* Duarte, Cal.: City of Hope Medical Center, 1964.

46. Hamovitch, M. B. Parental reactions to the death of a child. Mimeographed, 1962. Pp. 27.

    A discussion of interviews with parents of terminally ill children; the results show that the opportunity to discuss their feelings is valuable.

47. Heinicke, C. M. Some effects of separating two-year-old children from their parents: A comparative study. *Hum. Rel.*, 1956, *9*, 105–76.

    The presence of parents is necessary to maintain the balance between the two-year-old's impulses and controls.

48. Hilgard, J. R. Strength of adult ego following childhood bereavement. *Amer. J. Orthopsychiat.*, 1960, *30*, 788–98.

    "Loss of a parent in childhood is a serious blow for any child." Grief and mourning are affected by the age and sex of the child and by the sex of the lost parent. Dependence of the surviving parent upon the children may affect the maturity their egos can attain.

49. Kastenbaum, R. Multiple perspectives on a geriatric "death valley." *Community Ment. Health J.*, 1967, *3*, 21–29.

Little is known about the total situation in which aged patients find themselves as the prospect of death increases. This paper focuses on perceptions of "Death Valley," the intensive-treatment unit of a geriatric hospital. Information was gathered from a variety of sources, including patients who had survived a recent period of residence in "Death Valley" and attending personnel throughout the hospital. Differences between "official" and "unofficial" communications on the subject of death, modes of responding to patients' death verbalizations, and possible sex differences in response to a heightened prospect of death are among the topics covered. Alternative explanations for the findings are discussed.

50. Kirkpatrick, J., Samuels, S., Jones, H., & Zweibelson, I. Bereavement and school adjustment. *J. School Psychol.*, 1965, *3*(4), 58–63.

51. Klein, M. Mourning and its relation to manic-depressive states. *Int. J. Psychoanal.*, 1940, *21*, 125–53.

Mourning produces a temporary manic-depressive condition which recreates early developmental experiences for the child.

52. Kligfeld, B., & Krupp, G. Sexual adjustment of widows. *Sexology*, November 1966, pp. 230–33.

Death of a husband creates many problems for the social adjustment of the widow. Some of the problems are accentuated by social attitudes. "The paths to sexual adjustment for the widowed are many and sometimes tortuous . . . complicated by the confusing rules for sexual behavior set down by our laws, by religion, or by public opinion, which are frequently unrealistic and contradictory."

53. Krupp, G. R. Identification as a defence against anxiety in coping with loss. *Int. J. Psychoanal.*, 1965, *46*, 303–14.

This paper concerns the identification reactions to the loss of a loved one. The dynamics of identification and introjection mechanisms are reviewed, with illustrations added from the work of Eugene O'Neill. Three case studies are presented to illuminate bereavement problems—chiefly, the function of identification as a defense against anxiety. Four types of internalized mechanisms are distinguished.

54. Langer, M. *Learning to live as a widow*. New York: J. Messner, 1957.

55. Lehrman, S. R. Reactions to untimely death. *Psychiat. Quart.*, 1956, *30*, 564–78.

56. Levinson, B. M. The pet and the child's bereavement. *Ment. Hyg.*, 1967, *51*, 197–200.
    The death of a pet may provide an emotional dress rehearsal and preparation for greater losses yet to come. When a parent dies, the pet may also become a temporary crutch that helps the child hold on to life until the void can be filled and his shattered world can become whole again.

57. Lindemann, E. The meaning of crisis in individual and family living. *Teach. Coll. Rec.*, 1956, *57*, 310–15.

58. Lindemann, E., & Greer, I. M. A study of grief: Emotional responses to suicide. *Pastoral Psychol.*, 1953, *4*, 9–13.

59. Magazu, P., Golner, J., & Arsenian, J. Reactions of a group of chronic psychotic patients to the departure of the group therapist. *Psychiat. Quart.*, 1964, *34*, 292–303.
    The departure of a therapist creates some of the same responses as does the death of a therapist.

60. Marris, P. *Widows and their families*. London: Routledge & Kegan Paul, 1958.

61. Middleton, W. C. Some reactions toward death among college students. *J. Abnorm. Soc. Psychol.*, 1936, *31*, 165–73.
    A questionnaire was administered to 825 college students regarding death, dying, funerals, and afterlife.

62. Monro, A. Childhood parent loss in a psychiatrically normal population. *Brit. J. Prev. Soc. Med.*, 1965, *19*, 69–70.
    This study investigates childhood parent loss in a group of persons with no history of serious psychiatric disorder. The results suggest that parental bereavement may normally be a

much commoner event than generally assumed. In trying to establish a basis for comparability of study results, the author defines terms used in studies of childhood parental loss: parental bereavement, loss, deprivation; parental absence; disturbed relationship with parents; childhood. The findings indicate that parental bereavement per se is of questionable value in assuming a predisposition for mental illness.

63. Moreno, J. L. The social atom and death. *Sociometry*, 1947, *10*, 80–84.

    Discussion of the difficulties in adjusting to changing social patterns produced by death of those with whom the individual interacts.

64. Murphy, G. Discussion. In H. Feifel (Ed.), *The meaning of death*. New York: McGraw-Hill, 1959. Pp. 317–40.

    A summary and discussion of the salient points in the other articles in the book. Seven different systems of attitudes are listed.

65. Murphy, L. B. Coping devices and defense mechanisms in relation to autonomous ego functions. *Bull. Menninger Clin.*, 1964, *24*, 144–53.

    Discusses relationships between coping devices, defense mechanisms, and the autonomous functions of the ego in the early development of the child's capacity to handle his relation to the environment.

66. Natterson, J. M., & Knudson, A. G., Jr. Observations concerning fear of death in fatally ill children and their mothers. *Psychosom. Med.*, 1960, *22*, 456–65.

67. Opler, M. E. Reactions to death among the Mescalero Apache. *Southwest. J. Anthrop.*, 1946, *2*, 454–67.

68. Orbach, C. E. The multiple meanings of the loss of a child. *Amer. J. Psychother.*, 1959, *13*, 906–15.

    An intensive case history, indicating the need to accept shifts in the family structure and alterations in family roles.

69. Orbach, C. E., Sutherland, A. M., & Bozeman, M. F. Psychological

impact of cancer and its treatment: The adaptation of mothers to the threatened loss of their children through leukemia. *Cancer*, 1955, *8*, 20–33.

A psychoanalytic approach to the reactions of mothers to the loss or threat of loss of their children.

70. Osborne, E. When you lose a loved one. Public Affairs Pamphlet No. 269, 1958.

71. Osipov, N. Strach ze smrti (Fear of death). *Rev. Neurol. Psychiat.* (Praha), 1935, *32*, 17–25. (Obtained from *Psychol. Abstracts.*) A discussion of the reactions of children and adults to death, with some emphasis upon the etiology of fear.

72. Parkes, C. M. Effects of bereavement on physical and mental health —a study of the medical records of widows. *Brit. Med. J.*, 1964, *2*, 274–79.

Statistics indicate that grief produces an increase in the tendency of widows to visit their general practitioners; it may also lead to psychiatric symptoms.

73. Parkes, C. M. Recent bereavement as a cause of mental illness. *Brit. J. Psychiat.*, 1964, *110*, 198–204.

74. Pollack, G. H. Mourning and adaptation. *Int. J. Psychoanal.*, 1961, *42*, 341–61.

After object loss through death, the object replacement is a function of instinctual needs of the mourner, degree of energy liberation, and maturity of the ego and superego.

75. Rochlin, G. *Griefs and discontents: The forces of change.* Boston: Little, Brown, 1967.

Propounds a new theory of personality development which focuses upon the way in which humans cope with the inevitable losses and failures that occur in their lives.

76. Rogers, W. F. Needs of the bereaved. *Pastoral Psychol.*, 1950, *1*, 17–21.

77. Rose, G. Analytic first aid for a three-year-old. *Amer. J. Orthopsychiat.*, 1960, *30*, 200–201.

This study of a little girl's reaction to death points out the value of being aware of dynamic analytic possibilities in helping her adjust to the specifics of death as she encounters them.

78. Rosenthal, P. The death of the leader in group psychotherapy. *Amer. J. Orthopsychiat.*, 1947, *17*, 226–77.

A discussion of the reactions of group-therapy patients to the death of Dr. Paul Schilder, himself active in research on reactions to death.

79. Sandley, D. The study of bereavement. In K. D. Kroupa & D. Sandler (Eds.), Community mental health: Theory, practice, and research. Unpublished manuscript, Harvard University, 1962.

80. Shambaugh, B. A study of loss reactions in a seven-year-old. *Psychoanal. Stud. Child*, 1961, *16*, 510–52.

81. Strauss, A. L., & Glaser, B. G. The dying patient and his social loss. Unpublished report.
    The nurse tends to react to the dying patient in terms of how great his social loss will be to the community and to his family.

82. Strauss, A. L., Glaser, B. G., & Quint, J. C. The nonaccountability of terminal care. *Hospitals*, 1964, *38*, 73–87.
    Exact procedures in dealing with the terminally ill are unknown but may reflect the difficulty of medical personnel in coping with death.

83. Volkart, E. H. (with Michael, S. T.). Bereavement and mental health. In A. H. Leighton, J. A. Clausen, & R. N. Wilson (Eds.), *Explorations in social psychiatry.* New York: Basic Books, 1957. Pp. 281–307.
    The relationship between bereavement and mental health is a function both of ego strength and of the history of the relationship between the bereaved and the deceased.

84. Wetmore, R. The role of grief in psychoanalysis. *Int. J. Psychoanal.*, 1963, *44*, 97–103.

85. Wodinsky, A. Psychiatric consultation with nurses on a leukemia service. *Ment. Hyg.*, 1964, *48*, 282–87.
    Discussion of the results of a series of meetings with nurses working with leukemia patients.

86. Zinker, J. C., & Hallenbeck, C. E. Notes on loss, crisis, and growth. *J. Gen. Psychol.*, 1965, *73*(2), 347–54.

B. DEVIANT RESPONSES

1. Abley, X., & Leconte, M. Attempt to interpret manic reactions after sorrow. *Amer. J. Med. Psychol.*, 1938, *96*, 232–40.

2. Almy, T. P. Experimental studies on the irritable colon. *Amer. J. Med.*, 1951, *10*, 60–67.

   Healthy persons show disturbances of the colon during stress induced by experimental stimuli resulting in emotional conflict. Similar emotional conflicts, expressed in feelings of hostility, resentment, guilt, and self-reproach, were observed coincident with the colon disturbances of persons diagnosed as irritable-colon sufferers. Many experienced the emotional conflicts when mentally focused on lonely, helpless, or generally maladjusted life periods following deaths of key persons.

3. Archibald, H. C., Bell, D., Miller, C., & Tuddenham, R. D. Bereavement in childhood and adult psychiatric disturbance. *Psychosom. Med.*, 1962, *24*, 343–51.

4. Arthur, B., & Kemme, M. L. Bereavement in childhood. *J. Child Psychol. Psychiat.*, 1964, *5*, 37–49.

   A study of 83 emotionally disturbed children and their families.

5. Barnacle, C. H. Grief reactions and their treatment. *Dis. Nerv. Syst.*, 1949, *10*, 173–76.

6. Barry, H. Orphanhood as a factor in psychoses. *J. Abnorm. Soc. Psychol.*, 1936, *30*, 431–38.

   Among psychotic rulers throughout history, a disproportionate number were paternal orphans.

7. Barry, H. Significance of maternal bereavement before the age of eight in psychiatric patients. *Arch. Neurol. Psychiat.*, 1949, *62*, 630–37.

8. Barry, H. A study of bereavement: An approach to problems in mental disease. *Amer. J. Orthopsychiat.*, 1939, *9*, 355–59.

   Among a population of male Caucasian psychotics, maternal bereavement is statistically more common than paternal bereavement. Maternal bereavement, but not paternal bereavement, is more common among psychotics than among normals.

9. Barry, H., Jr., Barry, H., III, & Lindemann, E. Dependency in adult patients following early maternal bereavement. *J. Nerv. Ment. Dis.*, 1965, *140*, 196–206.

Characteristics of adult psychiatric patients, from both mental clinics and private practices, who had suffered a bereavement early in life (between 3 and 48 months old) were compared with those of other psychiatric patients who had suffered a later bereavement (between 11 and 17 years old). Comparison of symptoms, personality features, sex, age, marital status, and socioeconomic status showed a statistically significant difference in the dependency character. Dependency was a prominent characteristic of 13 of the first group and of only 4 of the second group (each group numbered 15 persons).

10. Barry, H., & Bousfield, W. A. Incidence of orphanhood among fifteen hundred psychotic patients. _J. Genet. Psychol._, 1937, _50_, 198–202.

11. Barry, H., & Lindemann, E. Critical ages for maternal bereavement in psychoneuroses. _Psychom. Med._, 1960, _22_, 166–81.

    Maternal bereavement was found significantly more frequently in psychoneurotics than in normals: earlier bereavement appeared more disturbing.

12. Beck, A. T., Sethi, B. B., & Tuthill, R. W. Childhood bereavement and adult depression. _Arch. Gen. Psychiat._, 1963, _9_, 295–302.

    Consistent with results reached by other researchers, this study reports a significantly greater incidence of parent loss in childhood in the high-depressed as compared with the non-depressed patients in a psychiatric ward or clinic. The author points out the variables which need to be controlled to produce comparable results in this area of research regarding loss of a parent or a disruption in the parent-child relationship and the incidence of subsequent depression in childhood.

13. Becker, E. Toward a comprehensive theory of depression: A cross-disciplinary appraisal of objects, games, and meaning. _J. Nerv. Ment. Dis._, 1962, _135_, 26–35.

    Mourning as a class of depression is explored in the context of everyone's problem of fashioning a coherent identity. Game-loss, encompassing one's view of the entire sociocultural world, is used to explain ego trauma resulting from loss of loved objects. The effect of this model of sharp changes in object relationships, such as death, is discussed from the viewpoint of "who you are" and "what you do." Finally, the implications for characterizing normal and abnormal mourning are detailed.

14. Beres, D., & Obers, S. J. The effects of extreme deprivation in infancy on psychic structures in adolescence. *Psychoanal. Stud. Child*, 1950, *5*, 212–35.

15. Bergler, E. Psychopathology and duration of mourning in neurotics. *J. Clin. Psychopathol.*, 1948, *3*, 478–82.

16. Blum, G. S., & Rosenzweig, S. The incidence of sibling and parental deaths in the anamnesis of female schizophrenics. *J. Gen. Psychol.*, 1944, *32*, 3–13.
    Female schizophrenics had a higher rate of sibling deaths than did female manic-depressives or normals.

17. Bowlby, J. Childhood mourning and its implications for psychiatry. *Amer. J. Psychiat.*, 1961, *118*, 481–98.
    Experiences of separation in the early years lead to defensive processes which may cause psychiatric illness.

18. Bowlby, J. Forty-four juvenile thieves: Their characters and home life. *Int. J. Psychoanal.*, 1944, *25*, 19–53, 107–128.

19. Bowlby, J. Separation anxiety: A critical review of the literature. *J. Child Psychiat.*, 1960, *1*, 251–69.
    A discussion of six main theories accounting for separation anxiety: transformed libido, birth trauma, signal anxiety, depressive anxiety, persecutory anxiety, and primary anxiety.

20. Brewster, H. H. Separation reaction in psychosomatic disease and neurosis. *Psychosom. Med.*, 1952, *14*, 154–60.
    Three patients with psychosomatic illnesses responded more severely to separation from their therapist than did three patients with neurosis.

21. Bromberg, W., & Schilder, P. The attitudes of psychoneurotics towards death. *Psychoanal. Rev.*, 1963, *23*, 1–25.
    Anxiety and hysteria cases are primarily concerned with object loss in death, but depressives are more disturbed by the thought of eternal destruction.

22. Bromberg, W., & Schilder, P. Death and dying. *Psychoanal. Rev.*, 1933, *20*, 133–85.
    A psychiatric interpretation of empirical data relating to the

problems of death in the attitudes of normal and neurotic individuals.

23. Brown, F. Depression and childhood bereavement. *J. Ment. Sci.*, 1961, *107*, 754–77.

It is hypothesized that depressive illness in older persons is often a reaction to a present loss or bereavement which is associated with a more serious childhood loss or bereavement.

24. Cain, A. C., & Cain, B. S. On replacing a child. *J. Amer. Acad. Child Psychiat.*, 1964, *3*, 443–56.

Parents who conceive a child shortly after the death of another child to serve as a substitute may induce severe pathological problems through their attitudes toward the later child.

25. Cain, A. C., Erickson, M. E., Fast, I., & Vaughan, R. A. Children's disturbed reactions to their mother's miscarriage. *Psychosom. Med.*, 1964, *26*, 58–66.

A discussion of the difficulties caused to an older child by the miscarriage of the mother during a subsequent pregnancy.

26. Cain, A. C., Fast, I., & Erickson, M. E. Children's disturbed reactions to the death of a sibling. *Amer. J. Orthopsychiat.*, 1964, *34*, 741–52.

27. Cochrane, A. L. A little widow is a dangerous thing. *Int. J. Psychoanal.*, 1936, *17*, 494–509.

28. Cohen, M., & Lipton, L. M. Spontaneous remission of schizophrenic psychoses following maternal death. *Psychiat. Quart.*, 1950, *24*, 716–25.

Case histories in which the death of the patient's mother appeared to relate to spontaneous remission of psychotic symptoms.

29. Dennehy, C. M. Childhood bereavement and psychiatric illness. *Brit. J. Psychiat.*, 1966, *112*, 1049–69.

Study of childhood bereavement in psychiatric illness, with control groups indexed at year of birth, or parental age at birth. Actual versus expected (per chance) bereavement volume was calculated for each mental illness investigated: depressives, schizophrenics, male alcohol addicts, male drug addicts; and for each sex.

30. Deutsch, H. Absence of grief. *Psychoanal. Quart.*, 1937, *6*, 12–22.

Cases are cited in which the reaction to the loss of a beloved object does not include mourning.

31. Earle, A. M., & Earle, B. V. Early maternal deprivation and later psychiatric illness. *Amer. J. Orthopsychiat.*, 1961, *31*, 181–86.
    Cases of early maternal deprivation are compared with a control group to investigate psychopathological differences.

32. Edelson, S. R., & Warren, P. H. Catatonic schizophrenia as a mourning process. *Dis. Nerv. Syst.*, 1963, *24*, 2–8.
    Presents a case for the catatonic syndrome as being a response to mourning.

33. Fleming, J., & Altschul, S. Activation of mourning and growth by psychoanalysis. *Int. J. Psychoanal.*, 1963, *44*, 419–31.
    A group research program entitled the Parent-loss Project studies the effect of object loss in childhood on adult personality structure. The adult patients have lost a parent by death in childhood and are being treated by psychoanalysis. A case study illustrates how reality-denial, a form of pathological mourning, has interfered with maturation and how psychoanalytic treatment was able to help activate the interrupted mourning process.

34. Freud, S. Mourning and melancholia. In *Complete psychological works of Sigmund Freud.* Vol. 14. London: Hogarth, 1957. Pp. 237–259.
    Melancholia and mourning are definitely related, since the former develops from the latter in some individuals.

35. Granville-Grossman, K.L. Early bereavement and schizophrenia. *Brit. J. Psychiat.*, 1966, *112*, 1027–34.
    Study to ascertain preconditioning to schizophrenia by bereavement. The conclusions are at variance with conclusions of previous authors, who reported that more schizophrenics are bereaved in childhood than are nonschizophrenics. In the opinion of the author, the present study was afforded superior matching, since the control group consisted of the nonschizophrenic sibs of the primary sample. Emphasis was placed on maternal-death bereavement.

36. Gregory, I. Studies of parental deprivation in psychiatric patients. *Amer. J. Psychiat.*, 1958, *115*, 432–42.

> Evaluates the literature related to the effects of parental deprivation upon later emotional illness.

37. Hilgard, J. R., & Newman, M. F. Evidence for functional genesis in mental illness: Schizophrenia, depressive psychoses, and psychoneurosis. *J. Nerv. Ment. Dis.*, 1961, *132*, 3–16.

> Among hospitalized women who had lost their mothers, a statistically significant relationship occurred between the age of initial hospitalization and the age at which the oldest child reached the age of the woman at the time of her mother's death.

38. Hilgard, J. R., & Newman, M. F. Parental loss by death in childhood as an etiological factor among schizophrenic and alcoholic patients compared with a non-patient community sample. *J. Nerv. Ment. Dis.*, 1963, *137*, 14–28.

> According to a careful evaluation of large comparative samples, parental death appears to be more frequent and occurs earlier among schizophrenics and alcoholic patients than among a control group of normals.

39. Hilgard, J. R., Newman, M. F., & Fisk, F. Strength of adult ego following childhood bereavement. *Amer. J. Orthopsychiat.*, 1960, *30*, 788–98.

> Interviews with adults who had been bereaved as children. The authors conclude that parental death is potentially extremely traumatic.

40. Hill, O. W., & Price, J. S. Childhood bereavement and adult depression. *Brit. J. Psychiat.*, 1967, *113*, 743–51.

> Study based on the hypothesis that there is an association between the diagnosis of depression and parental bereavement before the fifteenth birthday. Depressed patients were compared with patients admitted to the hospital for other psychiatric conditions. A significantly higher number of the depressed patients had lost their fathers by age 15 than had the control group; but the loss of mothers did not differ. Possible

reasons for some of the associations found in the study were discussed, especially the influence of the relative age of the father.

41. Ingham, H. V. A statistical study of family relationships in psychoneurotics. *Amer. J. Psychiat.*, 1949, *106*, 91–98.

    A comparison of psychoneurotic and normal students, based on responses to questionnaires. Family history is one of the variables investigated.

42. Keeler, W. R. Children's reaction to the death of a parent. In P. M. Hoch & J. Zubin (Eds.), *Depression*. New York: Grune & Stratton, 1954. Pp. 109–20.

    Cases are presented to establish that children are subject to pathological mourning, especially when the child held extremely strong feelings for the deceased.

43. Kirkpatrick, J., Samuels, S., Jones, H., & Zweibelson, I. Bereavement and school adjustment. *J. School Psychol.*, 1965, *3*(4), 58–63.

    Denial of loss and repression of grief may result in a delayed reaction in the form of restricted functioning. Underachievement is considered as a symptom of restricted reality functioning. Three case studies are reported.

44. Kraus, A. S., & Lilienfeld, A. M. Some epidemiological aspects of the high mortality rate in the young widowed group. *J. Chronic Dis.*, 1959, *10*, 207–17.

45. Lagrone, C. W. Developmental factors in relation to recidivism and nonrecidivism among military delinquents. *Amer. J. Orthopsychiat.*, 1947, *17*, 241–53.

    Three of the variables studied included death of a parent causing a broken home, occurrence of death among parents, and death of siblings. Recidivists are compared with nonrecividists on a total of 23 criteria.

46. Lifton, R. J. Psychological effects of the atomic bomb in Hiroshima: The theme of death. *Daedalus*, 1963, *92*, 462–97.

    A discussion of interviews with 75 bomb survivors, emphasizing the sudden and overwhelming encounter with death.

47. Lindemann, E. Modifications in the course of ulcerative colitis in

relationship to changes in life situations and reaction patterns. In H. G. Wolff (Ed.), *Life stress and bodily disease.* Baltimore: Williams & Wilkins, 1950. Pp. 706–23.

Discusses the relationship between grief and the onset of an organic disease.

48. Lindemann, E. Symptomatology and management of acute grief. *Amer. J. Psychiat.*, 1944, *101*, 141–48.

Delineation of bereavement reactions, both behavioral and organic, with emphasis upon acute and morbid grief indices.

49. Lipson, C. Denial and mourning. *Int. J. Psychoanal.*, 1963, *44*, 104–7.

Cites several cases illustrating denial of death of a loved one. Bereavement initially causes a splitting of the ego.

50. Madow, L., & Hardy, S. E. Incidence and analysis of the broken family in the background of neurosis. *Amer. J. Orthopsychiat.*, 1947, *17*, 521–28.

Relative to a normal military population, a disproportionate number of neurotic soldiers came from broken homes.

51. Meiss, M. L. The oedipal problem of a fatherless child. *Psychoanal. Stud. Child*, 1952, 7, 216–29.

A psychoanalytic view of the oedipal situation when the child must fantasize the father.

52. Meyerson, A. Prolonged cases of grief reactions treated by electric shock. *New Eng. J. Med.*, 1944, *230*, 255–56.

A brief report of four grief-precipitated depressions in which electric-shock treatment was successful.

53. Mitchell, N. D. The significance of the loss of the father through death. Paper presented at the meeting of the American Orthopsychiatric Association, Chicago, March 1964.

Several cases are reported in which the death of the father played a role in such problems as difficulty in sex-role adjustment, loss of self-esteem, and lack of creativity and productivity.

54. Moriarty, D. M. Early loss and the fear of mothering. *Psychoanal. & Psychoanal. Rev.*, 1962, *49*, 63–69.

55. Moss, L. M., & Hamilton, D. M. The psychotherapy of the suicidal patient. *Amer. J. Psychiat.*, 1956, *112*, 814–20.

    Bereavement was the precipitating factor in a large proportion of mental illnesses involving suicide attempts.

56. Oltman, J. E., McGarry, J., & Friedman, S. Parental deprivation and the "broken home" in dementia praecox and other mental disorders. *Amer. J. Psychiat.*, 1952, *108*, 685–94.

    Parental deprivation and broken homes occur more frequently for psychoneurotics than for patients suffering from dementia praecox, manic-depressive states, and alcoholism.

57. Parkes, C. M. Bereavement and mental illness: A clinical study. *Brit. J. Med. Psychol.*, in press.

58. Parkes, C. M. Recent bereavement as a cause of mental illness. *Brit. J. Psychiat.*, 1964, *110*, 198–204.

    The proportion of patients entering a mental hospital within six months of the death of a spouse is far greater than anticipated by chance.

59. Peck, M. Notes on identification in a case of depression reactive to the death of a love object. *Psychoanal. Quart.*, 1939, *8*, 1–17.

60. Pollack, G. H. Childhood parent and sibling loss in adult patients. *Arch. Gen. Psychiat.*, 1962, *7*, 295–305.

    A statistical description of the degree to which psychiatric patients seen by one investigator had suffered parental or sibling deprivation.

61. Rado, S. The problem of melancholia. *Int. J. Psychoanal.*, 1928, *9*, 420–38.

62. Rochlin, G. Loss and restitution. *Psychoanal. Stud. Child*, 1953, *8*, 288–309.

    Deals with the need for understanding of psychodynamics involved in loss of an object early in life of the child. A case history of relative absence of mothering process which established social isolation in early childhood.

63. Rosenzweig, S. Sibling death as a psychological experience with special reference to schizophrenia. *Psychoanal. Rev.*, 1943, *30*, 177–86.

    Schizophrenic patients reveal a higher incidence of sibling

deaths during their earlier years than do manic-depressives and general paretics.

64. Rosenzweig, S., & Bray, D. Sibling deaths in the anamneses of schizophrenic patients. *Arch. Neurol. Psychiat.*, 1943, *49*, 71–92.
    More schizophrenic patients than normals or other classifications of psychotics had lost a sibling in death before they were 19 years old.

65. Rosner, A. A. Mourning before the fact. *J. Amer. Psychoanal. Ass.*, 1962, *10*, 564, 570.
    A presentation of a case history in which mourning before actual object loss was utilized as a defense against the fear of actual loss.

66. Sanna, V. D. A comparative study of schizophrenics of different socio-cultural background (Protestant, Irish Catholic, and Jewish) : Parental loss and prognosis in terms of rehospitalization. *Revta. Psicol. Norm. Patol.*, 1966, *11*(1-2-3), 104–18.
    Major differences exist with regard to the extent of parental bereavement and rehospitalization rate of parents belonging to different social classes, ethnic groups, and subcategories of schizophrenia.

67. Schilder, P. The attitude of murderers toward death. *J. Abnorm. Soc. Psychol.*, 1936, *31*, 348–63.
    Questionnaires administered to 33 murderers indicated three groupings of personality and attitudinal types.

68. Schmale, A. H. Relationship of separation and depression to disease. *Psychosom. Med.*, 1958, *20*, 259–77.

69. Shoor, M., & Speed, M. H. Delinquency as a manifestation of the mourning process. *Psychiat. Quart.*, 1963, *37*, 540–58.

70. Spitz, R. A. Hospitalism: An inquiry into the genesis of psychiatric conditions in early childhood. *Psychoanal. Stud. Child*, 1945, *1*, 53–74.
    Institutionalization can lead to physical and psychological disturbances unless compensated for by adequate mother-child relations.

71. Stern, K., Williams, G. M., & Prados, M. Grief reactions in later life. *Amer. J. Psychiat.*, 1951, *108*, 289–94.

Tendencies toward somatic illness in elderly bereaved Ss are evaluated.

72. Yarrow, L. J. Maternal deprivation: Toward an empirical and conceptual re-evaluation. *Psychol. Bull.*, 1961, *58*, 459–90.

Maternal deprivation is divided into four types in this literature review: institutionalization, separation, multiple mothering, and distortions in quality.

73. Young, M., Benjamin, B., & Wallis, C. The mortality of widows. *Lancet*, July–December 1962, *2*, 454–56.

74. Zeligs, R. Death casts its shadow on a child. *Ment. Hyg.*, 1967, *51*, 9–20.

Traces the effect of the parental shielding of a six-year-old child from the facts of the sudden death of his one-year-old brother. Therapy with the boy unveiled guilt feeling resulting from a fear that death wishes caused the death; fear of rejection resulting from being shielded from family participation in the funeral; and fear of death during sleep. Applications of therapy helped the boy differentiate between sleep and death, advised him of the finality of death, and, together with parental cooperation, provided reassurance of his individual worth and some understanding of the concept of death.

C. RESPONSES TO THE DEATH OF A PRESIDENT OR OTHER NATIONAL FIGURE

1. Appelbaum, S. A. The Kennedy assassination. *Psychoanal. Rev.*, 1966, *53*(3), 69–80.

A group-dynamics class, meeting for the ninth time two weeks after the assassination, showed mourning, but with the group leader rather than the President as the object of the members' feelings of loss, guilt, anger, and fear. "The present paper offers an instance of overwhelmingly stimulating external events bringing about the hurried cathexis of a phallic-oedipal organization. The result was a confluence of experiences thrust on them by the present, aroused from their past, and expressed in the transference."

2. Banta, T. J. The Kennedy assassination: Early thoughts and emotions. Paper presented at the meeting of the Midwest Psychological Association, St. Louis, May 1964.

3. Fairbairn, W. R. D. The effect of the King's death upon patients under analysis. *Int. J. Psychoanal.*, 1936, 27, 278–84.
   Three cases are presented and interpreted, largely through dream analysis.

4. Greenstein, F. I. Young men and the death of a young president. In M. Wolfenstein & G. Kliman (Eds.), *Children and the death of a president.* New York: Doubleday, 1965. Pp. 193–216.
   Verbatim responses, plus the author's evaluation of a series of depth interviews with college students immediately following the assassination of President Kennedy.

5. Heckel, R. V. The day the president was assassinated: Patients' reaction in one mental hospital. *Ment. Hosp.*, 1964, 15, 48.

6. Johannsen, D. E. Reactions to the death of President Roosevelt. *J. Abnorm. Soc. Psychol.*, 1946, 41, 218–22.
   A sample of 128 college girls responded to a questionnaire regarding their reactions to the death of Franklin Roosevelt.

7. Krippner, S. The 20-year death cycle of the American presidency. *Res. L. Phil. Soc. Sci.*, 1965, 2, 65–72.
   Since 1840, every president elected at 20-year intervals has died in office. Several explanations are offered: coincidence (chi-square analysis indicates only one possibility in 10,000 that this is due to chance factors), synchronicity, expectancy set, gradual build-up of hostility among paranoid schizophrenics.

8. Nemtzow, J., & Lesser, S. R. Reactions of children and parents to the death of President Kennedy (digest of paper read at the meeting of the American Orthopsychiatric Association, Chicago, 1964). *Amer. J. Orthopsychiat.*, 1964, 34, 280–81.

9. Orlansky, H. Reactions to the death of President Roosevelt. *J. Soc. Psychol.*, 1947, 26, 235–66.
   An evaluation of the social-psychological phenomena displayed following the death of President Roosevelt, suggesting that people are simultaneously afraid of and deny death.

10. Sheatsley, P. Impact of the assassination of President Kennedy. Paper presented at the meeting of the American Psychological Association, Los Angeles, August 1964.

11. Sigal, R. Child and adult reactions to the assassination of President Kennedy. Paper presented at the meeting of the American Psychological Association, Los Angeles, August 1964.

12. Teahan, J. E., & Golin, S. Reactions to the president's assassination as a function of sex ideology, perceived parental attitudes and symbolic significance. Paper presented at the meeting of the Midwest Psychological Association, St. Louis, May 1964.

13. Wolff, K. H. A partial analysis of student reaction to President Roosevelt's death. *J. Soc. Psychol.*, 1947, *26*, 35–53.

14. Wrightman, L. S., & Noble, F. C. Reactions to the president's assassination and changes in philosophies of human nature. Paper presented at the meeting of the Midwest Psychological Association, St. Louis, May 1964.

IX.   DEATH AND THE LAW

1. Banks, A. L. Euthanasia. *Practitioner*, 1948, *161*, 101–7.
   > A revolutionary change in the minds of the profession and of the public at large is needed before the doctor is recognized in law as an executioner with introduction of legislation in Great Britain.

2. Carr, J. L. The coroner and the common law: Death and its medical imputations. *Calif. Med.*, 1960, *93*, 32–34.

3. Jakobovits, I. The dying and their treatment in Jewish law. *Heb. Med. J.*, 1961, *2*, 242–51.

4. Kevorkian, J. The eye in death. *Ciba Clin. Symposia*, 1961, *13*, 51–62.
   > "Eyegrounds may provide more accurate information on the exact time of death than can be obtained by any other means."

5. Rohrod, M. G. The meaning of "cause of death." *J. Forensic Sci.*, 1963, *8*, 15–21.
   > Cause of death is aggravated by the change in kinds of diseases we now have. Three principal purposes for wanting to know